D1568666

THE FUTURE OF BANKING

THE FUTURE OF BANKING

HENRY ENGLER
JAMES ESSINGER

Published by **Pearson Education**
London/New York/San Francisco/Toronto/Sydney/Tokyo/Singapore
Hong Kong/Cape Town/Madrid/Paris/Milan/Munich/Amsterdam

PEARSON EDUCATION LIMITED

Head Office:
Edinburgh Gate
Harlow CM20 2JE
Tel: +44 (0)1279 623623
Fax: +44 (0)1279 431059

London Office:
128 Long Acre
London WC2E 9AN
Tel: +44 (0)20 7447 2000
Fax: +44 (0)20 7240 5771
Website: www.financial-minds.com

First published in Great Britain in 2000

ISBN 0 273 65038 6

British Library Cataloguing in Publication Data
A CIP catalogue record for this book can be obtained from the British Library.

10 9 8 7 6 5 4 3 2

Typeset by Pantek Arts Ltd, Maidstone, Kent
Printed and bound in Great Britain by Redwood Books, Trowbridge, Wilts.

The Publishers' policy is to use paper manufactured from sustained forests.

CONTENTS

PROLOGUE: THE BACKGROUND

'In my end is my beginning', wrote the Anglo-American poet T. S. Eliot in his 1943 poetic masterpiece *Four Quartets*. He was using this arresting and thought-provoking aphorism to make a point about human life, but, in a curious way, what he wrote is true of the global banking industry, too.

Despite the enormous changes the industry has gone through during the past 20 years – let alone since 1943 – one factor has, crucially, remained the same: the fundamental nature of the need customers have for banking services. The framework within which these services are delivered has changed out of all recognition, but the need is still there.

For part of the 1920s, Eliot worked as a clerk at Lloyds Bank in the City of London. The banking services he and his colleagues provided then would readily be recognizable now. People's needs have not changed, and neither has the basic nature of the banking services people require, but the way banks meet those needs today is completely different.

To understand the future, we must first understand the past – not only *what* happened, but *why* it happened. To see just how far the banking business has travelled in what is, after all, a comparatively short time, we need briefly to visit the past – not the war years of the early 1940s, or the economically depressed 1920s, but the middle of the nineteenth century. Let us follow the successful and wealthy Swiss industrialist Johann Konrad Fischer as he makes a visit to a London bank one morning in 1851. The following reminiscence is from Fischer's journals.

> When I returned to the bank a little before nine o'clock, I was shown to a seat facing a counter where five cashiers conducted their business. At five minutes to nine the official to whom I had to give my cheque took his place behind the counter. I had it in my hand and showed it to him. He did not say a word but emptied several little bags of gold coins into a drawer. Then he produced the well-known little cash shovel that is used for coins in banks. And then he just waited. At the

> stroke of nine he asked me if I wanted gold or banknotes. I said I wanted gold. He did not count any of the sovereigns and half-sovereigns but simply weighed them on his scales and then put them on the counter without taking any further notice of me.

True, this was only an over-the-counter interaction with a cashier, and even today nobody would pretend that such transactions are carried out in anything other than a methodical and routine way, even 'in cold blood'. The journal entry, none the less, indicates a completely different type of banking environment, though. The point is that the attitude and interaction (if one can call it that), this silent, cold, grey attitude the cashier of 1851 displayed to Fischer, would have been representative of how the bank interacted with its customers throughout its organization.

Why? Because this, was, simply, how banks operated then. This was how banks thought, how they conducted themselves and how they felt they ought to behave. This was how they saw themselves culturally, and how they were sure they ought to be. What was true of banks was, of course, also true of every type of retail financial service provider, whether insurance company, savings institution or building society. (Incidentally, the very first building societies, which came to prominence in the nineteenth century, really were societies for helping their members have the means to build houses.)

Why did nineteenth-century banks and other retail financial service providers behave like this? Not because Victorian people were inherently any less lively, cheerful or fun than we are. The Victorians were, in fact, a good deal more lively, cheerful and fun than we often tend to believe.

Instead, the reasons for banks and other retail financial service providers not being very cheerful organizations back in the nineteenth century have more to do with the role they played in society and the expectations their customers had of them.

In his 1854 novel, *Hard Times*, Charles Dickens brilliantly captures the ultra-formal, strict, stubbornly masculine (it is true that banks were almost entirely all-male preserves during the nineteenth century) role of a bank as the hugely respectable pillar of society. Indeed, in a sense they were the very core of society, around which everything revolved. The crass, insensitive, wealthy (and, as it turns out, hypocritical) Josiah Bounderby – the epitome of the rough, callous, self-made man – discovers that his bank has been robbed. He breaks the news to a young aristocratic acquaintance (Bounderby, typically, does not have friends).

> 'Harthouse!' cried Mr Bounderby. 'Have you heard?'
>
> 'Heard what?' said Harthouse, soothing his horse, and inwardly favouring Mr Bounderby with no good wishes.
>
> 'Then you *haven't* heard!'
>
> 'I have heard you, and so has this brute. I have heard nothing else.'
>
> Mr Bounderby, red and hot, planted himself in the centre of the path before the horse's head, to explode his bombshell with more effect.
>
> 'The Bank's robbed!'
>
> 'You don't mean it!'
>
> 'Robbed last night, Sir. Robbed in an extraordinary manner. Robbed with a false key.'
>
> 'Of much?'
>
> Mr Bounderby, in his desire to make the most of it, really seemed mortified by being obliged to reply, 'Why, no; not of very much. But it might have been.'
>
> 'Of how much?'
>
> 'Oh! as a sum – if you stick to a sum – of not more than a hundred and fifty pounds,' said Bounderby, with impatience. 'But it's not the sum; it's the fact. It's the fact of the Bank being robbed, that's the important circumstance. I am surprised you don't see it.'

Bounderby's bluster, fluster and (despite his loss of £150) lustre would have no doubt been annoying, but, in his coarse and blurting way, he has indeed put his finger on the nub of the matter. The fact that his bank *could* be robbed, the fact that this crucial, core social entity could be illicitly deprived of funds, was so horrifying that it is irrelevant to this man – so typical in his boorish and insensitive hardheadness of so many nineteenth-century businessmen – that the amount stolen was fairly small. (In fact, in 1854, £150 was worth about £5,000 at today's prices.)

Bounderby's bank was not only the source of his money, it was also the centre of his moral universe, just as the thousands of city and town banks of the nineteenth century were the centres of the moral universes of the cities and towns where they were located.

The bank was, in an almost literal sense, the pillar of society and the human qualities that were praised in the nineteenth century – prudence, thrift, restraint, good sense, thoughtful caution – were also the qualities banks were expected to have. In George Eliot's novel, *Middlemarch* (1871–72), most of the citizens of the eponymous provincial town are heavily in debt to Bulstrode, the banker, whose web of influence, control and power spreads around the town like a pernicious creeping weed with steel tendrils, literally holding on to most Middlemarchers lock, stock and barrel.

Today, many people are no less mortgaged to their bank, yet the notion of the bank as the commercial epicentre of a community is as much a part of history as oysters and brown stout. Today, banks and other providers of financial services don't really have a moral importance at all, they are simply providing a service that they strive to provide at a profit. Indeed, when one considers the lengths to which banks will go to hammer home to customers – especially youthful customers – that banks can be youth-oriented and trendy, too, the whole idea of a modern bank being the moral epicentre of society starts to seem fairly farcical.

It is only by understanding how profoundly and completely the role of banks in society has changed between the relatively recent past and today that we can understand how momentous are the changes in the retail financial services industry that new, high-tech delivery channels have ushered in. Looking back at the nineteenth century is a useful preparatory exercise for investigating where banking has come from, but, to set the issues discussed in this book in their proper context in terms of the evolution of banks, we need to look at a much more recent period: the past 20 years. This is a particularly useful period to scrutinize, because the careers of many senior people working in banking today were already well under way 20 years ago. One can therefore bring one's own personal experience as a banker to bear when this period is under consideration.

Before considering the key changes that have taken place in banking during this period, we need to give some thought to geographical matters. *The Future of Banking* looks at the future of banking from a global perspective, but nobody lives in a country called 'global' – it is just a convenient term to discuss the sum of all the world's countries, each of which have their own prevailing national social characteristics, economic conditions and challenges. This book, however, deliberately sets out to provide a global perspective on an industry that, by definition, is based around national banking industries that operate within national regulatory and procedural frameworks, which vary from one country to another, although not usually to a significant extent.

The past 20 years have seen enormous, wide-ranging and permanent changes to the face of the world's banking industry. The days epitomized by the entry in Fischer's journal or by numerous portraits of bankers in Victorian novels, the days when banking was a genteel, formal, even snobbish, business carried out by people who were trained almost solely in manual calculation and fiduciary practice, are over.

Retail and corporate banking has had to adjust to the changing needs of societies, where people not only regard a bank account as a *right* rather than a *privilege*, but also are aware that their business is valuable to the bank and, if the bank does not look after them, they can easily take their business elsewhere.

Wholesale banking has also had to adjust to a marketplace that is similarly knowledgeable about the various deals that different banks are offering; a marketplace that can, for maximum transparency, see these deals presented simultaneously on a computer screen; a marketplace that has access to a dazzling range of financial instruments in which to invest and that can be set to work in a great number of ways to make money do what its owners want it to do. Specialized areas of wholesale banking, such as asset management, have seen enormous changes – from the ubiquity of technology providing a bewildering range of screen-based valuation and analytical information to the introduction of important new regulatory measures, such as the Global Investment Performance Standards (GIPS), which came into force on 1 January 2000 and compliance with which is increasingly important for asset managers wishing to be taken seriously in beauty parades. Meanwhile, in the United States, recent passage of the Gramm-Leach-Bliley Financial Services Modernisation Act is expected to transform the financial landscape, allowing banks, insurance and securities firms to merge and become truly diversified and full service financial services organisations.

Indeed, technological and regulatory changes have had such an impact on the banking industry during the past 20 years that a good case can be made for saying that they are the most important changes to have occurred in the industry, apart from ones that are directly due to the changing nature of society itself. The interview subjects in this book, not surprisingly, have plenty to say about technology – indeed, it is of such great importance that they tend to take its impact for granted.

The precise nature of the impact technology has had on the banking industry since the early 1980s is difficult to assess, because the intimacy of the relationship between the industry and its technology means that it is impossible to separate the two. Technology is as much part of the banking industry today as a ship's engine is part of the ship. And, like a ship's engine, technology drives the whole thing forward.

Some time during the early 1980s, technology in banking ceased being simply a convenient tool for automating processes that had traditionally been carried out manually by clerks condemned to spending much of their working lives on extremely tedious ledger work that had to be carried out with the utmost accuracy. This application of technology as a way of automating formerly manual processes was of the greatest importance and, of course, it still is, but it does not represent the real cutting edge of technological implementations in the banking industry today. What does is the use of technology as a revolutionary means of delivering services to customers. This way of using technology was first explored seriously within the retail banking industry during the late 1970s in the United States and the early 1980s in the rest of the world.

Someone somewhere realized that the way in which automated teller machines (ATMs) were being used – as an additional convenience for privileged, wealthy customers – was all wrong. The bright spark in question realized that the people who most needed access to ATMs were not, in fact, wealthy individuals who could visit a town centre whenever they wished, but, rather, blue-collar workers working out of town in factory complexes during the day, who had real problems ever visiting their bank at all during their somewhat primeval opening hours. After all, let us not forget that, until even the late 1980s in some countries, banks often shut their doors during the week at three o'clock or half past three and did not open at all on Saturday. For blue-collar customers, ATMs were a godsend, giving them access to cash around the clock, at least once the people running banks cottoned on to the fact that if ATMs really were to have a chance of fulfilling their potential, they had to be open, ideally, all the time, including of course public holidays.

Once ATM use was made available to the majority of a bank's customers, rather than only the privileged and wealthy few, the enormous popularity of this way of delivering services to customers made even the most old-fashioned bankers sit up and realize that a whole new dimension in customer service had opened up to the banking world. Nor did it take long for bankers to realize that the cost of giving a customer a cash withdrawal facility via an ATM was very significantly lower than the cost of such a transaction taking place in a branch – up to a sixteenth of the cost.

Not surprisingly, banks wasted no time in implementing more and more ATMs and, before long, they also realized that they could create collaborative ATM networks with other banks and allow customers to share these networks. The enormous benefits of the shared network approach was that banks were able to offer customers a nationwide (and, eventually, international) network of ATMs at a fraction of the cost of deploying such a network entirely by themselves, even had they been able to afford it. Sophisticated transaction switching services meant that it was possible for a bank to give the impression to the customer (not that any deceit was involved) that the customer was only dealing with his or her bank, even when using an ATM installed and operated by a competitor.

The lesson that banks learnt over ATMs meant that they were extremely receptive to new types of approaches to delivering services and payment facilities remotely. Electronic funds transfer at point of sale (EFTPoS) was also taken up enthusiastically, both by banks and their customers, as soon as the technology became readily available in the mid 1980s. A few years later, telephone banking systems began to be deployed, although some banks insisted on giving their customers access directly to live operators rather than using automated response systems. Today, Internet banking is becoming more and more popular, as is banking via digital television. Beyond doubt, a substantial part of the future of banking business lies in a banking environment that is less and less branch-based and where customers access banking services remotely.

This does not mean that the branch is completely dead. Indeed, the future fate of the bank branch is one of the most hotly debated issues in today's banking industry.

With the exception of pathological misers, people do not interact with their banks for fun. Instead, they do so in order to obtain access, in various ways and in various manifestations, to money and payment facilities they need in order to live their lives. Banks, in fact, offer only what might be termed a secondary level of utility to customers: customers use the money access that banks provide as a means of buying the things they really want from retailers who offer them a primary level of utility. This, incidentally, explains why banks have so much to fear from retailers who decide to move into the banking industry. The very fact of the retailers' experience and reputation in providing customers with a primary level of satisfaction means they often have a head start when it comes to competing with traditional banks. The real point here, though, is that, because banks only offer a secondary level of utility to customers,

customers naturally want to get the interaction with their bank over as quickly as possible and then get on with doing something they really want to do or with buying something they really want to buy. Consider your own experience as a customer. When you 'pop to' your bank as part of the things you are doing in town, how often is the popping in the highlight of your excursion?

Of course, it isn't, it's something you do on the way to having lunch with a friend or buying something you want at your favourite consumer electronics shop or whatever else. It is precisely this fact – that customers want to carry out their banking transactions with maximum speed – that explains why new types of delivery channels that allow rapid, convenient, accurate delivery of banking services to customers are so popular: customers enjoy being able to get their banking chores done quickly and easily.

The question of the role of the bank branch in the future of banking is more difficult than it appears at first sight.

Certainly, it is true that, in general, customers use bank branches less and less. Many customers visit their branch only about once a month or, even, much less, while some hardly bother going into their branch at all. Yet, while the demand for branches is certainly reducing all the time, this does not mean that it is necessarily fated to disappear entirely, any more than the increasing proliferation of mobile telephones mean that landline telephone kiosks will disappear completely. It is possible, though not certain, that, just as there will always be people who need to use telephone kiosks (apart from anything else, people may have lost or mislaid their mobile telephones or may have left them at home), there will always be people who need to visit their branch.

Furthermore, branches remain comparatively popular to organizations with corporate accounts (including small businesses), mainly because businesses like to be able to discuss things in person with a banker in a branch. Also, some older people (including some older, wealthier people) like to be able to 'pop in' to their branch. There is a need for some good research about why this is: if it is simply that older people are less adept with new-style technology than younger ones, then, of course, in time, by a natural process, the need for branches will start to erode. However, if, as may well be the case, older people *inherently* feel more comfortable with being able to do their banking at a physical branch, this may limit the extent to which banks can afford to get rid of branches entirely, especially branches that cater to wealthy customers.

On this particular point, in April 2000, the UK retail bank Barclays suffered considerable bad publicity stemming from its decision to close more than a hundred branches, almost all of which were, tellingly, located in economically depressed areas. The whole thing was a public relations disaster for Barclays Bank, which seems to have misguidedly thought that it should close all the branches within a short time frame and get the bad news over with quickly. The public outcry that followed may tempt one to believe that there was a backlash against branch closures, but, in fact, the branches remained closed and the story soon died down.

If Barclays had managed the PR side of the development more adeptly, it might have taken steps to emphasize what was, in fact, the case: that, in most of the towns in question it was the last bank in town anyway. For example, between 1988 and 2000, the UK clearing bank the NatWest cut its branch network from 3,086 branches to 1,712, while HSBC (formerly the Midland Bank in the UK) cut its UK branch network from 2,090 branches to 1,622.

Barclays, whose closed branches were located mainly in Britain's less than profitable remote, rural communities, attributed this phenomenon of branch closures to the fact that fewer and fewer customers were visiting their branches and preferring to conduct their banking business by telephone and, increasingly, via the Internet. The story of what has happened at Barclays Bank is being repeated every day at banks throughout the world.

The kind of enormous and far-reaching developments in banking discussed above have gone hand-in-hand with the blurring of demarcations between different types of banking and financial industry activity. Five particular reasons can be identified for this blurring having come about.

Still, there are emerging signs, particularly in some northern European countries, that the tide towards internet banking and, therefore, the demise of the local branch are rising faster and faster. Aided by the popularity of WAP mobile-phone technology, Swedish-Finnish Merita Nordbanken now has 1.2 million commercial and private internet customers in Finland and Sweden, more than 20% of its total customers. Some 62% of all equity trading by the bank's customers was done via the internet in December 1999, while 16% of all consumer loans were negotiated electronically. The expectation by the bank is that this number will reach 30% by year-end.

First, governments have implemented philosophies and policies based on effecting an increase in competition in order to maximize efficiency, both at a domestic level and for international competitiveness. These policies have had a particularly heavy impact on the banking business, and have tended to create new regulatory frameworks that take any mystique out of what constitutes the qualifications for entry into the market. New players can enter the marketplace as long as they have the money to do so and conform to entry requirements. This has, naturally, tended to encourage the creation of large new financial institutions (whether created out of traditional players, newcomers or a combination of the two) that have sufficient presence and financial muscle to operate simultaneously in several financial sectors, such as retail banking, wholesale banking, insurance and asset management.

Second, the prodigious impact of information technology on the banking industry has tended to make old demarcations less relevant because the new technology creates infrastructures that allow a player to carry out a wide range of banking and financial services, again simultaneously.

This powerful technology is extremely expensive, which explains why an important consequence of the blurring of demarcations is the creation of enormous global banks that have the capital needed to invest in the customer service frameworks and the technology required to compete in the new dispensation.

Third, banks have had to respond to the increased prosperity of their customers and to customers' desire to get the best deal possible. This has tended to encourage banks to extend their activities into other areas. Thus, the traditional demarcation of a bank as an institution that simply takes deposits and operates current accounts no longer applies.

Doubtless customers would, in an ideal world, prefer to bank with just one bank and buy all their financial services from it. In reality, though, customers know they can get a better deal from shopping around. Today, customers have less loyalty to their bank than they have ever had, many customers having relationships with several institutions.

Fourth, banks have had to develop and extend their services to accommodate the fact that their customers are now far more mobile – both nationally and internationally – than they have ever been before. An example is the creation of international ATM networks, which allow customers to draw funds in local currencies when abroad using their domestic ATM cards. Not only are demarcation barriers breaking down at a national level, they are doing so internationally, too.

Fifth, banks have every motivation to move into new sectors of activity in order to try to deal with the problem that, if they only offer banking services, they are condemned forever to provide only a secondary level of utility to customers. Facing up to this problem is closely related to dealing with the threat of *disintermediation*. This term means the omission of an intermediary – usually a traditional intermediary – from a process. It can happen in almost any industry, but it is a particular problem for traditional banks, precisely because, as organizations only offering customers a secondary level of utility, there is a serious danger that retailers offering a primary level of utility may be able to muscle in on the banks' territory and win substantial amounts of business from them or even make banks completely redundant.

Banks have three basic ways of dealing with the threat of disintermediation. They can:

- maximize the appeal of their products and services and the efficiency, speed, convenience and usefulness of the means by which these products and services are delivered;
- team up with retailers offering primary levels of utility and create mutually beneficial joint ventures (or even mergers) with them;
- extend their activities into new areas, whether these are areas of the financial sector (for example, a bank decides to go into the business of selling insurance direct) or non-financial areas (say, a bank decides to acquire an estate agency chain, (again, this last development tends to blur demarcation barriers between financial institutions)).

PART I

AN OVERVIEW

THE INTERVIEWS

This book contains detailed interviews with 26 people whose specializations cover many aspects of the retail and wholesale banking industry. Where do they think banking is going in the future? What do they want to see from the regulators of their particular niche of the banking industry? What do they expect customers to want from the new and exciting delivery channels that are coming into being? What major trends are going to matter during the next five and ten years? How do they see their own financial institution's future?

These are just some of the probing questions that Reuters journalists posed to the interviewees. In this overview, we profile many of the ideas and beliefs that were most widely held by the respondents.

What exactly will be the nature of the future of banking? These pages and the interviews themselves, to be found in Part II of the book, provide you with comprehensive insight into where banking is going.

For your convenience, and to aid the obviously demanding task of summarizing the content of 26 interviews in a relatively small space, we present this summary of key viewpoints under a series of headings. The headings arise naturally from the nature of the responses. We have arranged the headings in a logical order that takes you from general issues relating to how banks organize and structure themselves on to areas more connected with operational strategy. The headings are as follows.

CONSOLIDATION

The material presented under this heading looks at the phenomenon of banks merging to create organizations that are both larger and more streamlined.

GLOBALIZATION

This follows naturally on from the issue of consolidation. The material here discusses issues arising from the creation of banks or banking groups that literally bestride the world or at least aspire to do so. It should again be emphasized, though, as mentioned above, that nobody lives in the country known as 'global' – every global bank must, first and foremost, be an expert in all the national markets where it operates. Customers are not interested in its global strengths, but, rather, in its strength in the national market where they run their lives.

THE ROLE OF IT

When one analyzes the role of IT in banking, it soon becomes clear that it is a force that both makes change happen and is a response to change. In many industrial and commercial sectors, technology is only implemented in direct response to customer demand, but the dynamic of the use of technology in the banking industry is more subtle than this.

One cannot really say, for example, that Internet banking came about because there was a customer demand for it. Until customers saw an Internet banking system in action, they had no way of knowing whether or not they wanted to make use of such a thing. The same applies to all other new types of channel for delivering services to customers, whether these are automated teller machines (ATMs), electronic funds transfer at point of sale (EFTPoS) or debit systems, telephone banking systems and, indeed, any kind of remote banking mechanism. In these cases, technology has to be seen as a sort of driver of demand rather than a consequence of it.

Yet, if we take a deeper view, it is clear that technology is a response to profound changes in customer demand. In retail banking, for example, the actual specific implementation may be driven by what has become available at a technical level, but the overall *need* for the implementation has stemmed from sweeping changes in customer expectations, lifestyle, ambitions and prosperity. In wholesale banking, the enormous impact that technology has had during the past 20 years is more of a direct response to customer demand for rapid, accurate and global access to information and funds.

INFORMATION SECURITY

The importance of this issue in banking today and in the future can hardly be overstated. It is as intimately related to the operational side of a bank's IT as an airplane's wings are related to the safety of the passengers. In any event, the best kind of IT systems for banks come complete with built-in security. Such security is an absolute necessity.

INTERNET BANKING

This is a term on every retail banker's lips and the dangers of getting left behind by the competition in this area are giving many bankers sleepless nights. It is incontestable that Internet banking has yet to achieve its potential. In many countries, the initial take-up of many Internet banking systems has actually been disappointing with the exception of countries such as Finland and Sweden where its use is rapidly growing. What is also incontestable, however, is that we have so far barely glimpsed the possibilities of this new delivery channel for retail banking. It is perfectly feasible that by around the year 2010, the majority of people in developed countries will carry out most of their banking via the Internet, possibly even using remotely loaded stored value cards that can be loaded via the Internet and thus act as a facilitator of a form of remote cash withdrawal.

RISK

The past 20 years have seen great advances in banks' ability to understand the nature of the risk that faces them and develop methods for assessing it. Following on naturally from this are methods that enable risk to be minimized.

Risk impinges on most areas of a bank's activities. Examples of types of risk with which they must concern themselves on a daily basis are:

- credit risk;
- interest rate risk;
- currency risk;
- custody risk;
- market risk, that is, the risk that a stock market in which the bank invests will fall;
- technology risk – the risk that a particular implementation of technology will not live up to expectations;
- indeed, any other risk that may involve the bank in possible loss.

Modern economic theory and investment science, such as modern portfolio theory, has furnished banks and other types of financial institutions with a wide range of methodologies for assessing and evaluating risk. These are designed to allow banks to assess the risk both of specific areas of their activity and also provide a composite picture of risk throughout their organization. The methodologies themselves are extremely ingenious and often make use of algorithms that have been worked out by academics specializing in risk management. However, no matter how clever the methodologies are, there is never any gainsaying the fundamental fact that risk and return are proportional to each other and that a higher return always goes hand in hand with higher risk.

Nor have experts at risk management ever achieved much success at forecasting calamitous events such as shock falls in a particular stock market index. However, condemning these risk management experts for this failing is a little like blaming doctors for being unable to abolish death. Risk can, unquestionably, be reduced and, above all, understood using these modern techniques and every bank, very sensibly, wants to make maximum use of them.

The interview subjects provide abundant evidence of the importance of effective risk management. Increasingly, it is being realized that risk management is the hub of what banking is all about.

BLURRING OF DEMARCATION BETWEEN FINANCIAL FUNCTIONS

We have already seen that this is an important phenomenon in the banking industry today. Indeed, it is a major trend and it is getting more and more important. Ironically, perhaps, it is going hand in hand with the continual trend towards customers being increasingly ready to 'buy' their financial services from a range of different institutions. This should not surprise us unduly – after all, changes in government regulations have been substantially responsible for making this blurring of demarcations happen and the government regulations were introduced in the first place in order to encourage competition.

COMPETITION

It should be self-explanatory, from all the above discussion, that competition in the banking industry has increased dramatically over the past 20 years. Government initiatives to increase competition, combined with the democratizing effect of technology (anybody who can afford the technology can implement it and new players may even have an advantage in this respect as they are not encumbered with dated, even obsolete, 'legacy systems'), have meant that the level of competition has reached unprecedented heights. Indeed, there is presently excessive competition, which explains the large numbers of mergers, takeovers and consolidations generally in most niches of the banking industry, especially over the past few years.

NEW ENTRANTS

Many bankers would be inclined to call these new entrants 'gatecrashers'. They, however, regard themselves rather more neutrally, as 'newcomers'. This latter term encompasses any organization that does not have any history of activity within the financial industry sector in which it chooses to compete. They are the most virulent competitive threat of all to traditional banks. Newcomers are here to stay and the impact they have on the traditional banking scene is only likely to increase in the future. They need to be considered in some detail.

Newcomers generally come in a great variety of shapes and sizes, as do the particular type of newcomers that are entering the banking industry today.

Of course, to call them newcomers at all is slightly to beg the question as far as their status is concerned. From their point of view, they are not gatecrashers, but are simply exploiting an exciting and potentially profitable commercial opportunity. However, no traditional type of bank can afford to be so philosophical about the challenge posed by these newcomers: the challenge is a frightening one and believe the banking system offers significant opportunities.

In terms of the nature of the organizations that are coming into this industry, they could potentially consist of almost any type of organization that has the financial resources to launch a workable virtual banking resource, maintain it during the first couple of years when profitability is likely to be low or non-existent and believe the banking system offers significant opportunities.

We should not rule any large organizations out as potential entrants. After all, if General Motors can buy and make a success of an organization such as Electronic Data Services (EDS), which is in a very different business from that of making motor cars, it should not be difficult for any large organization to move into banking.

As one might expect, the type of organization most likely to move into banking is the large retailer with a substantial customer base and high profile among the general public. After retailers, the next most likely class of organization to move into banking is the financial services organization (such as insurance companies and investment companies) that already has a track record – often a very lengthy track record – of supplying financial services to the public. With the repeal of the Depression era Glass-Stegall Act in the US, which strictly circumscribed the activities of banks, investment and insurance companies for decades, banks are expected to face even greater competition from the insurance and investment sector. The next most likely class of organization to get involved in banking appears to be telecommunications organizations, which already have networks set up that can be used to deliver virtual banking services.

Real-life experience suggests that telecommunications companies are unlikely to enter the banking business without first teaming up with a business partner with access to some of the know-how associated with marketing retail or financial services to the general public. However, the first two categories of organization mentioned above are usually perfectly happy to enter the banking industry themselves without forming any joint venture, although they may need some additional expertise. Sometimes retailers do join forces with a bank in order to provide a major new range of banking services, but, where this is the case, the retailer will usually avoid promoting the bank that is the business partner, but will ensure that the new banking service is seen very much as being associated specifically with the retailer's own name.

Whatever the nature of the newcomer, it will obviously have decided that entering the banking business makes sense to it from a commercial standpoint. In order to investigate the nature of the competitive threat posed by these newcomers, we need to confront the precise reasons for their being so well placed to become bankers and also look at problems they face in their endeavour.

Reasons for newcomers being well placed to enter the banking business

Assuming that we are talking here about a newcomer that fits into one of the three categories listed above (large retailer, large financial services company, a large telecommunications company), the reasons for entering the banking business are as follows, in descending order of importance.

They will have a known brand name
It is infinitely easier for an organization to win the public's confidence in relation to a new venture if it has already won their confidence with another type of venture. Large retailers have, by definition, a considerable number of loyal customers who associate them with the generally positive experience of doing their weekly shopping on the retailer's premises. The notion of the experiences being positive is important. The importance of weekly visits to supermarkets and superstores is being increasingly recognized by sociologists as an important part of the fabric of modern life. Some are even going so far as to argue that these visits replace an earlier generation's visits to church.

In the case of financial services companies, the association with agreeable weekly shopping visits will not be there in the same way, but this should be readily compensated for by the solid reputation the financial services company will presumably have built up.

Telecommunications companies have the least advantage in this respect as, even though their name is likely to be well known to the public, there will be little truly advantageous brand association. Most people take their telecommunications companies for granted and do not think much about the name of the company that supplies this basic utility. One might say that telecommunications companies are handicapped by the fact that their service is supplied in a virtual way from the outset!

They will have a large customer base to market the new service to
This point is fairly self-explanatory. Next to the brand name, its customer base will be its most valuable resource, both in terms of its entry to the banking sector and of its commercial activities generally.

Furthermore, modern marketing methods – including a variety of methods that enable the buying potential of different customers to be assessed with considerable accuracy – greatly assists with maximizing the success rate from marketing new types of services – such as banking services – to customers.

They will have the financial resources
Entering the banking business is extremely expensive and, as we have seen, is unlikely to produce much in the way of return for the first year or so. Consequently, it is essential that the organization entering the market is well funded. The organization also needs financial credibility and creditworthiness to a level beyond any suspicion that it would ever default on its liabilities. All developed countries nowadays have extremely stringent regulatory requirements that any organization entering the banking sector or, for that matter, already in it, must comply with.

In the case of large retailers, financial services organizations or telecommunications companies, the possession of the requisite levels of financial resources will almost always be in place. Furthermore, these types of organization frequently have better credit ratings than many traditional banks (this is particularly true in the United States). While the average customer is unlikely to be aware of the credit rating of a traditional bank compared with that of a newcomer – or, indeed, be aware of credit ratings of large organizations at all – organizations with better credit ratings can borrow money (by issuing bonds) more cheaply than those with less good ratings, which gives the former an in-built commercial advantage.

They will be experienced at operating in a competitive environment
In the vast majority of developed countries, the banking industry has been extremely competitive for at least ten years. Prior to that, restrictions on who could enter the industry, coupled with the persistence of traditional ideas that having a bank account was some kind of privilege, meant that many traditional banks were not all especially effective at operating in a highly competitive environment.

Even though the time when banking was, arguably, too respectable and uncompetitive for its own good has past, many traditional banks still, to some extent, appear to regard fierce competition as somewhat below them and consider that they have a God-given right to their customer base.

Newcomers to the industry, especially if they are in the three categories identified and, consequently, used to operating within highly competitive markets (admittedly, this is less true of telecommunications companies, but it still applies to some extent) will be adept at competing fiercely, so they have an edge over traditional banks in this respect.

Problems newcomers may face

In addition to the advantages newcomers are likely to enjoy from the perspective of competing with traditional banks, they will also inevitably face some problems. These, listed in order of severity, are as follows.

They will not have a track record
This is an obvious problem for newcomers. It amounts to just about the only thing the traditional banks have going for them in a competitive sense in relation to the threat posed by newcomers. The public will not automatically associate the newcomer with being a provider of banking services so the newcomer will have to launch a vigorous marketing initiative to project itself in this way to its customers.

However, there is ample evidence from newcomers that have already started to succeed in the banking industry that customers quickly get used to the idea of a new organization offering banking services, especially if the organization is one they are already familiar with.

Furthermore, the point that newcomers will not have experience of offering banking services and delivering them is not really a valid one, as the whole point of the virtual banking revolution is that an organization can buy in the requisite delivery technology, as well as specialized banking expertise (from a consultancy or simply by hiring banking specialists), and set up a bank from scratch.

They may only have unprofitable customers

This is not such an obvious problem as the first, but it is likely to be more persistent. The point is that newcomers to any banking industry frequently find themselves landed with customers who are not particularly creditworthy and not especially rich. This is because more creditworthy and wealthier customers are likely to have their banking arrangements already deeply embedded in a relationship with a traditional bank. As such, they are unlikely to want to change those arrangements, unless a very good incentive is offered to them for doing so. Of course, newcomers will, from the outset, offer products that provide the very incentive that may be required, but this does not greatly alter the fact that the more profitable types of customers are unlikely to be successfully wooed by newcomers.

There is also the status factor, especially in countries such as the United States and United Kingdom, where personal status – and implicit differences in status among different people – is an important part of general culture. For example, a London-based customer of Coutts Bank is unlikely to want to become a customer of Sainsbury's bank without a great deal of persuasion. While this is a fairly extreme example (as Coutts is a particularly traditional and exclusive bank) the status issue is always likely to be a big factor for people who do not like the idea of banking with an organization they usually see as a supermarket.

Some newcomers might agree that this problem is not as severe as it might seem at first sight, because there is plenty of money to be made from less wealthy customers, as long as stringent credit testing procedures are put in place. Furthermore, wealthier customers might move to the newcomer in time if the newcomer is perceived as offering a consistently good deal.

The rapid growth of international private banking is another example of wealthy individuals preferring a tailor-made approach to financial services rather than the impersonal and mass-market strategy of new entrants. In Europe, the private banking market is conservatively estimated in the hundreds of billions of dollars, with Switzerland occupying a premier position in attracting such wealth. UBS and Credit Suisse are Europe's top-two portfolio managers, in terms of volume managed, and are global leaders in the management of crossborder money for wealthy international investors. UBS manages in excess of Swfr 1.57bn for institutional and private investors; Credit Suisse, more than Swfr 930bn.

Their entry will only be credible if they use reliable and staff highly trained in customer service
This is not so much a problem as a warning. Clearly, a newcomer's technology and remote delivery systems will have to work to the highest level of efficiency if the competitive credibility of the newcomer is to be established and maintained.

Similarly, customer service staff deployed by the newcomer must be of the highest calibre in terms of their personal qualities and highly trained in the often difficult and sensitive business of handling bank accounts and providing advice regarding financial matters.

Fortunately for their customers and themselves, newcomers understand that the technological infrastructure and staff capabilities need to be of the utmost quality, that this is essential. If you are delivering a banking service via remote channels and making use of telephone staff to assist customers, these are your only resources and they have got to be superb.

The competitive power of newcomers around the world

The role of newcomers in competing with traditional banks by using virtual financial services varies considerably around the world, depending on a variety of factors relating to the commercial and academic conditions in the country in question.

Generally, the factors dictating what level of competitive power the newcomers are likely to enjoy will be as follows.

How much scope the traditional banking system has left
This may seem a fairly tautological factor, but there has to be some slack in the banking industry if any newcomer is likely to have a chance. Experience shows that the major area of potential opportunity is simply the relative slowness of traditional banks to offer virtual delivery channels, because they are still branch-based. This, unquestionably, creates an opportunity for newcomers to move into the market by offering such services, which, for reasons we have already seen, are extremely attractive to customers.

There are also, clearly, opportunities for newcomers to offer services that meet customers' needs more precisely than those being offered by traditional banks and products – such as new types of accounts – with benefits (mainly in the area of access, interest on deposits and banking facilities) that customers may prefer to existing products offered by traditional banks.

Their brand strength in the market

We have already seen that the newcomer's brand strength is an essential resource. Clearly, it is not impossible for a completely unknown newcomer to launch a successful market initiative, but this is much more difficult than it is for a newcomer that already has a name that is familiar to people. The additional financial expenditure necessary to become known may prove an overwhelming disincentive to the would-be newcomer.

The strength of their existing customer base

Similarly, it will be much easier for a newcomer to make an impact in the market if it has an existing base of customers who can be targeted as prospective customers of the new products and services.

A benign regulatory climate

Clearly, no newcomer can make an impact in a country's banking sector if the newcomer is forbidden by regulation from entering the sector. The fact that, in most developed countries, the regulatory climate is, generally, favourable for such incursions by newcomers should not blind us to the fact that this is far from the case in every country. In many developed countries – especially areas with lower populations – there are extremely good reasons for the number of service providers in the banking sector being kept relatively small and for possibly unscrupulous outsiders to be kept out.

THE EURO

The euro was first introduced on 1 January 2000, and is now locked into an implementation schedule that seems to make it inevitable that, by around 2010, even countries that are not especially euro-friendly (such as Britain) will have yielded to the inevitable and will be using the euro as a principal currency, if not as *the* principal currency.

REGULATION

No bank that wishes to compete successfully can afford to ignore the role of regulation in the forward thrust of the industry. The point is that regulators – which are, by definition, adopting an industry-wide view – are always going to be 'bigger' and more influential than banks themselves, which are only one player in the industry.

There are two major types of regulators, the activities of which are important to the banking industry. First, there is the national government itself, which acts as a kind of 'regulator of last resort' to all industrial and commercial sectors. The government's word is, literally, law.

Recent years have, however, seen a distinct increase in the trend for governments to take steps to encourage industries to regulate themselves, especially professional sectors where the activity embodies a high cerebral content. This has stemmed partly from a growing belief that the best regulator of a profession is usually the profession itself, the members of which are most in tune with what the profession needs by way of regulation and are likely to be the first to spot malefactors. Another increasingly important factor here is a general perception among politicians that governments ought not to spend time regulating professional industries.

The second type of regulator is the industry body – either national or international – that creates new regulations, standards or other types of measure and then launches an industry-wide initiative to foster its implementation, again either nationally or internationally.

Industry bodies within the banking business have always been extremely resourceful and often highly creative. This has been especially true during the period since around 1980, which has seen, for example, the formation of the highly influential Group of 30 – the recommendations of which have led to sweeping changes in the clearance and settlement procedures of the world's securities industry – and the more recently formed group of industry figures, which implemented with remarkable promptness the Global Investment Performance Standards (GIPS) for the asset management industry.

DEVELOPMENTS IN ASSET MANAGEMENT

The importance of this last niche sector of the financial industry was well represented in the responses that several interview subjects made to the questions. What is interesting about the asset management business is that active management continues to be extremely popular, despite the continued use of indexation and the curious fact that few active managers succeed in beating the index on a regular basis. The clients of active managers, it would seem, provide continual proof of the poet Alexander Pope's maxim that hope springs eternal in the human breast. On the other hand, maybe their asset managers are simply still getting away with providing highly selective details of active fund performance. This is precisely what compliance with GIPS is designed to prevent. It will be most interesting to see what effect widespread compliance with GIPS has on the willingness of pension funds and other clients to trust their money to the difficult and unpredictable business of active fund management.

The discussion here now moves on to looking at the above topics in detail. The quoted comments all come from the interviewees. The interviews themselves are given in full in Part II.

CONSOLIDATION

The interviewees clearly took it for granted that, in banking, they were engaged in a battle to maintain, or establish, supremacy in an increasingly competitive market, and that the consolidation of their resources with other banks could play a major role in achieving this. What reasons are the banks themselves giving for their desire to acquire other banks and increase in size?

Angel Corcostegui, Chief Executive, Banco Santander Central Hispano (BSCH), remarked:

> The consolidation taking place in the banking industry is a strategic response to a business background demanding greater competitiveness and efficiency. Banks are seeking greater size precisely to compete better in a market transformed by globalization, the demographic transformation and a technological revolution, but the creation of more and more large banks increases competition. If we look at the world bank ranking by assets, we find that the five leading firms are financial groups created from 1998 and 1999 mergers, and they are, on average, four times as big as the top five entities just ten years ago.

Peter Wuffli, Chief Executive Officer, UBS Brinson, commented:

> We see several forces that favour continued consolidation. One of them is certainly globalization – of client needs and of assets and asset classes.
>
> The second reason I believe consolidation will continue is based on the breadth of resources needed to solve client problems. Breadth is needed in terms of portfolio consulting, education, marketing and the fund-structuring capabilities necessary within portfolio management.
>
> The third factor, which is also tied to size and resources, is talent development. People with a lot of talent want to work with other talented people. You need to have that strength, a certain global scope and a certain level of breadth in order to attract, retain and motivate the most talented people.

He concluded:

> So, I think there are forces that support size, scale and global reach. This does not imply a need for large bureaucratically led rigid organizational structures. I think the challenge will be to capture the benefits of size, while at the same time staying alert, entrepreneurial, client-centric and global in thinking.

BSCH's Corcostegui said:

> There is a limit to consolidation advantages in terms of economies of scale, but size is not just important for achieving lower costs through economies of scale. Size is also necessary to enable risk diversification, improved service quality to an increasingly global clientele and attract the best human resources.
>
> Once the laws and regulations of EU member countries do finally become harmonized, I think there's going to be vastly more consolidation. It's just beginning and that's because there really isn't harmonization of laws and regulations.
>
> Consolidation in the European banking sector is proving fast and intense. The euro pushes our sector to remodel itself in European terms, as it has eliminated national currencies as a barrier between domestic markets. For this reason, banks first seek size in order to compete on a European level.
>
> There has been continuous news of bank mergers since the beginning of the year [2000]. It is true that the sector is in the full throes of transformation. Probably, by the time euro notes and coins arrive, we will have a significantly different European banking map than the one we know today.

Emphasizing that the road to consolidation of an integrated European bank sector was not free of obstacles, Corcostegui said:

> There are technical barriers, too, such as the different tax, accounting, good management and supervisory systems. These technical barriers, however, will be gradually resolved as European bank consolidation advances.

He added:

> The creation of a European banking industry is also being hampered by some national authorities' insistence on championing the domestic nature of their financial sectors. This is delaying the creation of pan-

> European firms capable of efficiently producing and marketing financial products throughout the European market. Transnational consolidation is the natural tendency of banking in an integrated monetary area. We are already seeing this in the US, where the elimination of the restrictions on inter-state bank mergers have given way to an unstoppable process of mergers and acquisitions.

For Corcostegui, the pan-European financial environment created by European Monetary Union (the EMU) offers the European financial system the chance to compete with the North Americans on a global scale. However, he stipulates that there is an important proviso:

> For this to occur, it is necessary to create leading European banks that are sufficiently large and competitive. In short, protectionist attitudes only hamper the process of consolidation in European banking, which is not just a natural response to the new size of the market, but would also raise the financial sector's efficiency and its international competitiveness.

With the regards to consolidation among American banks, Roger Ferguson, Federal Reserve Board Vice Chairman commented:

> ...I don't think the US will reach a stage where we have a small handful, or two handfuls, of universal banks covering the nation. There's still room for very vibrant community banks and regional banks. Their comparative advantages have to do with their ability to understand the needs of their customers and to serve them in a way that is more, if you will, 'high touch'. I think large institutions will have some advantages of scale and the ability to invest in technologies.

Dick Kovacevich, Chief Executive Officer of Wells Fargo, was very conscious of the practical, commercial issues resulting from consolidation:

> As we do more and more with fewer customers, we can do it more economically and give better value to the customer. The potential negative is that if you become so big and so removed from the customers, you don't serve them well, but, in a way, I don't see that as a negative. If that's what happens, the customers are going to go somewhere else. I think there's nothing but positive from the customer's standpoint of consolidation. It might be negative from a particular company's standpoint because if they fail to deliver good service or fail to be customer-focused, they'll die and there'll always be someone to take their place.

Alessandro Profumo, Chief Executive Officer of UniCredito Italiano, discussed the specific way in which consolidation had happened in his own country:

> Consolidation in Italy happened very quickly. Italy's banking system was extremely fragmented, so it started to react ahead of other European countries, which waited until the birth of the euro.

The general consensus was that consolidation was more an economic and cost imperative than an operational necessity. For example, Marshall Carter, Chairman and Chief Executive Officer of State Street Corporation, when asked if technology leads to more efficient ways of servicing financial needs and thereby reduces the need for the formation of mammoth organizations, answered, 'yes ... yes, definitely.'

What about the future of the consolidation trend? Katsuyuku Sugita, President and Chief Executive Officer, Dai-Ichi Bank, said:

> The trend towards consolidation will continue for at least the next ten years, and the pace will likely accelerate for the next five years. The investment in information technology will increase and the need to offer a wider range of financial services will get stronger. Against this backdrop, mergers and acquisitions, initiated primarily by major banks, will continue for some time, but it is not desirable for companies to become too big because they would be more difficult to manage.

Of course, the practical aspect of actually managing an organization that has been created as the result of consolidation must never be underestimated. All the same, experienced senior managers of banks are used to managing large organizations anyway and, ultimately, whether the organization they are managing employs 50,000 people or 100,000, the management challenges are similarly formidable.

The real threat to the momentum in favour of consolidation surely stems from the problem of getting the fit right and making all the pieces yield the synergies they are supposed to yield, especially in terms of the personnel issues, which have tripped up the initially most enthusiastic merger or takeover plans. This, as one might imagine, is a particular problem when it comes to cross-border consolidation.

As William B. Harrison, Jr, Chief Executive Officer of Chase Manhattan, observes:

> Cross-border consolidation in the financial services sector has not happened very quickly because there are huge cultural differences

> and, more importantly, different return-on-equity requirements, so it's just not as attractive to do.

Dr Henning Schulte-Noelle, Chief Executive of Allianz Insurance, comments:

> Consolidation is being driven by three key factors: the need to provide competitive pricing, which is clearly a function of investment size; the growing sophistication of investors, both on the institutional as well as on the retail side; and, hence, the increasing demand for more international investments and the need to accompany clients into whatever markets they go.

What of the after-the-event practical experience of those who have had to live through consolidation? In the United Kingdom, one of the most successful mergers of recent years is reckoned to have been that between the Lloyds Bank and the TSB, which an earlier generation knew as the Trustee Savings Bank. Sir Brian Pitman, the former Chairman of Lloyds Bank and now Chairman of Lloyds TSB, said:

> I think you could get to such a complicated Byzantine organization that diminishing returns would set in. If you wanted to be everything to every person, then I think you could get yourself into a point where you wouldn't be a very efficient organization and there is plenty of evidence that the most effective mergers are those that have been really thought through to say where all these synergies are going to come from because bigger doesn't necessarily mean better.

Indeed, he added:

> It's not size that Lloyds TSB has been after. If you measure it by total assets, we're certainly nothing like as big as some banks. We've been after performance.

In all these comments on consolidation, it is, perhaps, difficult not to feel that, on this occasion, the thoughtful, considered framework of the interviews somewhat masked the urgency of the cost and competitive imperatives that made the mergers desirable or even essential for survival. As we discussed above, newcomers have many inherent potential advantages over traditional banks – of these, sheer size is a particularly important one – and these advantages must be combated with great vigour and determination.

Ultimately, considering the newcomers' financial, branding and operational muscle ranged against them, banks have little choice but to engage in dialogue with other players in order to create large organizations that have the financial power to deploy the resources needed to fight off competition from powerful newcomers such as retailers and telecom companies. The cost of technology is especially formidable – this cost alone can be more than sufficient grounds for consolidating.

For these reasons, consolidation has been particularly in evidence in the global custody industry, where there are now barely half a dozen major global players, about 20 fewer than just 10 years ago. The cost of implementing technology to deliver global custody services to a literally worldwide client base has been a major reason for the reduction in the number of players, as they have had to merge to create larger entities that can afford to do this. Incidentally, not all of the reduction in the number of global custodians can be accounted for by mergers or takeovers. Some players, such as Morgan Stanley (which previously took over Barclays Global Securities Services), have simply found the market unprofitable and have left it.

The bottom line is that consolidation is a result of banks having had their backs to the wall. Banks talk about it as if it were a sort of considered strategic plan, but that's not true. It's done out of desperation. Just because the chief execs seem magisterial and strategic in what they say, mustn't conceal the fact that banks are desperately trying to cut costs. The fundamental business axiom that 'you make money by not spending it' applies with particular force to banks.

The point is, retail banking is not inherently an extremely profitable activity, but it can become very profitable if you get everything right. For a bank to be profitable it has to be comfortable with its size – 'comfort' here meaning that its size is allowing it to have the critical mass it needs to optimize its business effectiveness without becoming unwieldy.

Banking is not like selling computer software, where you can sell millions of copies for a quite high per unit cost. Banking is a service industry and it is actually quite labour-intensive, even with electronic banking frameworks.

It's also, in the past, been a very wasteful industry. This is especially true of the retail sector. What possible justification can there be for a typical high street to have, say, 20 ATMs operated by, say, a dozen different banks? This is a particular absurdity in today's retail banking industry, when ATM-sharing arrangements between different banks have become so extensive that most ATM cards work in most ATMs. Even with the consolidations of the past few years, the situation in many towns and cities remains faintly farcical, with unnecessary spare capacity staring one in the face. For 'unnecessary spare capacity', of course, read 'wasted expenditure on overheads'.

The situation in many high streets – especially in countries such as Britain, which have banking industries with numerous players – bears a resemblance, even now, to notorious historical wasteful commercial situations, such as the nineteenth-century scenario of three major railway stations in North London that were the termini for the three big railway companies.

There is every motivation for banks to consolidate. Especially in the retail sector (this is less true than in the wholesale sector), they can't differentiate themselves too much in terms of the quality of service they offer. In other words, it's not as if one bank has such a huge advantage over another bank that it wouldn't want to merge with it. Essentially, banking is a commodity. This is also becoming evident in the wholesale market, where trading in government bonds, foreign exchange and other securities markets, is becoming increasingly commoditised.

The consensus viewpoint of the interview respondents is that consolidation almost always makes sense for a bank.

Only a big bank is, ultimately, going to have the money to consistently and energetically, throughout its entire (possibly global) operations, carry out certain essential functions, namely:

- win itself a global or national marketing profile;
- buy the state-of-the-art technology it needs;
- recruit really top-class people;
- invest in the Internet and develop electronic banking channels.

The advantages of economies of scale are unarguable. These are always of great importance in a service industry. If, for example, you're paying a manager anyway, you may as well have him or her managing 20,000 accounts as 5,000 accounts – you've got to pay the manager's salary either way.

Advantages of specialization are also a big reason for consolidation being the sensible option. Almost every branch of a bank will need to employ someone who is an expert in financial services. In smaller branches, these people are not always very busy. However, in big branches they are and, as they are specialists, and the more business they have, the better they will become at their jobs. So, creating a big bank lets people specialize in what they do best and use that knowledge.

The need for substantial capital reserves is another reason for big, in banking, usually meaning beautiful. Big banks can weather storms that smaller ones can't. This is especially true of wholesale banks, which can only take profitable trading positions on their own account if they have the capital reserves to do so. Unquestionably, substantial capital reserves enable a bank to handle risk better than would be possible without such reserves.

In the future of banking, consolidation is bound to play an even bigger role than it has already.

GLOBALIZATION

What is a global bank? Inevitably, it is not a bank that sees its customers as members of a great monolithic community. John Bond, Chairman of HSBC Holdings, emphasizes this when he says:

> I think tailoring your products to suit your different markets is terribly important. What you do get out of size are economies of scale ... but in the final analysis you want to treat each individual in the way they want to be treated. I ask myself every evening on my way home – , 'How many clients did you meet today?'

How does he decide which countries to operate in? As he explains:

> We think we need to be in countries where we can make sense of it for our shareholders and where we can make a contribution to the host economy ... that means that you're unlikely ... to see a truly global bank. If global is 225 countries in the world, we're only in 80, [but] HSBC is as international as any financial institution in the world today.

It is important to bear in mind that global banking is based on joint ventures as much as on mergers and takeovers that lead to the creation of enormous global players.

For example, in April 2000, while *The Future of Banking* was in preparation, HSBC and Merrill Lynch, for example, announced a standalone Internet joint venture to offer banking and brokerage services to affluent individuals around the world. The two banking giants pledged a total of $1 billion to set up the company, a name for which has not yet been chosen. Bond said on the day of the launch, 'At a stroke, this makes HSBC and Merrill Lynch a major player – maybe the major player – in global on-line financial services.'

As if by way of demonstrating that 'global' joint ventures need to be put together with an intelligent awareness of which national markets really will be receptive to the idea and which won't, the two players announced that the 50:50 joint venture, which will be headquartered in London, would not cover the world's largest financial services market – the United States – as there was too much conflict there with existing offerings that the two players were operating in that market.

This particular joint venture provides two other important levels of insight. First, it shows that there is potential for joint ventures even between banks that have very disparate profiles in the industry. Second, it shows that banks are increasingly basing joint ventures on intelligent and creative responses to changing customer needs. Firmly denying speculation that the joint venture was the first step towards a broader alliance or even a merger, they said that it would be aimed squarely at a class of people in Europe and Asia that the banks describe as the 'mass affluent' – individuals with between $100,000 and $500,000 of assets to invest. Roberta Area, Head of Global e-business at HSBC, said, 'The real story is diversification; people want to do more with their wealth than simply put it into a bank account. It's the growth of the equity culture, people arranging their own pensions and so on.'

This leads on to a point that clearly has enormous implications for the future of banking, especially in relation to the future of global banking and joint ventures such as the one between HSBC and Merrill Lynch. Customers are not only becoming increasingly savvy about the deals available to them, they are also, increasingly, making use of the Internet to 'design' their own banking and financial services packages. This should remind us of one particularly important point about the Internet in this context: it is so easy to access and so adept at facilitating the display of competing products on offer that, in fact, a perfect or near-perfect market is created in which customers are relatively indifferent to the name of the institution offering the deal, but, instead, are mainly alive to the deal itself. In this context, it is useful to bear in mind research that HSBC and Merrill Lynch quoted at the time of the launch of their joint venture. By the year 2004, there will be 50 million on-line banking customers outside the US, with 14 million in Europe, they said. Whether this prediction is optimistic or accurate remains to be seen. If it *is* accurate, though, that adds up to an enormous potential market for forward-thinking banks.

A comment regarding global banking made by one of the interview respondents seems particularly prescient in the light of the announcement of the HSBC and Merrill Lynch joint venture. As Dr Henning Schulte-Noelle of Allianz remarked:

> US firms will likely have to partner with European banks and insurance companies and vice versa. In the global asset management business, it will be necessary to have access to a minimum level of distribution in any geographic region. Efficient transfer of know-how, sharing of distribution networks as well as equity linkages are basic parameters for success in this financial sector. The business is highly dependent on economies of scale, integration bundling effects.

He added:

> The trend will be the same in the investment banking sector. A handful of very large asset managers will dominate the business, among them insurance companies. There are still more than 4,000 insurance companies and fierce competition will force many of them to merge or disappear. Potential competition may be lessened by careful building of strong investment performance franchises, coupled with excellent multiplatform distribution channels. A couple of years from now, the markets will be less determined by geographic differences and more by customer attitudes. If we look at Europe, however, there is a nascent trend for a more open approach within traditional sales channels via specific products. In the near future, some clients will prefer basic financial insurance coverage and others will ask for full problem-solving services. Some will want to buy their insurance from the Internet or through telephone and others will want to talk about it with a financial expert, either working for one company or acting as a broker. Some will prefer 'one-stop shopping', others will build their own menu of financial services providers. There is, however, a critical sales volume that an asset manager must have before it can concentrate on exploring these new trends. Asset managers have to maximize their comparative advantages. Therefore, they have to define their core businesses and answer the question, 'Which financial product range will be the best?'

Whenever global banking is discussed, questions of size are inevitably raised. How big is big enough? When is a bank too big? Similarly, when is a bank definitely too small to make the most of crucial opportunities? Peter Wuffli of UBS Brinson commented:

> In the end, banking is a people business, no question about it. I think there will always be boutiques which have either a specific concept, or are built around very specific, charismatic personalities. What will be difficult to maintain in the future is a position in the middle where you have a strong, heavy infrastructure in one market – geographically, for example, or in one asset class or specific capability – but where you may not have the breadth to address the various needs of a client's franchise, and I think this will be a relatively difficult thing for some firms to manage.

He pointed out that globalization was taking place at different speeds in different sectors of the banking industry, with retail banking lagging behind in the globalization stakes compared with investment banking. He also said:

> I think in Europe we will also see – as in the investment banking industry – that the strong relationship-based traditional networks, operating on a national scale, will be eroded. We will see specialists operating globally, in a globally competitive environment, gaining market share. This will result from clients demanding specialists with professional resources and the ability to harness the synergies of an integrated global platform. That will put purely national players at a structural disadvantage. I think the trend here is clear. The question is, how quickly will this process take place and that is a very difficult thing to forecast. It also depends on the legislative velocity of the various markets in Europe – allowing for things like defined contribution plans, for example, which obviously creates a push for a more competitive industry than one dominated by a defined benefit structure.

He went on:

> So, it depends on the velocity of this break-up of the traditional network-based national models and how quickly they are replaced with models favouring global specialization and focus, but we should expect a globally competitive setting with, perhaps, ten or so leading global players dominating the industry.

Sir Brian Pitman of Lloyds TSB emphasized that global banks are sometimes much less responsive than smaller ones:

> There will undoubtedly be some nimble, niche players that will give everybody a rough time. It will be very difficult for big companies to match that because they are very quick on their feet. They will be great competitors. At the other extreme, there will be big specialists.

Robert Pozen, President and Chief Executive Officer of Fidelity Management & Research, commented on the continued opportunities for small players in the investment management industry:

> I view the structure of the industry as the large players getting larger. I also think there is still a tremendous opportunity for small players because everybody is willing to make deals with people to act as distributors through structures like mutual fund marketplaces. Also, if you're a small fund company and you get a good performance record, you can get plenty of marketing. But I think the middle gets squeezed.

One interesting matter that arose from the interviews was the comparison between the extent of the market share achieved by even the largest banks compared to that attained by big retailers and other international conglomerates – that is, precisely the sorts of organizations with the financial muscle, customer base, branding and knowledge of customer service to move into the banking sector and make a killing. Wells Fargo's Kovacevich, for example, commented:

> Citicorp only has a 3 per cent market share of financial services. It's really not huge, compared to Wal-Mart, which has a 40 per cent market share and Home Depot with an 18 per cent market share and General Motors with 30 per cent. Financial services just happens to be a huge business, but the big players have really quite small market share from the perspective of other products and services. That's why it has to get bigger. Why should financial services be different? The only difference was laws and regulations, not what the customers want.

Hank Paulson, Chief Executive Officer of US investment bank Goldman Sachs, emphasized that, even in a banking industry that favours size, establishing and maintaining a niche presence can, literally, pay dividends:

> A strategy that I think works very well is the niche business. As long as you have very good people, niche businesses are going to do well. It really comes down to talent – that's where there is always a shortage.

He adds:

> The commercial banks bought up the boutique securities firms in the technology era and you see new ones emerge because there is a need for

> that. The world is filled with very large financial institutions that do nothing particularly well – that's why I don't think just being big does it.

Dr Henning Schulte-Noelle commented:

> As a result of globalization, investment firms must be able to provide clients with more international products in their domestic market and, now, increasingly, must also be able to provide these products on a cross-border basis. This does not mean that small boutique firms will disappear, however, but the trend is moving toward smaller, niche product firms – as demonstrated by the proliferation of small independent hedge funds in the 1990s.
>
> The middle market or purely domestic players will increasingly face problems in remaining on the cutting edge in this rapidly changing industry. Mid-market firms will have difficulty maintaining the level of systems investments that are an important part of providing products and services to an increasingly demanding client base.
>
> On the investment side, building a robust investment factory requires attracting and retaining top investment professionals. For a pure investment company, such as Allianz Asset Management, the development of a proprietary buy side research team is a substantial investment, as is retaining top investment professionals. Furthermore, as the need to provide global products increases, firms which cannot point to the capacity to manage across all markets will find it difficult to retain sophisticated clients. On the institutional side, global investment capacity for large multinational clients with various asset and liability requirements is essential. Developing added-value products and services is, more and more, capital-intensive business, which argues strongly for size and diversity of market reach in order to best leverage these investments.

Banks operating in Europe are more than ready to take part in profitable globalization, but they are conscious of the need to master their European regions first. Ernst Welteke of Bundesbank remarked:

> The supervisory authorities need to be coordinated at the European level. We need a level playing field. We need single standards. It's certainly also important that, in view of the continuing breakdown of the divisions between securities operations, insurance and traditional bank business, the supervisory authorities for these activities cooperate closely with one another. They may even have to be integrated in the long run.

What about foreign players aiming to master the European market as part of their global operations? Katsuyuki Sugita, President and Chief Executive Officer of Dai-Ichi Kangyo said:

> Since the euro's introduction, the integration of money and capital markets has proceeded smoothly, but, given that there still exist differences in tax systems and regulations, it may take more time before financial institutions can operate freely within the euro zone. Differences in culture and languages also hinder cross-border mergers.

This is perhaps the nub of the matter. Globalization is an aim, certainly, but it is no good banks trying to manage it as if it were a vast, overreaching, worldwide aim. It has to be both managed and expressed at a regional, national and even local level. Somebody once said that all politics is essentially local and, in many respects, the same is true of banking. How can a bank build a global empire if it can't run its local customer bases and win real customer loyalty there?

THE ROLE OF I.T.

As we have seen, the importance of the impact of technology on the global economy and on the banking industry worldwide cannot be doubted. It has changed the face of human civilization over the past 50 years and there is no doubt that this sweeping change is going to continue its momentum, at least for the foreseeable future. The dawn of the Internet – which, in barely a decade, has moved from being a largely unknown technology designed to link North American university libraries together to being the basis for the greatest telecommunications revolution since the invention of the telephone – has created a completely new delivery channel for industry and commerce. It is a delivery channel with almost unlimited potential and we are only at the start of the revolution it has caused.

William B. Harrison, Jr, Chairman and Chief Executive Officer of Chase Manhattan, an organization that has pioneered many of the banking industry's most innovative applications of technology, commented:

> Technology has been one of the key drivers of the global economy. The whole Internet phenomenon is furthering a trend that had already begun, and will continue to have a huge impact on our industry. The Internet has caused a technology revolution that, when history is

> written, will have had a greater impact on change than the Industrial Revolution. If you believe that, then you want to make sure you're part of that process, doing whatever you can to get your company to understand the importance that the Internet carries.

The views of BSCH's Corcostegui provide convincing support for this perspective:

> There is no doubt that technological development is one of the main motors of change in the financial system. In our sector, technology is allowing new competitors all over the world to rapidly develop numerous e-businesses to exploit the rapid growth of potential customers and the low per-transaction cost.

He adds:

> Technology is an even greater source of opportunity for the large banks, who already have an immense client base and brand image the new competitors do not possess and could take years to acquire. [From an operational and cost perspective, of course,] e-business is a volumes, not margins business, and volume is determined by the number of clients. The Internet is a classic example of a technology that is ideally suited to mass market applications. Firms applying this technology that already have a wide client base can win an almost unassailable competitive advantage. So technology, far from representing a threat to the leading banks, is an instrument that, if exploited well, can boost their efficiency and competitivity even more.

Hank Paulson of Goldman Sachs, which is internationally renowned for its energy, the legendary hard work of its executives and its single-minded pursuit of profits, had this to say:

> The growth of our profitability was largely the result of big breakthroughs in technology. ... To take just one example, in 1990 we had about 190 people in our foreign exchange area. We didn't rank anywhere in the top ten in terms of foreign exchange trading. We weren't even a price giver, we were a price taker. If a client wanted to do a big foreign exchange trade with us, we had to go to one of the big commercial banks.
>
> We were forced to develop superior analytics, we created a very complicated option pricing model and technological link-ups with our clients.
>
> Then the market changed. You can now get foreign exchange quotes right off your screen. The banks went through a tough period, their

> distribution force was disintermediated. We still have about the same number of people in foreign exchange, but, for the last three or four years, we have been well in the top ten and it's been one of our most profitable areas.

Paulson continued:

> I would expect, looking ahead, that technology is going to bring about a very significant change in our industry. Financial services lend themselves to the Internet, so I would expect that there are going to continue to be very big efficiencies coming out of this.

Paulson's views on technological evolution are characteristically forthright. As he explained:

> The businesses that will change the most will be the sales and trading businesses. There are certain businesses, what I call the commodity-type businesses (small stock orders and government bond trades), where trading should be done largely electronically. The revenues we would reap would come down, but the cost would also come down.
>
> I think we will see disintermediation in sales and trading. It really comes down to adding value. As a firm, we get relatively high revenues per transaction.

He summarized Goldman Sachs' approach to technology:

> As an investment bank, technology has helped us a great deal to date. I don't think we could have been as profitable or as effective without it. Technology has made a huge difference. ... We're in an information business. Some of it is in numbers. There's no doubt that technology helps us gather that information and transfer it to the client in a way the client understands. Naturally enough, the sheer benefit of access to a new breadth and depth of customer information is one of the most important benefits banks perceive technology as offering. Traditionally, banks have been conspicuously bad at gathering and using customer information. The problem has not been due to any lack of inclination on their part to do better, but, rather, to their lack of adequate technology to achieve this aim. In particular, the legacy systems of the 1960s and 1970s were notoriously poor at permitting the effective gathering – let alone storage and retrieval – of precisely the kind of information banks needed to make the most of their competitive potential.

> Today, however, technology is giving banks access to a whole range of systems that permit them to obtain a handle on their customers – given the constraints of national data protection legislation – that is enabling banks to solve the thorny problem of acquiring and managing customer information.
>
> Datamining systems – which allow data to be stored, analyzed and retrieved according to a wide variety of analytical techniques and criteria – are especially important here. Almost all banks in developed countries – and many in developing countries – are now engaged in implementing datamining techniques in order to bring a completely new dimension to their mastery of customer information.

Jacob Wallenberg, Chairman of SEB Bank, commented:

> Information plays a very important role in the new business model. More specifically, customer information – individual as well as corporate – is extremely valuable. This information would probably be used to improve the services to each customer, but not necessarily become an information product. However, customer information can be bundled and turned into a sellable information product to other players interested in getting access to the specific customer base. The higher the quality of information, the higher the purchasing power of the customer base.

Dick Kovacevich of Wells Fargo – an institution widely respected for its skill at understanding customer needs and meeting them – emphasized the need for banks to respect their customers' need for privacy:

> Protecting our customers' privacy is a very important goal. It's all about trust. I think we need to distinguish the use of information of a single entity and ensuring that we keep that information private and only use it for the purpose of helping our customers. If we don't, we'll lose the trust and it will be bad for us and the customers.
>
> Some people are saying that, within the whole corporate family, we shouldn't share information. I don't think that would serve the customer well. It's all about knowing more about the customer. Let's assume we have a customer that we believe has too much money in low interest rate CDs and believe that some of that money should be in stocks or bonds or something to get higher returns. Some would argue that to go to that customer and suggest it is an invasion of privacy. But not 1 per cent of the *customers* in the country believe that. Most people want us to do this. Giving CD balances and so on to

> ten investment banks would be an invasion of privacy, in my opinion. There's the difference. I think we should publish our privacy principles and adhere to them and the customer can decide whether they want to do business with this firm or not.

Yet, he also said:

> To make it hard to use data would be a big step backward. We have to distinguish between true privacy and better information and advice and customer service. I think they're getting mixed up. I think it would be a disaster for the customers if an entity is not allowed to share information among its affiliates, its companies that it controls, in order to better serve the customers and give them advice and optimize their financial balance sheets.
>
> If some corporation is not protecting someone's privacy, then the customer should go somewhere else, but to pretend that we can somehow write laws that would work in every situation is absurd. The world is moving too fast. In fact, customers often call us and get very upset if someone on the other side of the phone doesn't realize what a good customer they are or are treating them in a very narrow fashion.

He concluded:

> There is going to be a privacy issue, which is coming up big in this country, which may or may not come up outside the United States. The privacy issue is, if one of these new financial services companies owns an insurance company, credit cards, a bank, mutual fund, healthcare processor, used cars, leases, how much exchange of information about the customer can you allow between these areas?

INFORMATION SECURITY

The intimacy of the link between technology itself and information security has already been discussed. Information security is always a problem for organizations, especially those that operate in industries where information is inherently valuable. Clearly, the banking industry is the classic example of such a business, although it is by no means the only example. Wherever information is valuable, there will always – almost by definition – be the danger that fraudsters will try to obtain funds illegally by gaining illicit access to the information systems that are storing and handling that information. Perhaps the most hazardous type of system of all is one that is specifically used for electronic funds transfer. Such systems can easily give computer criminals the opportunity to make millions illicitly in just a few seconds.

The Internet introduces a completely new level of information security challenge. It is an unfortunate truth that whenever a new technology becomes available, there will always be people who want to use it to make illicit gains. Not only is the Internet no exception, but the very fact that, in principle, the Internet is not a regulated technology and it is readily accessible to millions of people from relatively inexpensive terminals, naturally makes it especially attractive to computer criminals.

The first aspect of Internet security is the problem of ensuring that the data communicated across the Internet retains its integrity – that is, that it cannot be read by someone who has no business seeing it and it cannot be changed or manipulated by unauthorized persons in any way.

Ultimately, the problem of Internet security is actually fairly straightforward. It is a problem, in essence, of the security of computer data and it can usually be solved by implementing well-tried and reliable security solutions, such as encryption (which prevents the message from being read by any unauthorized persons) and message authentication (which prevents any unauthorized person illicitly interfering with the message or manipulating it in some way).

A more difficult problem to solve in the area of secure use of the Internet is the problem of Internet trust. This is the challenge of ensuring that a counterparty (who may be an individual, a corporation or any other party using the Internet) is who they say they are. This problem is, at heart, the problem of authentication – that is, the establishment of the truth or genuineness of a person or organization.

The problem of authentication via the Internet has many very serious implications, especially in the banking industry. The Internet security problem is basically one that can be solved fairly easily, but, the very nature of the Internet means this does not apply to the problem of Internet trust, because there is never any face-to-face contact in Internet transactions. Thus, it is probably impossible for one counterparty ever to be absolutely 100 per cent certain that the person they are dealing with is who they claim to be. The Internet is always going to be a virtual, electronic medium and that is really all there is to say about it. All that can be done is for the process of Internet authentication to be made so sophisticated that it ceases to be worth a would-be criminal's while to try to pretend to be someone they are not.

Naturally, this problem of Internet trust is a very serious one for banks. Banks deal in valuable information all the time and even the simplest Internet banking system requires that some procedure be implemented to prevent private details of a customer's account or accounts being given to an unauthorized person.

There is clearly a hierarchy of banking services available over the Internet, starting with services that merely provide information about the state of an account and going on to those that provide customers with facilities to make funds transfers to prearranged accounts and, indeed, to any account at all. It is no exaggeration to say that the problem of Internet trust is the major reason for, as things stand now, most banks being very cautious in the extent to which they allow their Internet banking systems to give customers a facility to make funds transfers to prearranged accounts (from which there might be expected to be some comeback if fraudulent transactions were made), let alone any account at all, from which the possibility of comeback would be very slight. No doubt, the problem of Internet trust will be rendered a less grave problem in the future than it is today, but, at the moment, banks retain their caution about it.

So how can authentication be established over the Internet? The best way to think about this is to consider how authentication is established in a face-to-face situation. After all, it is only relatively recently that people and organizations have had to worry about authentication in a situation where they cannot see the other party or have any direct physical contact with them.

The first time this problem reared its head was in the 1970s, when banks started to realize that they could cut down enormously on costs – and give better service into the bargain – if they delivered some routine banking services remotely, via ATM networks. It is only during the past few years that the Internet presented particular authentication challenges, with this new communications system creating a serious authentication problem by virtue of its completely virtual operation.

Compared with the history of the human race, ATM networks and the Internet are extremely recent events. This does not, however, mean that authentication is a recent problem. It has always been necessary to authenticate people, from our earliest days in primitive tribes. In essence, there have always been three principal ways of authenticating an individual.

First, a person can be authenticated by attention being given to what they are. With this type of authentication, the individual, in effect, proves their genuineness (or is revealed to be fake) by virtue of what he or she is. This has undoubtedly been the most important authentication system and, in any physical meeting between people, is as important today as it ever was.

Psychologists studying human perception have found that the human brain has evolved a particularly effective perceptual mechanism for allowing us to recognize people we know, even among a vast sea of faces. In practice, the thought process behind this identification is so rapid that we hardly notice it. It is, however, remarkable that we are able to identify friends and loved ones so effectively and so rapidly. Incidentally, this ability seems to be more effective when applied to people of our own racial type. It is easy to see how evolution, acting during thousands of years when people only ever met other members of their own racial type, did not find it necessary to develop a facility for cross-identification of other racial types.

Identification of faces is not, of course, the only type of identification that relies on us assessing the physical nature of somebody. Build, height, and other features are also relevant in this type of authentication. Eyes are particularly important. It is a well-known fact that eyes constitute a large element of the facial identification process. In some circumstances (though presumably more in the past than in these hygiene-conscious days), smell was presumably also an important physical identification method. However, faces were always the most important, and will no doubt continue to be so.

Second, a person can be authenticated by what they know. On the face of it, this seems like a more modern type of authentication process, but we can readily imagine our forebears requiring this secondary authentication method during dark nights when it was simply impossible to assess the genuineness, or otherwise, of somebody by their face before they got so close to one that if they were hostile they might have delivered a fatal blow. It is impossible to know exactly when passwords were first used, but, very likely, they, like language itself, evolved with the rise in intelligence that marked man from mere primates. Some linguists believe that the very evolution of language came about because our distant forebears wanted to comfort each other with intelligible sounds during dark nights when they could not see each other and it proved so useful for this purpose that it was eventually used during the day as well.

In the Bible, in Judges 12.5-6, one reads that the genuineness of people claiming to be from Gilead was tested by the genuine Gileads asking them to say the word 'shibboleth' (the Hebrew word for an ear of corn). The Ephraimites – the Gileads' enemies – could not pronounce the first consonant and said 'sibboleth' instead. As the Bible explains, the Gileads took each man who failed the test 'and slew him at the passages of Jordan, and there fell at that time of the Ephraimites forty and two thousand'.

This violent and dramatic story has given a word to the English language. A 'shibboleth' means a custom, doctrine or phrase that distinguishes a particular class or group of people. If you think passwords are a modern invention, think again.

In the case of the shibboleth, one might see this password as a kind of test that incorporates both what they are and what they know. A password like that is particularly effective.

Language itself is a kind of elaborate password. We recognize that someone who speaks our language correctly is at least one of us, even though this is only very much a preliminary authentication test. In modern usage, passwords are employed in an extremely subtle way to indicate that a particular person has the privileges associated with a particular status, such as that enjoyed by a customer of a particular bank. In practice, although passwords are still widely used as authentication devices, passnumbers are more practical, partly because they can be more readily digitized and because they can be changed more easily.

The third way to authenticate someone is to focus on what they have. Again, this is far from being a modern technique. The classical world made considerable use of special seals and other tokens that indicated the genuineness of the bearer. In modern times, tokens such as bank cards are so widespread that there are few people in the developed world who do not have at least one, and many people have several.

It is interesting to note that all these authentication devices, while useful in themselves, only become really effective when used in conjunction with another one and, ideally, when all three are used. For example, one might make a mistake in identifying someone's face at dusk, especially if one only has a brief glance at them, but if they also know the password, one is likely to be more inclined to confirm the authentication and if they bring with them the broken half of a seal you gave them the previous week that matches your own seal perfectly along the join, you are hardly likely to disbelieve that they are who they say they are.

This principle of authentication requiring two indicators rather than one is at the heart of most authentication in business today. The core of the ATM authentication process, for example, is the use of two indicators – the Personal Identification Number (PIN) and the relevant bank card. Most PINS are four-digit numbers that are designed to be easy to memorize, an attribute furthered by customers having the opportunity to change the PIN they are issued with to something more readily memorable. Some customers have different PINS for different cards, others prefer to have the same PIN for all their cards. In any event, the PIN and card system is extremely effective, at least if the following procedures are adhered to:

- The card must be issued to the recipient in such a way that it is difficult – ideally, impossible – for an impostor to use it. This is increasingly often achieved by the individual being invited in to the branch to pick up the card, in which case physical identification by the branch staff will confirm the genuineness of the recipient.
- The PIN must also be issued in a confidential way. Today, this is usually achieved by the recipient only being issued with the PIN after he or she has signed and posted an acknowledgement of having received the card. The PIN itself is issued automatically, by a special machine that prints PINs on a slip of paper without any human intervention. The PIN is held in encrypted form inside the computer system (such as the computer operating the ATM network) and never appears 'in the clear' to anybody but the bona fide user.
- The PIN must be memorized by the user, not written down. Unfortunately, this rule is often not obeyed, because people find memorizing a four-digit PIN more difficult than they expected, especially as they are urged by the card-issuing organization not to choose an obvious PIN, such as 1111.
- The PIN must not be disclosed to any other party, nor must the user allow anybody else to use the card.

We have now seen how these three authentication methods are used in face-to-face situations and also in the much more recent development of the ATM network. Let's now look at how they work in connection with the Internet.

The Internet, like the ATM network, is a virtual delivery system. However, there is a big difference. The Internet tends to work on what are essentially open telephone lines, while the ATM network almost always uses a financial institution's proprietary lines.

The fundamental problem facing any retailer or other organization seeking to use any of these three authentication methods is unpleasantly straightforward: there is a danger that the authentication process may be intercepted by an Internet criminal. This problem casts each of the three methods in a somewhat questionable light.

The first – what they are – is interpreted by modern authentication methods as the biometric type of authentication. The literal definition of biometrics is the application of statistical analysis to biological data. The specific use of biometrics in authentication involves the physical identity of the bona fide person being evaluated and stored in some form and 'sample' authentications being presented and tested against it.

For example, an individual's fingerprint or thumbprint may be used in a biometric identification system to permit or deny him or her access to a physical location. In this case, the individual would press his or her finger or thumb against a pad, which will then assess the sample either by an analogue method or digitally. Retina scanning is also an important biometric authentication technique, although its relatively low acceptability to customers means that it is only usually employed in extreme high-security systems where bona fide persons do not object to having their retinas scanned.

How useful are biometrics in Internet authentication? The answer is that they are less useful than might be imagined. The problem is that the very nature of the Internet means that the sample can only be assessed digitally at a distance and this is a vulnerability that makes the whole authentication method of dubious value. It is comparatively easy for an Internet criminal to intercept the authentication (which, again, is only being sent in digitized form) and to imitate it, thereby providing authentication of the Internet criminal.

As far as the Internet is concerned, the very sameness and constant nature of the genuine biometric sample restricts its usefulness. It means that the digitized version of the sample will always be the same, so that, in effect, the biometric sample is simply a complex digitized value sent across the Internet.

What about passwords sent via the Internet? Here, there is a similar problem of the password being essentially a constant, at least throughout the duration of its acceptability. Even if, in a highly secure application, passwords were changed every day, they could still be intercepted by Internet criminals who would then be able to use them and authenticate themselves. The password also creates the problem that it is difficult to distribute to genuine users without its security being compromised. Furthermore, apart from special applications, customers are unlikely to accept the inconvenience of having a new password issued more than very rarely.

As far as tokens are concerned, these are easy to distribute and, once distributed to a user, can be employed for considerable periods. Furthermore, the use of smart cards – plastic cards that incorporate a computer chip (the memory capacity and speed of retrieval of which will vary from one model of card to the other, but is continually increasing) – means that a considerable amount of information about the user can be embodied on the card. Also – even more exciting from an authentication perspective – the chip can be programmed to generate many essential elements of the authentication technique, particularly the password.

The California-based organization ActivCard, which also has a major presence in Europe, has pioneered the use of Internet authentication based on the use of a smart card and what it calls a 'dynamic' password. The dynamic password is a password or number that is continually changing, but which is recognized by the sender card and the recipient computer system because both card and computer system make use of the same password encryption system. This encryption system is based on a number of factors, including the time when the transaction is made, so it is comparatively straightforward for both card and recipient system to generate the same password – straightforward, that is, for the bona fide authentication system, but almost impossible for an Internet criminal to crack.

It is important to bear in mind that, at the time of writing, the ideal Internet authentication systems, profiled above, are exactly that – an ideal, but not yet used in practice. This is because the infrastructure that supports them is not yet in place, nor are many of the tokens necessary (such as smart cards) currently issued to users in sufficient numbers. However, this situation is bound to improve in the future. Beyond doubt, an enormously important element of the future of banking will be the implementation of major initiatives to make the extension of trust over the Internet genuinely feasible, rather than something that is fundamentally risky.

Ultimately, banks are never going to be able to become complacent about the threat posed by computer criminals. Dick Kovacevich, of Wells Fargo, no doubt spoke for all bankers when he observed:

> All banks are at risk from hackers. New technologies and new procedures are always being developed to protect this, but it's a concern we take very seriously and spend a lot of money and effort testing to make sure our systems are as secure as possible. Thus far, we have not had any problems, but I can't guarantee that it would not happen. It's a very difficult situation.

It is indeed and it isn't going to get any easier. This does not mean that banks are without resources in the fight against Internet criminals. On the contrary, banks are getting access to more and more resources every day, with hundreds of extremely resourceful and ingenious software vendors devoting a vast amount of time and effort to ensuring that the financial institutions that are their clients can win the battle against the computer criminal. On balance, it is a battle the banks should win – they have far more money and man hours to devote to the problem than do the computer criminals, many of whom are extremely odd individuals working alone and for motivations that, even to them, must, on occasion, be fairly obscure. Yet, these people have showed that they can sometimes score surprising victories. The only safe way for a bank to proceed is to assume that there is a permanent state of war between them and these people.

Figure 1 shows how security remains the biggest barrier to the adoption of internet commerce.

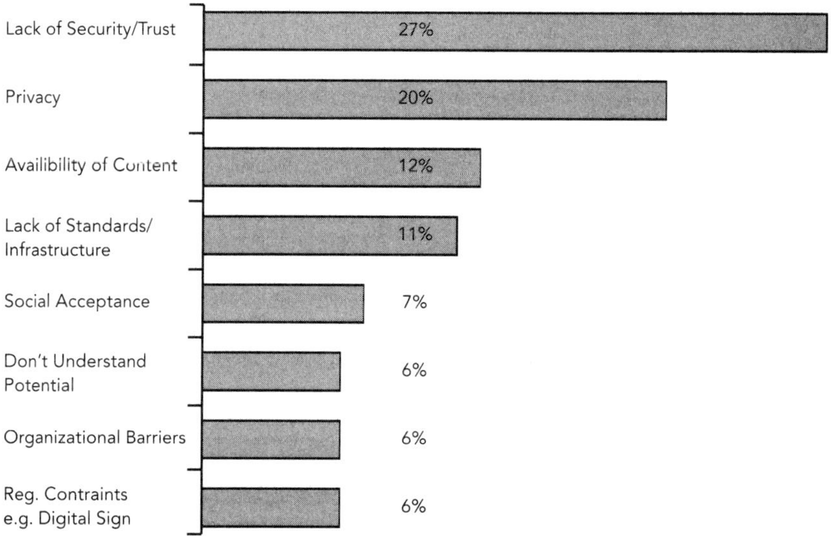

FIGURE 1 Barriers to Adoption of Internet Commerce
Source: Giga Information Group/AD Little

INTERNET BANKING

Few bankers would doubt that Internet banking is going to be playing a crucial role in the future of banking. It is true that some Internet banking ventures have been much less successful than the banks launching them hoped, but this is more a reflection of the technical and security teething troubles the banks are experiencing than any indication that the whole idea of offering a banking service over the Internet can, ultimately, do anything but succeed. The possibilities of mobile Internet banking – where the banking service is offered via a mobile Internet link, such as a specially modified cellular telephone – are particularly exciting. Jacob Wallenberg, Chairman of SEB Bank, commented:

> Internet penetration – or new technology penetration – primarily drives the future of Internet banking. As the Internet becomes more commonplace, so does transparency in terms of comparing different services. Culturally, the customer segments are quite homogeneous in terms of the 'innovators', 'early adaptors' and 'early majority' in each country. Hence, the customer demand is out there, but it is in different phases depending on the country/continent.

He added:

> Regulatory and legal obstacles to the proliferation of Internet banking still prevail. However, the pressure will increase to abolish these obstacles – above all because of the transparency that the Internet provides. However, a new legal/regulatory framework will need to be put in place once you have players that have one Internet banking solution, with one offering serving customers in any country in the world. Technically and culturally, this is doable today.

Naturally enough, the proliferation of Internet banking is expected to go hand in hand with the proliferation of Internet use generally. In fact, bankers are not necessarily well placed to be certain of how rapidly Internet proliferation will develop – their trust in this is mainly a leap of faith. However, they do have confidence that the Internet will certainly continue to proliferate and nobody could really doubt that this could happen. As Sir Brian Pitman, Chairman of Lloyds TSB, commented:

> The growth of on-line banking will be pretty rapid all over the place because, if you look at the percentage of the population, you can see how it wouldn't be long before 20 per cent of the population will be on the Internet and then it will continue to grow. It doesn't mean to say that we'll use it exclusively.

The profitability of Internet banking is still a matter for discussion. Naturally, profitability tends to vary between retail banking and wholesale banking, and a bank's individual profitability in this area will depend on its own internal efficiencies and the way in which it is using the Internet. The dynamic of profitability from on-line wholesale banking is that commissions tend to be reduced due to competition, but that costs are also reduced because the cost of delivering a service on-line is much less than delivering it via physical branches. In the banking industry generally, virtual delivery is usually reckoned to be between one sixteenth and one sixth of the cost of physical delivery. Alessandro Profumo, Chief Executive Officer, UniCredito Italiano, explained:

> From trading on-line, commissions will tend to get squeezed, while interest margins should improve. Interest rates and lending spreads in Italy are very low compared to other European countries. Total assets will increase and the spread will widen, while commissions will be under pressure.

He also observed:

> On-line trading is provided at a low cost or even for free and profits come from other services. The important thing is to understand what is a commodity and what is a value-added service.

Profitability is a particularly important issue for new-style on-line brokerages, which are frequently extremely attractive to investors, but, as Profumo observed, often not very profitable:

> On-line brokerages are seeing their bourse values soar because they're the flavour of the month with investors, but the day of reckoning will come for them, too, when they have to start showing profits. There's a lot of confusion about prices right now, as there is in all moments of discontinuity, but, in the end, we need to make a profit.

The precise nature of customer acceptability – or otherwise – of on-line banking services is a hotly disputed matter. Some banks have unquestionably lost status by trying too hard to make their Internet sites seem 'trendy' and so likely to appeal to the younger market. There is a general consensus within the banking industry that this is not the way to do it, that there is no point pretending a bank, which is, after all, a deadly serious type of business, is unduly trendy or should mainly appeal to younger customers. In fact, the people who constitute the base of a bank's profitable customers are not young people – who teeter on the borderline of solvency, but may become profitable customers in the future – but older people with fairly stable financial lives who may wish to partake of a full range of the bank's services. That said, banks obviously do want to attract customers to their websites and this requires a considerable element of sensitivity on the bank's part in order to attract the widest range of customers without alienating anybody. As John Bond of HSBC explained, a working relationship between the bank and the customer via the Internet requires a fair amount of trust on the customer's part:

> So, your virtual bank, you're talking about just having a website and people putting money on it and using the Internet to move money around. Even that is an act of psychological faith by the client. We've always believed that people would be much quicker to borrow money from Internet sites – because nobody minds where they borrow from – than they will to launch their savings into cyberspace.

Bond also emphasized the importance of trust, a matter discussed fully above:

> Trust is the key issue with Internet banking. [We have] 33 billion dollars-worth of capital and a track record for having been one of the strongest financial services companies in the world. Whether you measure by market capitalization, total assets, total capital.

Dick Kovacevich, Chief Executive Officer of Wells Fargo, was very conscious of the need for banks to allow Internet technology to go where the technology wants to go. It is refreshing to find a banker who is so enthusiastic about this technology – too often, bankers are in awe of it, despite publicly professing its importance:

> I think there are obstacles to the proliferation of on-line consumer banking, but the world is recognizing that it's important to use this technology. I think we have a good chance of getting it right around the world. Right now there are too many restrictions, but I think people are addressing that. It's important that we do not put handcuffs on this wonderful new technolog, that allows us to do so much. Although there are legitimate restrictions, there's got to be a balance. With any laws, you have to be careful not to stifle the creativity and advantages.

Kovacevich also considered Internet banking from the wholesale perspective. Certainly, the potential of the Internet for facilitating rapid investment decisions and 'day trading' appears close to inexhaustible. As he said:

> I think there is no lack of information for investors on the Internet. Certainly, it is both easier, cheaper and faster to obtain information today then ever before, and that's one of the great things about the Internet, but you can be so overwhelmed by information, it still doesn't help you to make an intelligent decision. I do not believe that providing advice to people on financial matters is going to disappear, by any stretch of the imagination. If anything, it will become more valuable because the world is becoming more complex and is moving faster. We're in a worldwide economy, not just domestic, but people will have a choice. People had less of a choice before because less information was available. There will be a bifurcated market, but advice will continue to be extremely important.

The question of whether or not Internet banking will always take place over the Internet is very much a point of debate. In the United Kingdom, for example, the customarily innovative Abbey National bank has pinned its colours to the mast by opting to base its initial big push into on-line banking on digital television rather than PC-based Internet banking. One certainly sympathizes with this view, which was echoed by Marshall Carter, Chairman and Chief Executive Officer of State Street:

> I don't think on-line consumer banking is going to make a big splash in America – and it is pretty popular now – until all of this stuff comes across a single pipe into your house and into your TV.

Such a perspective makes sense. For one thing, almost everybody has a TV, but – even in this highly computer literate age of ours – only about one in three households has a PC. There is also the psychological consideration that people like television and associate it with leisure activities, whereas people do not see PCs in that light – even if they have one at home, they often associate it with work.

What is indisputable is that the Internet has the power to effect a major increase in the level of competition within the banking industry. Just as the advent of shared ATM networks in the 1980s allowed small financial institutions to compete on a nationwide or regional basis with larger institutions by the simple expedient of joining a shared network that would give their customers access to all the ATMs of the network, Internet banking is levelling the playing field by making it relatively cheap for newcomers to launch their own virtual banking service.

After all, there was always a limit to the virtuality of ATMs – many of them are sited in the walls of physical branches and are really a limited way of extending a physical branch's opening hours. Of course, many ATMs are situated in other locations, but, even then, people tend to view them psychologically as a kind of mini-branch rather than a dynamic, on-line banking facility in their own right. Internet banking, on the other hand, is a completely different matter. It is possible for a bank to be entirely virtual and, indeed, new banks with this characteristic are being launched every week around the world. With no overheads for bricks and mortar branches to worry about, many of these new, virtual banks can afford to offer extremely good deals to customers. David Li, Chairman of Bank of East Asia was surely spot on when he said that he thought that the Internet and cyberbanking are going to level the playing field a great deal. More subtly, he gave a recipe for success in the Internet banking stakes:

> Banks can stay competitive with the Internet by investing more, knowing the market and jumping in before everyone else, and adding content so that people come to your website and having bonus points that people can earn by buying things through you. The Internet is basically a quick leveller, but having a cyberbank alone is not enough. You also have to have bricks and mortar, so the customers are aware of what you are doing. You have to advertise on television and in newspapers so that people know that you have bonus points or other incentives to come to your website. We are adopting a multichannel approach.

He was unequivocal about the need for serious up-front capital expenditure to make the most of the opportunities being provided by the Internet. His perspective was fairly unconventional in the sense that he questioned whether or not smaller banks can make an impact over the Internet if they don't have a customer base already. However, this seems to place too little emphasis on the fact that customer loyalty in the banking industry has changed radically over the past 20 years and, nowadays, customers will use almost any institution as long as it offers them a good deal. There is no question of customers ignoring a virtual bank simply because they haven't heard of it before. On the contrary, its very novelty could be an important selling point. Admittedly, the bank needs to have credibility and it certainly helps if a well-known retailer or bank is responsible for launching it, but there is no reason to believe that its novelty should be a drawback:

> I basically believe that the more you spend [on Internet initiative], the better it is. And that is the reason why some smaller banks may be prevented from going into it. If you don't have the customer base, what is the point? Even if you have a group of banks going in together on a homogeneous [Internet] product, how are you going to make certain that they all agree to the same policies when one is prepared to go lower than the others in price? The costs of an Internet banking system are pretty much fixed, regardless of the size of the bank, so if you are a very small bank, it's probably going to be unbearable. It will encourage consolidation.

At a strategic level, the Internet is playing an enormously important role as a means of helping all kinds of organizations – especially banks – to create new business models of all kinds. According to William B. Harrison, Jr, Chairman and Chief Executive Officer of Chase Manhattan, this is a particularly important issue with business-to-business models because they continually suggest new types of approaches to conventional forms of business practice:

> The Internet's impact on the business-to-business model will be huge because the Internet is all about doing things differently and enabling you to think and leverage yourself differently. All of this creates huge opportunities.

He added:

> We are seeing those opportunities. ... It is more difficult in the business-to-consumer space to come up with business models where you can easily convince others that you can make money on a sustainable basis than in the business-to-business space. A lot of people are in the consumer space and it is hard to see how you can create a huge competitive advantage. Although people will do it at some point, nobody in the banking business has really created a business-to-consumer model that is taking a big market share yet. People have created business models that are enabling them to gain some market share and provide better fulfilment to their clients while creating a cheaper delivery system. But nobody has come up with a leapfrogging business-to-consumer model in consumer banking yet, so far as I can tell.

A particularly interesting angle to Harrison's comments concerns the way in which physical business models in the banking sector are being affected by the drive towards virtualization. This is a common phenomenon when a new technology starts to become extremely important – it tends to affect the way in which previous technologies are viewed. Very often, the new technology will first be presented as a mere adjunct of the old technology. For example, ATMs were first seen as part of the branch rather than as a new technology in their own right. Similarly, when televisions first became consumer products, they were designed to look not like modern entities, but like nineteenth-century cupboards or old-fashioned pieces of living room furniture. Today, the simplicity of much living room furniture derives, to some extent, from its need to look right alongside televisions and other high-tech domestic gadgetry. As Harrison said:

> We are seeing cannibalization of the physical by the virtual. Any smart management team has to encourage cannibalization of their business. If you look at past history, quite often the inability to let new processes and new thoughts cannibalize existing business has created major problems for a lot of companies. We are great believers in cannibalization because the view is, if *you* don't do it, somebody else will, so you might as well do it yourself and get out in front of the curve.

It is certainly refreshing that a banker of Harrison's calibre is so willing to put his reputation on the line by declaring himself not only in favour of Internet banking, but extremely enthusiastic about it.

The first question a leading bank has to ask itself is, 'Do we really believe that there's an Internet revolution going on, is it real and is it going to change our competitive position?' My answers are, 'I do believe in the Internet revolution. I do believe it is sustainable and real and I do believe it will have a major, major impact on our business and our future.' So, what do you do about it? In a big company, unless you get the whole company engaged – not just pockets of the company or a few senior people – you won't be successful. This is all about major change, as a strategic matter and as a cultural matter.

I am sure that all readers of *The Future of Banking* will agree that one of the gems of this book is Harrison's lucid and highly revealing account of how one of the most famous banks on the planet started to look closely at Internet banking and how it decided to mould the Internet culture into its organization. As he explained:

> This is all about major change, as a strategic matter and as a cultural matter. After we announced the importance of the Internet, we announced steps to reinforce the process of becoming more Internet-driven as a company. It started with the creation of Chase.com, which is our greenhouse incubator, with talented people who have venture capital kinds of backgrounds and experience. Their job is to Internet-enable the business, to take Internet ideas and make them come alive fast.
>
> Parallel with that, we went to 15 key businesses and said we would like each one to take one of their top business people – not a staff person or an IT person, but a businessperson who really understands the business at a senior level – and pull them off their jobs to devote 100 per cent of their time to developing an Internet strategy and Internet-enable that particular business.
>
> We have tied this approach together with the Internet council that I chair. On that council, we have the 15 businesspeople, the Chase.com people and a few other senior people. The council is meant to be the repository, the gatherer of inventory, for what's going on at the company with the Internet. The council members share information with each other as they develop business ideas and thoughts to create common platforms so we do not have to reinvent the wheel every time we come up with a new idea. Over time, I will look to the group to help prioritize strategic investment decisions that Chase will have to make as we develop Internet ideas.

> Imagine a big company like us. If the process works, you will have a huge amount of thoughts arising from the different businesses about Internet strategies for particular products and services. At some point, if that's happening, you can't do it all. You have to prioritize, based on your view of how you can win.
>
> The second piece involves making sure we have a window to the external world, in terms of financial returns, expertise and knowledge. Chase Capital Partners, our private equity arm, created a special Internet group about four years ago to invest in the dot.com space. We own 100 dot.com companies. Not only are we getting substantial financial value there, but we also hope to incorporate and integrate some of the products, thinking and talent at these companies into processes going on at Chase.
>
> The third leg involves our acquisition of Hambrecht & Quist. This not only gets our investment banking business into the Internet space in a serious way, but also provides a wonderful external window of expertise and knowledge into the Internet phenomenon, which is absolutely critical.

The reason it is courageous for a bank to effect such a huge transformation of its organization in favour of the Internet is that precisely how profitable Internet ventures are going to prove in the future is by no means certain. As Robert Pozen, President and Chief Executive Officer of Fidelity Management & Research, explained:

> There's no doubt about it, the Internet is putting downward pressure on prices, both because it's allowing more productivity and because it's providing a great degree of transparency. However, contrary to what some people think, the segment of the industry that Fidelity is in has been reducing prices over the years and is probably already pretty price-competitive.

He went on to question the whole idea that the Internet is a distribution channel:

> I wouldn't say that the Internet is a new channel of distribution; it is a more efficient way of delivering information and doing transactions for an existing channel.

Thinking about the role of the Internet in relation to his own industry, he observed that the Internet had created many competitive opportunities that had not previously existed. As he explained:

> There's plenty of room for people to come into the fund industry through the Internet as a small player; whether people can really become big players with the Internet, I think that's a more difficult question. I would say the factors against it are, first, that, basically, all mutual fund companies are already adapting to the on-line environment.

Despite the increasing importance of the Internet, many bankers believe that the branch is far from doomed. As John Bond of HSBC commented:

> The evidence at the moment suggests that people like to talk face to face about investment products and more complicated insurance products and they will only buy over the telephone, over the Net, those products which are fairly straightforward and plain vanilla; but that will change.

This seems an insuperable obstacle to the idea that branches may completely disappear. It is important to remember that, even though a technology becomes extremely sophisticated, some fundamental aspects of the customer service relationship are too essential to be dispensed with. Does anybody really believe that branches are going to be dispensed with entirely? Surely even the most computer-literate customers like to be able to meet their banker face to face when a problem needs to be discussed or a complex financial service, such as a mortgage, pension plan or permanent health insurance, is being taken out? Banks, too, surely like to be able to meet their customers face to face. Indeed, one of the first things a bank does when a customer is clearly unable to meet their financial commitments is invite them in for a face-to-face discussion.

There can be no doubt that the number of retail bank branches will decrease sharply in the future – both because of consolidation between banks and banks wanting to run fewer branches generally – but it is highly unlikely that branches will disappear altogether: they are just too necessary. An analogy can perhaps be drawn with the retail photographic industry. Despite the extraordinary sophistication of modern cameras and their ability to make the taking of a good photograph an almost foolproof activity, we still take our photographs in to a laboratory to be developed, just as we did a century ago. The development process is simply too complex to be done by the average consumer and it is difficult to imagine how this would ever change, especially as colour photographs are particularly difficult to develop at home. Technology is always subservient to customers' needs. Customers need branches and are almost certainly always going to.

RISK

Federal Reserve Board Vice Chairman, Roger Ferguson, encapsulated the changing face of risk in the financial sector when he commented:

> Be it consumer credit cards, auto lending, fancy underwriting of hot IPOs, whatever it may be, the nature of risk is changing. It's changing because the products and services are becoming more technologically enabled and so institutions are capable of slicing risk more thinly; they're creating layers of risk, they're doing credit enhancement. But all of that means that the ability to recognize risk, measure risk, manage risk, offset risk, the entire world of risk control is going to become an even greater challenge for institutions.
>
> Whether or not the net risk in the system is greater is hard to say because certainly the ability to take riskd has gone up, but then the risk-management skills have gone up, as well. The same IT that allows for the introduction of riskier products and services allows for us to understand that risk.

Figure 2 shows trends in the switching of payments value from cash to electronic channels.

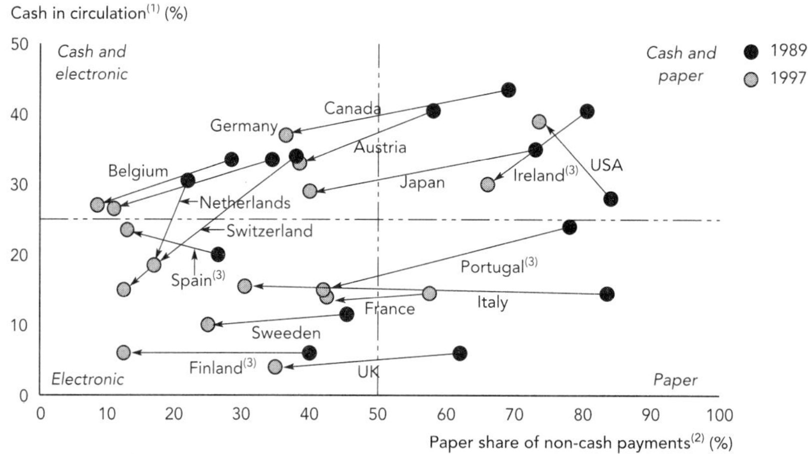

(1) As percentage of M1 except Sweeden (M3) and the UK (M2)
(2) Japan: Share of paper = (clearing of checks and bills)/(clearing of checks & bills + domestic funds transactions systems + consumer credit
(3) 1990 figures for Austria, Ireland, Finland and Spain; 1991 figures for Portugal

FIGURE 2 Leaving Cash and Paper Behind.

Source: Bank for International Settlements, ECB Bank, Bank of Japan, Post Finance, Japan Credit Industry Association, BCG

Between 1994 and 1997 over $180 trillion of payments value, 12 percent of the 1994 global total, switched to electronic channels. The US, the UK, Germany, France, and Italy represented nearly 90 percent of this migration. In Japan, by contrast, the dollar value of electronic transfers actually fell because of the devaluation of the yen, though in local currency, there was modest growth.

If the collapse of Barings proved anything, it is that nothing is sacred in the banking world. The fact that one of the world's most famous merchant banks could be obliterated relatively quickly by the trading decisions of one young man also demonstrates that today's financial markets are so potentially volatile, and have so much money in play, that a large asset base deriving from even a couple of centuries of successful trading offers little protection.

Of course, as a merchant bank, Barings was inevitably more vulnerable than a clearing bank would have been. It is difficult, for example, to imagine that the British Government would have been able to allow a bank such as Barclays or NatWest to fail – the political implications would just have been too great. Indeed, many risk assessment systems for banks attach an extremely important weighting to the likelihood that the threatened collapse of a bank would be staved off by government intervention – not that shareholders should ever feel that this means that a bank in which they have invested money can ever fail. As Howard Davies, Chairman of the FSA in London, observed:

> The lender of last resort is able to provide liquidity to the market when necessary. But I think it's important to recognize that that might not necessarily be support that would do a lot for the institution which failed. ... I don't think support would be available for the shareholders of an institution that has failed. From a shareholder point of view, it's very important that people understand that there is no institution that is called too big to fail.

The reason no institution is too big to fail is partly that nothing is sacred in the world of risk and also that, even with diversification, a big institution will almost certainly have a big exposure to many potentially hazardous areas of business. As Sir Brian Pitman, of Lloyds TSB commented:

> It's perfectly rational to think that markets are just too powerful and point the finger at some companies that are too big. The basic point is that markets act very abruptly. The Asian crisis almost brought the world to its knees. I am very much in favour of free markets, but we

> do have to find a way of avoiding these intensely abrupt movements that can destroy people's lives. We will learn from this process, find a mechanism that will get the best of both worlds – free markets but ones that have more information about things.

David Li, Chairman of the Bank of East Asia, also supports the view that any bank can potentially fail in today's highly demanding financial market environment:

> I don't think we are getting to the point where we have banks that are too big to fail. I think with the Internet and cyberbanking, it is going to level the playing field a lot more. To say that no bank can fail is like saying that no country can default on their debt. It's not true.

Henry Kaufman, President of Kaufman & Co., a New York-based international economic consulting and investment management firm, raised the point that a large institution has an obligation to install and implement so many frameworks and behavioural codes that, while its failure can never be ruled out, in practice, this is hardly ever going to happen. It is certainly true that many failures of banks – just as many failures of commercial organizations – are due to hubris, the feeling that nothing can go wrong and that the institution leads a charmed life. However, just as Macbeth discovered that he did not lead a charmed life when he came face to face with Macduff, no bank or any other organization can, in fact, lead a charmed life. However, if they are good at what they do – really good – they stand an excellent chance of being able to ward off disaster indefinitely. As Kaufman said:

> You have to put in place all kinds of supervision and certain codes of behaviour in large institutions that make them too good to fail, instead of too big to fail.

Generally, despite the occasional disaster, such as the fall of Barings, there is a perception that most large institutions are, in practice, unlikely to fail. They have the money to deploy state-of-the-art risk management systems and employ brilliant people who understand how to minimize risk. As Frank Zarb, Chairman of NASD, said:

> I think that's less and less of a problem – the industry getting so much bigger. The bigger firms are well-regulated, they're well-managed. Smaller firms, generally speaking, are run by businesspeople who live by their wits and they are smart guys and honest guys. ...

> There are always 2–3 per cent that are overextended – you know, gone too crazy in terms of margins and what they have lent customers, and when the market breaks, their capital is insufficient. We try to watch out for those and catch them before they become a problem.

Having said that, banks only make money in two ways:

- by delivering a service to customers that they can charge for;
- by accepting levels of risk that they are prepared to take on.

They can never be certain that a person or corporation to whom they lend money is going to pay them back, nor that certain positions they take in a wholesale market will not lead to serious losses, but they can use their experience of risk from the past to have a good idea of what level of loss is likely to arise from taking certain positions and decide whether or not this is a level they are prepared to accept. Hubris is indeed always a threat and it is frequently the apparently most gifted senior manager and most successful trader who is a source of potential disaster.

The belief that one simply can't fail is particularly evident in a bull market. Some of this is due to sheer fundamental human psychology. Making money is exciting, even desperately exciting, and it is extremely easy to get caught up in the thrilling scenario of money-making, continually escalating bonuses and generally great success. In banking, pride has all too often come before a fall. As Dick Kovacevich of Wells Fargo said:

> I think the greatest danger to a systemic issue is the belief that some institutions are too big to fail and therefore should be supported in the case of failure. This belief gives a false security to those in the marketplace. The market is a much better monitor than a regulator. We've seen evidence in the US where very small banks – with $500 million or a billion dollars – have lost 35 to 40 per cent of their assets.

Kovacevich continued:

> I think the market has this impression that we're going to be bailed out if there's a problem and they don't have to use appropriate due diligence and they can rely on regulators and supervisors, and I think that's very dangerous.

He sounded a warning, however:

> I think people are not pricing for risk. They are assuming the economy is going to go up forever. They are loosening covenants, particularly on

> commercial lending, beyond prudent means and not pricing for risk. Eventually, when the economy doesn't bail us out from these bad decisions, there will be significantly higher credit losses. We've been in an unprecedented [span] of low losses and this cannot continue.

Kovacevich suggested that there is a kind of multiplier effect in lending, which swings too far on either side:

We [the industry] go too far in both directions. In good times, we lend too easily and in bad times, we shut our doors. That's why, generally, you have recessions in this country. The banks have done too much or too little and this has exacerbated the situation. ... If everyone else is pulling in and your bank is getting out to the customers, you can really gain market share.

Andrew Crockettt, Managing Director of BIS, had the following to say:

> It has always been the case that the difficulties of large financial institutions pose public policy issues and, in some cases, necessitate some kind of public intervention. Presumably, as more institutions get larger and more complex, the public policy issues that are raised by those difficulties themselves become more complex. That doesn't mean to say that a large institution, just because it is large, is going to be protected. It can fail in different ways: it can be merged or it can, in certain circumstances, be wound down through official action. The owners of the institution are always liable to lose their money and the managers their position. No institution is guaranteed to survive in its existing form if, through bad management, it makes losses. We have got to be very careful about how we deal with large institutions. It is a question of striking a balance between protecting the system and avoiding moral hazard that protects people from the consequences of their own actions.

Crockett also provided some practical advice when he observed:

> You have to make sure that the issuers understand the nature of the risks they are running – hopefully their customers do, too – and be prepared in cases where you think risks have been inadequately reflected in the firms' activities.

He paid particular attention to the need to develop workable bank models that accurately reflect the enormous changes in the banking industry over the past few years:

> Even in the big banks, the models have been developed on the basis of relationships observed to have held in the past. There is a need for

> imagination to be exercised, and say, 'Let's not look at what has happened in the past as a guide to the future, but let's imagine how the future could be different from the past, in ways that would pose dangers and risks, and then manage or adapt the models to take account of that.'

Federal Reserve Board Vice Chairman, Roger Ferguson, agreed:

> We know that models, even the most well-developed models, are by definition backward looking. We know that they build coefficients and relationships that have historically been the norm, but we also know that, as we saw in the LTCM and Russian crises, that once in a while improbable outcomes actually can, because of external shocks, occur. And so that means that we've got to be mindful not to put too much of the supervisory weight on risk modeling because models by definition are imperfect.

Ernst Welteke, the President of Germany's Bundesbank, was very much a supporter of the view that any institution has the potential to fail if things go wrong. As he said:

> From the point of view of the supervisory authorities, there is generally *no* institution that is too big to go bankrupt. The responsibility must lie with the management of the individual institution.

He also raised the important point that the very existence of the euro has enormous risk implications for the European financial community. The importance of the euro in the future of banking is discussed below, but, at this point, it should be said that it may turn out to be the most momentous financial development in Europe since the invention of the modern banking system:

> Europe now has a single money and capital market and that fosters a tendency to create larger institutions as well. If we consider the trends towards more investment banking and securitization that are emanating from the English-speaking countries, it has to be said that those institutions, which in the past benefited from interest rate margins, are today faced with enormous competitive pressures. They need a very different customer profile to offset the enormous costs required for information technology.

Peter Wuffli, of UBS Brinson, observed:

> Financial services have always been vulnerable to risk, because there is a huge interconnection between one financial institution and the other. Why? Because we all have learned over the centuries that

> maintaining liquidity is very important for depositor confidence. How do you maintain liquidity? You lend it in the bank. There are many financial institutions whose largest risk exposure is to our own industry, which tells you of the interconnectivity of banks and financial institutions around the world. There is no such thing as risk-free banking, but I think it's more there in that it exists less in the cash markets and exists more in the derivatives markets.

Hank Paulson, Chief Executive Officer of Goldman Sachs, placed a particular importance on liquidity and this certainly makes abundant sense. After all, when an institution collapses, the real problem is that it does not have enough liquidity at the moment to pay its debts. The money does not really vanish from the financial system completely because there is almost always another institution that will take over the debt if the overall deal is right:

> We worry a lot about liquidity risk. When investment banks fail, they fail due to liquidity problems – not enough cash on hand. We always worry about our funding, staying liquid. We think a lot about reputational risk, legal risk. Every time I speak to a group of partners and they ask me, 'What do you worry about?' I say, 'Because ours is such a great firm, every one of us has a lot more potential to hurt the firm than they can ever help it.'

The development of tools for monitoring and managing risk is of enormous importance for the industry. As Robert Pozen, of Fidelity Management & Research, commented:

> I think people have become much more sophisticated since 1987 about volatility. I think we are used to more day-to-day volatility, and intra-day volatility, on all markets. To deal with this higher level of volatility, we have developed more tools and we all monitor market movements pretty closely. But in the end it's always the unanticipated that gets you. ... While we have good tools, I can't guarantee that there's nothing that could happen that would really throw us.

Important devices to reduce risk are being developed all the time, from subtle and synthetic derivatives, to abstruse portfolio diversification theories based around the work of the currently fashionable academic guru. Perhaps the most spectacular recent example of a academic theory gone wrong in practice was the dramatic downfall of Long Term Capital Management, the US hedge fund founded by John Meriwether – a fomer Salomon bond trader – and managed by a team of Nobel prize winners, Myron Scholes and Robert Merton.

Merton and Scholes, who developed the famous Black–Scholes options pricing model, depended on a key assumption in LTCM's trading strategies – that markets were both continuous and liquid. This assumption was a key element of their risk management approach, known as value-at-risk (VAR). VAR aimed to avoid financial disasters by monitoring the volatility of a bank's positions; as volatility increased, banks could either cut positions or increase capital. But in August 1998, when the news of the Russian debt default broke, VAR limits were breached and most banks decided to cut positions. The trouble was that many of them were making the same type of arbitrage plays as LTCM. As investors raced to cut their positions, the result was massive illiquidity and prices that breached all precedents in LTCM's models. There is no necessary correlation between the subtlety of the risk management approach and the likely success of that approach, but in an ultra-competitive scenario, such as today's global banking industry, even establishing an edge in the risk management stakes that persists for a couple of months, can add billions to a bank's profitability. Again, no bank should allow itself to start believing that all the risk in the world can be diversified or intellectualized away. As Richard Medley, Chief Executive Officer and Chairman, Medley Global Advisors, commented:

> The lessons of that crisis were that very simple fundamentals in terms of risk management and conditions of the marketplace will always end up catching up with you, no matter how thorough you are and how much you think you are hedged. You can't hedge the entire world.

Hank Paulson, Chief Executive of Goldman Sachs, concurred:

> If another firm blows up in the mortgage area because it takes all kinds of imprudent risks, you can run your mortgage desk very well and do a lot better than they will, but when they get into problems and have to sell everything they've got, it hurts the market and it hurts you.

To avoid that hurt, it is important not to forsake tried and tested risk management devices, such as diversification and the taking of a long-term view. As Dr Henning Schulte-Noelle of Allianz said:

> A lesson of 1997 and 1998 is that, while volatility can be high in any single investment or during any short time period, investors with a longer time horizon and a diversified investment portfolio will reduce volatility in their results and attain attractive risk-adjusted returns. Good risk management requires good controls at a local as well as global level. Good risk management requires qualitative as well as quantitative know-how.

He added:

> Risk-management techniques should give an overview of the current risky exposure of a firm and estimate performance of this exposure in the near future as well as in the long term. This represents an enormous task as a typical financial services company faces various kinds of risk, like interest rate, liquidity, market or credit risk. All of those must be monitored not only independently, but also on an aggregated level. ... Models only create a rather simplified picture of [the] world.

He paid particular attention to the importance of ensuring that risk management techniques are matched to the type of exposure in question:

> Risks originating from different kinds of services, like insurance, asset management or banking, should be measured and controlled, each by its appropriate means and methods.

The risk management industry – and it *is* an industry today – has developed extremely subtle tools for measuring and monitoring risk that are mainly the province of specialists. 'Quant' investment management techniques that attach a mathematical value to risk and return and play around with these figures in a variety of extremely ingenious ways are reckoned on diversifying away much of the risk inherent in a portfolio. However, they are not foolproof, as Henry Kaufman of Kaufman & Co. emphasized:

> Quantitative [risk management] techniques have weaknesses. If you come out with risk management tools that are quite conservative, and someone else will have risk-management tools that are somewhat more liberal, then you don't get the business. There's a tendency to be romanticized by analytical tools that try to give you answers that are stretched into several decimal points which tend to reflect mathematical accuracy, rather than accuracy in analytical judgement.

BLURRING OF DEMARCATION BETWEEN FINANCIAL FUNCTIONS

Naturally enough, banks want their customers not only to bank with them, but also to buy a wide range of other financial services from them. Bankers adhere to a certain optimism that 'one stop' customers are highly prevalent, although, in fact, experience suggests that customers have less and less loyalty to their banks and are, instead, only too happy to shop around for the very best deals. Many retail and wholesale customers have relationships with several financial institutions simultaneously and there is no reason to believe that the tendency for this to happen is declining, but this does not remove the optimism. As Sir Brian Pitman of Lloyds TSB said:

> I don't think there are significant drawbacks from customers having all their financial needs serviced by one company, as long as you are willing to shop around so as you're getting very good value for money [from one supplier].

This view was corroborated by John Bond of HSBC, who observed:

> I think any company that offers each [type of financial service – be it insurance, banking or investment service –] in a competitive, good-value way will attract the business. I think it is perfectly possible for a customer to do all of that financial business with HSBC, provided we make certain that we offer good products at fair value.

Marshall Carter, Chief Executive Officer of State Street, was alive to the potential conflicts of interest caused by the creation of monolithic one-stop shops, but was no less optimistic about the appeal of these organizations to customers. As he explained:

> On a global level, the bundling of various financial services, such as insurance, securities and deposit taking, all under one roof is causing a conflict of interest, but, in today's financial services world, everybody is a competitor, a counterparty and a customer with each other, and the most sophisticated companies have no trouble dealing with that. From the customer's standpoint, having all of one's financial needs served by one organization has the benefit that the customer only has to divulge his or her information to one source and the source should be able to meet your needs. The risk, of course, is if that company gets in trouble, you have all your eggs in one basket.

Katsuyuki Sugita, president and Chief Executive Officer of Dai-Ichi Bank, sounded a well-expressed warning that, despite the acceptability of the one-stop shop among many customers, there are always going to be customers who have the money and influence to be entitled to a more personalized and specialized service:

> The point is what kinds of services individual customers would want. Average customers would normally prefer the 'one-stop shop' concept, because it is convenient in most cases, but certain customers, such as those who are very wealthy, would prefer more specialized financial services to meet their specific needs.

Angel Corcostegui, Chief Executive of BSCH, reminded us that many mergers and consolidations are designed not just to create a more muscular entity, but to form an organization that has fingers in more pies. As he said:

> Mergers in the financial sector are not limited to banks, but, rather, seek to create large financial groups active in retail banking, insurance, asset management, pension funds, etc. Multiproduct integration aims to offer a global response to all the customers' financial needs through creation of large 'financial service supermarkets'. This strategy enables substantial cost savings and efficiency gains, which undoubtedly benefit consumers. The groups' greater size will increase their ability to offer cheaper products and services and invest in new services or improve existing ones, raising customer satisfaction.

He also delivered a timely reminder that a wide range of products and services is no substitute for knowing how to keep customers happy:

> Along with a wide range of products, it is crucial to offer customers global and very personalized advice. In an ever more complicated and opportunity-filled financial world, consumers will value the convenience of retaining one or a few advisers offering global solutions to their multiple specific requirements.

Henry Kaufman, President of Henry Kaufman & Co., raised the important issue that diversity of products and services is all very well, but tends to cause problems in the risk management department. As he said:

> I don't think risk can be adequately measured in institutions engaged in a great diversity of financial activity. I think we are creating financial conglomerates where you have banks, insurance companies, security firms, finance companies, leasing companies – all under one umbrella. The dependence of the senior management on these various arms of activity … in turn, is heavily dependent on the middle management of those subgroups is probably greater than at any time in the post-war period. The middle management has become all powerful because that's where both the risk sits, that's where the reward sits.

He also made an observation that surely needs to be taken seriously as a warning:

> I do not believe you can really have a senior management that can be fully conversant in the magnitude of these risk takings of the financial conglomerate.

Robert Pozen of Fidelity Management & Research had evidently given a great deal of thought to the question of whether or not one-stop shopping really works. His own view is that, in one particular area, it doesn't:

> I am still of the view that one-stop shopping is not very attractive to most of the high net worth customers. The high net worth investor – who everyone wants – is very sophisticated about his or her use of financial services, they want the best deal in every financial service. While they may be willing to buy some closely related products from the same firm, the idea that they're going to do all of their insurance and all of their brokerage and all of their money management at the same place seems unlikely.

However, he conceded the obvious attractions of a one-stop financial shopping opportunity:

> A big attraction of a financial supermarket is that it's very convenient when one person can give you all these financial services, so you don't have to go to a lot of different places. But the Internet makes it very convenient to buy from several providers. Another important aspect of a financial supermarket is that the consumer will say, 'Oh, this is a reasonable price for the other product and, as you are a nice guy, I'll buy this other product from you,' but, once you have the Internet, consumers do not develop a personal relationship with the seller. Also, consumers can very quickly see the offerings of many financial service providers, and they can see pricing for everybody. So, I don't believe that customers are going to stick with one firm for all financial services – the transparency of products and pricing has been so enhanced by the Internet.

Yet, he accepted that, when all is said and done, one-stop shops do not necessarily always work and that there is another more plausible future scenario:

> I think that what will happen is that you'll have clusters of firms – firms will concentrate on a few related products.

COMPETITION

This section is somewhat smaller than might be expected, because, in fact, competitive issues are considered throughout the entire range of interviews. Almost by definition, anything to do with banking is also to do with competition in the banking industry.

Jacob Wallenberg, Chairman of SEB Bank, believed that flexibility and speed of adjustment to change are what bring banks their maximum competitive edge:

> Execution, execution and execution are the sources of competitive advantage. The firm that can drive and adjust to change the fastest has the leading edge. Change forces banks to rethink their current roles. However, banks do have significant advantages in the financial services arena compared to other players in terms of credibility, trust and the ability to understand and price risk. Yet, new intermediaries will emerge, focusing specifically on individual pieces of the existing value chain and create new value chains.

Andrew Crockett of BIS accepted the importance of competition from the consumers' point of view, but sounded a warning note:

> We like competition in the economy, because it produces greater service to the consumer. But, on the financial side, competition driven by the need to improve returns for shareholders can sometimes induce greater risks to be taken. There are cases where competition is driving financial institutions to take unjustified risks.

What is undeniable is that US banks have the size, money, confidence and sheer credibility to out-compete rivals in almost any area where they choose to be players. In the future of banking, the role of American banks in moving even more into Europe than they have already, is surely going to be increasingly important. As Angel Corcostegui of BSCH said:

> European banks are still behind US firms in size and profitability, due mainly to the intensive bank sector concentration undergone over recent years in North America. From Europe we are competing with the large US banks for global clients, a segment proliferating as a result of globalization and consolidation in industrial sectors. We are also competing with US investment banks in the capital markets.

NEW ENTRANTS

This overview of the interviews has already elaborated in detail on the role of new entrants in the banking industry, so not a great deal remains to be said here. Jacob Wallenberg of SEB summarized the whole situation succinctly when he said:

> Intermediaries will come from all industries – retail, media, heavy industry – as well as brand new Internet players trying to capture a share of the consumer surplus that exists in financial services. You could certainly envision a future where technology is the intermediary.

Nor are newcomers restricted to the retail banking industry. As Wallenberg explained:

> The major US asset management houses have been making marketing pushes into the European markets for several years, sometimes directly, at other times through acquisition of local companies or via joint ventures. It is, or can be, a slow process and overall success can be elusive.

The extent to which newcomers are prepared to take on every aspect of banking activity is very much a moot point. As Marshall Carter of State Street observed:

> I think [competition from outside the industry] is only an issue in certain areas. We carry a certain amount of fiduciary risk which requires us to have a capital base. These dot.coms might be able to be our competitor in providing information technology-based services, but we don't see them wanting the fiduciary risk.

THE EURO

At the time of writing, attitudes towards the euro among the world's bankers are, to put it mildly, ambivalent. For one thing, several European Union countries have opted not to be involved with the euro at this stage and, consequently, the banks in these countries only see it as an issue relating to foreign transactions. Inevitably, the euro was always going to be a controversial issue. Many countries have a nationalistic, even rather sentimental, attachment to their own currency, although this seems fairly irrational because many of the currencies these countries used in the past are not used any more and nobody seems to mind. Even the most rabid anti-euro Englishman, for example, does not lose any sleep over the passing of the groat or the farthing. Why should the possibility of the passing of the pound really be any different? Nor are French bankers too worried about the disappearance of the *livre* (originally the value of one pound of silver, although inflation did reduce its value over time). One can understand an attachment to one's language, because language transmits culture – nobody can be surprised that Esperanto has never really caught on – but currency? It really does seem a fairly superficial element of culture.

Even without wishing to be unduly partisan, it is surely inevitable that the euro is bound to become the dominant currency of Europe. It really makes very little sense for nations locked into a single European market to have different currencies. The enthusiasm with which some euro nations have embraced the concept is both refreshing and encouraging. Finland, for example – a fiercely (and justly) patriotic country with an exquisite and subtle language, a profound culture and an extremely energetic business community (the Finnish telecoms giant, Nokia, supplies the world with mobile phones) – has embraced the euro with great enthusiasm. The bankers interviewed for this book were more circumspect about the euro – no doubt partly for political reasons. Sir Brian Pitman of Lloyds TSB, was at best lukewarm about it. As he said:

> Whether or not the euro requires a more centralized system of banking supervision depends on how politically integrated these countries become, and it's difficult to predict how integrated these companies will become. I don't think we are going to find ourselves in a world where people want more choice, that everything will be standardized.

Angel Corcostegui of BSCH observed:

> National authorities and central banks have an essential role to play in the European financial system's integration. Seeing that the process is unstoppable and knowing the advantages integration holds for firms' competitiveness and for their customers, the authorities' aim should be to facilitate full exploitation of the opportunities opened up by monetary union. In general, what is needed is that all the authorities, institutions and the private sector of member countries wake up to the new realities of the European market. In this sense, the responsibility of national and European authorities is to ensure their companies and citizens know and benefit to the full from the opportunities offered by the new market.

REGULATION

Howard Davies, Chairman of the FSA in Britain, made an extremely important general observation about the role of regulation in the banking industry, both of today and in the future:

> Industry consolidation both domestically and internationally has created institutions which are very large and very complex and that

> are very challenging to regulate effectively. We believe that it's very important that there should be consolidated supervision of these major international institutions and that the lead supervisor in the relevant jurisdiction should take responsibility for it with good relationships and good information sharing systems with the supervisor in the 'home state'.

The interviews discussed at some length the potential for a global regulator to appear in the banking industry. It is certainly true that, in some areas of wholesale banking, certain 'think tanks' provide what is almost a global regulatory role. For example, the Association for Investment Management Research (AIMR) in the United States – a key force behind the implementation of the Global Investment Performance Standards (GIPS) – can almost be said already to play a kind of global regulatory role in the area of fund management performance reporting, but is there scope for a real global regulator to appear in the banking business? Howard Davies of the FSA in the UK doesn't think so:

> I think it's inconceivable for the foreseeable future that countries would be ready to hand over control of their financial institutions to a global regulator. There is no legal basis for that and I don't think we are anywhere close to it, frankly.

David Li of the Bank of East Asia observed:

> I think it will take some years before global standards can be achieved. Even today, the European and American standards of accounting are very different and the two giants are not getting together. The American standards are getting ahead of Europe, but Europe doesn't want to adopt the American standards.

Henry Kaufman, of Kaufman & Co., on the other hand, is very much an optimist as far as global regulation and standards are concerned:

> I have long advocated a centralized body. I call it a board of overseers of major financial markets and financial institutions globally. We need uniform accounting, reporting, rating and capital reporting standards for major financial markets and major financial institutions. We now try to accomplish this on an *ad hoc* basis. It's a very slow, imperfect process, waiting for the next crisis to happen. We don't have anyone that does this on a centralized basis, but, nevertheless, we have global markets and money moves from one country to another country and financing is done in a global sense.

Andrew Crockett of BIS made the interesting observation:

> I think regulators have been moving in the direction of more pre-emptive action. It is always better to close an institution when it still has a positive net worth, because the liquidation of a financial institution, by its nature, involves losses. ... I don't think of it as being more interventionist. A number of regulators have been looking at the issue of what to do when the capital of regulated institutions falls below the prescribed minimum. There is, it seems to me, a good case for regulatory intervention at an early stage. You may call that more interventionist, but it avoids a situation arising where an institution is likely to fail with losses that are spread beyond the losses of shareholders and managers.

He also said:

> Regulators will increasingly be paying attention to the qualitative aspects of risk management. ... In the future, supervision will become less a quantitative exercise of adding up certain elements of the liability and asset sides of the balance sheet, and comparing the size. It will become a much more analytical and qualitative exercise of trying to assess how well a bank is protected against unexpected events, how well its risks are hedged, priced, traded and so on. ... Regulators also have a responsibility, where banks are being driven by their models, to take a second look and say if the model being used is adequately robust, and not just a model that tells you, 'Everything will be all right in the future, because it was all right in the past'.

In the context of changing financial services companies, Federal Reserve Board Vice Chairman, Roger Ferguson commented:

> The first implication is that regulators and supervisors have to build skills. Supervisors in particular have to build a new set of skills to deal with this broad range of institutions. That, I think, is going to mean deeper specialisation. We're probably moving away from the general bank examiner model. We're obviously going to have to build skills in areas of technology, for example, which had not been key historically, though obviously important always.
>
> The second is that regulators are going to have to recognise that in some places they are going to be catching up with the fast-moving market, and we're going to have to be able to do that much more quickly. We're going to have to be able to learn how to spot risks before they become crises.

> When all is said and done, human regulators are very good, but the market is still the better regulator. Therefore, we need to understand how to enhance the ability of the market to work by encouraging transparency, and we need to improve our skills at readng the market signals that come back.

Angel Corcostegui observed:

> Institutions are more and more global and complex. Deregulation of the international financial industry has boosted the trend towards disintermediation, tightening the connection between banking business and the capital markets. These changes alter the nature of risks in the international financial system and make regulatory and supervisory reform necessary in order to offer a sufficient guarantee in the new context. This has been recognized by the regulators themselves, who propose a review of the 1988 Basel Accord, the main basis for international financial regulation. As this proposal states, apart from better integration and internationalization in supervision, the reform should take into account the chance of advancing towards greater bank auto-regulation, given two fundamental factors: the greater discipline demanded by ever more efficient and competitive markets and the growing development of highly sophisticated research and risk control systems in the banks themselves.

Dick Kovacevich of Wells Fargo was adamant that, ultimately, regulation is only truly effective when it *is* global:

> I think there are aspects of regulation that need to be global. Certainly, from a competitive standpoint, you can't have different laws and regulations that would give one entity a competitive advantage over others because people are dealing in a global environment. From an information transfer standpoint, again, multinational companies and multinational individuals need the information and data readily available without restrictions. So there is a need for some things to be globally regulated. I see an overview of global regulations and the primary part of regulations will be country-specific. I think we're moving that way. We have these standards that apply to all financial institutions – standards of information and communication – but about 95 per cent of our regulations are country-specific. I think risk standards, capital standards, information and communication standards ought to be globally regulated – those kinds of things level the playing field. But the actual details of supervision and regulation need to be country-specific.

CONCLUSION

This overview of *The Future of Banking* started by quoting the poet and banker T. S. Eliot. It is indeed true that the end of the banking industry is always going to resemble its beginning in many extremely important ways. Life changes, people's living standards improve or fall depending on circumstances, technology transforms many aspects of the world, but people still need approximately the same kinds of banking services they needed in the 1920s, the nineteenth century and even the Middle Ages.

Yet, it is indisputable that the banking industry has changed to an extraordinary extent since the morning in 1851 when Johann Konrad Fischer visited a London bank to cash a cheque. Banks are infinitely more than mere custodians and lenders of money nowadays. They not only have their pulse on the world's finances, but, in a very real sense, *are* that pulse. The banking profession has also changed to an enormous extent – management and interpersonal skills are required now much more than has ever been the case. As for the myriad lowly, poorly paid clerks who spent up to 12 or 14 hours a day drawing up ledger books and making tedious calculations, they have gone the way of Bob Cratchit, who had his salary doubled by a reformed Ebenezer Scrooge and never looked back. Today, a single Intel Pentium III processor does more in a second than a million Bob Cratchit's could have done in a day.

So much for the past. As for the future. It has been discussed at some length in this overview and features in even greater length in the interviews you are about to read. As far as a summary of the major trends is concerned, one London-based banking consultant – Nick Masterson-Jones of the management and e-business consultancy, Charteris – offered a blueprint of the way things are going and provided the kind of provocative predictions consultants are more likely to offer than bankers, who always need to be careful about what they say in case they expose too many of their future plans.

Masterson-Jones provided comments that any knowledge of the global banking scene today reveals as being shared by many observers and players in the industry. He started by considering the future role of the cheque:

> Cheques are going to disappear. In ten years, expect the cheque to be as rare as a banker's draft is today. The issues of authentication and repudiation will get sorted out and, in ten years' time, we will be paying each other by direct credit. The drive for this will come from the States, where the inefficiencies of their fragmented clearing systems

> mean that there is a strong and natural business case for getting rid of cheques. Who knows, in the UK, we might even have managed to catch up with countries like Mexico and be able to offer same-day instead of three-day clearing!

What about the future of cash?

> Don't expect cash to disappear. It was forecast ten years ago that, by 2000, we would all be using electronic purses. This ignores the fact that there is still – and for the foreseeable future is going to be – a demand for completely untraceable, unauditable transactions.

He might also have added that the whole idea of cash disappearing is patently absurd anyway, because many types of transactions – small transactions, children's transactions, transactions where you are in a hurry and need to toss a few coins on the counter for a newspaper before catching a train or even a hyper-space plane that takes you from London to Sydney in 30 minutes – are always going to be cash-based. Again, people who don't believe this are forgetting that human needs don't really change all that much.

What about bank branches? Nick Masterson-Jones predicted:

> The branch network will continue to shrink as the bulk of the population switches to Internet banking. The 14,000 branches of retail banks will probably reduce by anything up to 75 per cent. The only branches that will survive will be those that satisfy normal retail business hurdles, such as sales per square feet or metre. The idea of a branch as a place that a bank provides to allow its customers to carry out simple banking transactions will seem laughable.

He also forecast a much greater depth of on-line functionality:

> Expect the banks, under competitive pressure, to open up their banking systems to allow customers much greater flexibility in areas such as cash management (setting up cash sweeps, etcetera). Also, expect the appearance of new mechanisms for storing value – such as on-line purses that allow consumers to spend on-line without (as is the current case) the heavy security overhead implicit in revealing debit or credit card details.

A particularly interesting prediction he made was that there would be an introduction of mass, technology-enabled personalization of banking services:

> In a few years time, I expect to log on to my bank's website and be greeted by an intelligent and friendly interface. The interface will demonstrate that my bank has a clear grasp of my banking needs, will remember the types of transactions I tend to make, will prompt me that it is my wife's birthday in a week – in fact, the on-line interface will give me a customer experience similar to the one I used to get many years ago when I first opened a bank account at my local branch of the Midland.

On the wholesale banking front, Masterson-Jones observed:

> The traditional investment banking model is dying. In the States recently, fees of 3 per cent, 5 per cent or even more were demanded by lead managers for pushing out a debt or equity issue. The reasons for this enormous fee were reach and capital – only the investment banks could get to the institutions and retail customers and get the issue away, and only the investment banks had the financial clout to underwrite the issue. Does anyone believe that is the case today? The Web means that any issuer can reach the mass market and low-cost Web brokers will undercut the banks to get to the institutions, offering two-way prices. Even underwriting will be less important. If a borrower can tap the market several times a month, because the transaction cost of so doing is so small, then the need for an underwriter is reduced. Also, expect the emergence of techniques whereby demand for a particular name is tested out on-line within financial Web communities.

He believes that many current wholesale banking professions are going to be de-emphasized or even eliminated by new technological applications. On the foreign exchange trading front, for example, he said:

> Don't expect to make much of a living as a straight forex [foreign exchange] trader. Margins, already horribly thin, are going to get tighter. The forex desk will need to be replaced, as is already happening, by Web-based dealing tools, whereby bank customers can carry out forex transactions through their on-line banking systems.

On the dealing front, he said:

> The shift towards complexity on the dealing floor will accelerate. In ten years' time, the leading banks will have incorporated risk management techniques that will allow the flows in any trade to be instantly modelled for their impact on a portfolio. The days of the risk manager stalking the dealing floor the day after a new position has caused his or her VAR (value at risk) to balloon, excitedly waving a 'capital at risk' report at the

> secondary bond desk, will go. Instead, the principles of ROVAR will be incorporated into the dealing process.

He also predicted continued consolidation of exchanges dealing in financial instruments:

> As anyone who has ever dealt in emerging or small markets can testify, the most important characteristic of a market is liquidity. By coming together, the exchanges in stock, commodities and financial instruments will provide the greatest possible mass of potential purchasers and sellers. Expect some well-publicized IT disasters *en route*, but, by 2010, if I want to unload a portfolio of Brazilian shares, I would not be surprised to find that the consolidated exchanges will facilitate a purchase in Frankfurt.

Mired in the present as we are, the future is something we can only glimpse and make inspired guesses about. Even those of us who make our livings from the banking industry are, ultimately, restricted to inspired guesswork rather than certain knowledge of what will happen.

Ultimately, the future of banking is the future of human society and nobody knows exactly how society will turn out. The only absolute certainty is that people will need banking services, will want those services delivered quickly, conveniently, at a time of their choosing and in a format they can understand and can use. Banks that make real, creative and concerted efforts to respond to this need have every right to expect profitability and success – and are likely to wind up enjoying them.

PART II

THE INTERVIEWS

SIR JOHN BOND

Chairman, HSBC Holdings

INTERVIEW BY BERNARD HICKEY

Does achieving a brand name mean being all things to all people or are there markets where one can carve out profitable niche opportunities?

Well I can think of brands that are one product, so I don't think there's anything that links having a brand with being all things to all people. I mean, Coca-Cola would be a one-product company, so I don't think it means being all things to all people. What I think it does is give clarity to clients and potential clients. I make no bones about it in HSBC – I think the Internet was perhaps one of the most powerful forces behind moving towards a global brand.

There are a billion pages on the Web and it's growing at 150 per cent per annum, and if you want to be in front you had better give your clients and potential clients around the world a little bit of a prompt, and the prompt is the brand, and it also enables you to go direct in terms of search rather than conduct a protracted scan.

This is interesting because the Internet seems to crystallize for people who are thinking about global financial services the idea that you could really market a global brand fully globally .

I couldn't leave you with the impression that it was *solely* the Internet. The Internet was the final driver, I mean it was something that we had debated for a period of time and we start all debates in HSBC by asking ourselves 'What is the customer's perspective?', and we found that our colleagues – in any form of business that crossed more than one international boundary – were spending time explaining HSBC Group to the client before they began to discuss the client's needs. We just felt that in today's world you need to be talking straight away about the client's needs and not sitting there doing a ten-minute introduction about all of the various constituent parts of HSBC Group.

That must have been a difficult decision to make because you've got some very strong brand names in the places that you're in, which you've invested money in, no doubt, in either buying or building those brand names up. What made you decide to finally go for the international, global brand?

I think we had name recognition in some countries, and we had brands in other countries. The rationale of moving to a global brand really started by trying to get outside HSBC, as I said, and look at it from a customer's perspective. But today's customers – particularly our most valuable customers – travel the world, and we had I'm going to talk a little at length here I mean usually had examples of customers of Midland Bank who'd been on holiday in Thailand, had a problem, and returned saying they wished we had a branch in Thailand. Little did they know that we were the first bank in Thailand, and that we happened to have the name the Hong Kong Shanghai Banking Corporation. We had a customer, a Canadian customer, who left southern Ontario, crossed into New York State and saw Marine Midland Bank with the logo and called up Hong Kong Bank of Canada and said, 'You've got somebody who's imitating your logo in New York State.' I mean, there was beginning to be quite a lot of of anecdotal evidence that we were not achieving clarity in the eyes of our customers. Brands, the study of brands, is, in my judgement, an art rather than a science. We conducted, in key markets, customer studies which said what would happen if we changed the name. The message we got back fairly consistently was 'I won't change my financial relationship with you if you change the name, unless I already have some grievance, and this could be the final straw.'

The evidence also suggested to us that, in eight years, First Direct had created a bigger brand name than Midland Bank had over a hundred years. And that, if anything was the crucial test, because if you can create a brand in eight years in a country where 70 per cent of the people already have a banking relationship, we wondered if we wanted to go the Hexagon Bank route and create a brand new name. But we decided that we had enormous recognition around the world in the name of HSBC, which was the name of our stock, which has 160,000 shareholders from 90 countries, it had been the nickname of the Hong Kong Shanghai Banking Corporation for a number of years and already in the wholesale markets in treasury and trading we were already known as HSBC.

That's fascinating that over eight years you can create a bigger brand than a bank that's been around for a hundred years.

And that . . . that is the fine point between brands and name recognition. First Direct was related with a very positive experience – good service, 74 per cent of their clients recommended them to somebody else for convenience, friendliness, etc.

That First Direct experience seems to me like almost a warning sign of what could happen to the established banks in the future, that someone else could come along and create such a bank.

This is what happens; Sainsbury's, Tesco, Virgin. We then decided HSBC was powerful, then there was a debate about whether or not we should include the main bank and we decided against, because we're much broader than a bank. We do insurance, investment banking and a whole array of financial services, so we decided that a bank still, in many people's eyes, has a restricted view. We then debated whether initials were better than words. We found evidence in our research that having a brand that is linked to geography could be inhibiting. It can work both ways, but there was the potential for it to be inhibiting, whereas letters were absolutely neutral. So these are all of the reasons why at the end of the day we decided to go with HSBC and the logo. We'd already done it – we'd put the logo across everything – and we were told that 'h' doesn't pronounce in Spanish, but actually, a brand is a visual and a tactile experience. It isn't so much that you talk about it, it's what you see. So, we made the decision. We clearly recognized that there were risks, so we watched attrition rates very carefully to see whether or not we were losing clients and all of the evidence that we have from our key markets around the world shows, that there was absolutely not a blip and, in fact, we had a slight up-tick in the UK market in new business attracted. There were smarter effects, which I have found some of the most interesting. We've found that we were dealing with 75 different advertising agencies around the world. We'd had 67 campaigns. So we could pay for a large amount of the conversion cost that we'd estimated at 50 million dollars by actually curtailing these campaigns: if we had a dozen corporate image advertising, we could eliminate 11. And that helped funding. We found it created a new homogeneity in the human side of the bank. Everybody was on the HSBC team. It wasn't a Midland customer being received into the Hong Kong Shanghai Banking Corporation; it wasn't a British Bank of the Middle East customer being received in the Marine Midland Bank New York; they were HSBC customers, they belonged to us.

> “It's clear to us that the brand is the experience ... what we wanted to be recognized for was integrity, fair dealing – i.e. good value for our clients, and service.”

On the issue of creating a financial services bank, because some people would say that financial services are different from soft drinks or Big Macs, you have to do different things to create a brand. How did you go about thinking about creating a financial services brand?

It's clear to us that the brand is the experience. And we believe HSBC was a long way down the road, but what we wanted it to be recognized for was integrity, fair dealing – i.e. good value for our clients, and service. Because, if you look at some of the most successful brands in the world – I suppose you could look at Coke or McDonald's or even here, some people would say Virgin – a lot of them are very specifically customer-oriented businesses and very service-oriented businesses. And there've been some people that have said that banks worldwide haven't been as customer-focused as others.

And, therefore, it'd be more difficult for a bank to create a really strong brand in the same way that you'd have a really strong brand of soft drinks or . . .

Well, we wouldn't share that viewpoint. We think today we are differentiating HSBC on the high street in the UK, for example, and we will show you evidence of that through *The Daily Telegraph* article that said HSBC is head and shoulders above the rest in terms of the complaints that they receive, in terms of the IBAS survey, which is the Independent Bank Advisory Service. Out of the 20,000-odd complaints they looked at, I think it's 1998 now, only 4 per cent came from HSBC, whereas 35 per cent came from the leading institution and 25 per cent and 22 per cent for the next.

What does somebody want from their bank? They want integrity this is their money, these are their hard-earned savings, they want somebody that looks after it with total integrity. They want fair dealing, they don't want charges introduced without any proper warning or explanation. They want fair dealing in all aspects of their financial affairs, and they want service. So we actually think that HSBC – before we moved to establish the global brand – was a long way down this track, that it was deeply imbued in the culture of HSBC from a long time ago.

It must help to . . . your not having to weld together two different cultures.

Absolutely.

One of the things I'm interested in is how you're going to leverage this brand across the world using the Internet. I mean, what specifically have you go planned?

Well, we will identify our top – personal clients – just in the same way as we had done a while ago in the corporate world the major thousand multinational companies that we dealt with. Nearly all of our private banking top clients from around the world are people who travel and we will find a way of identifying them on an international basis so that they can walk through any one of the 5,500 offices we have around the world and be recognized and looked after in a way that gives them the attention that they deserve.

What about the idea of setting up a single Internet banking plan and a single Internet bank, if you like, that traverses all boundaries?

Well, we need to be very precise when we talk about the Internet because there is a lot of hyperbole around – some stunning facts and some very misleading facts. There are people who do one-product Internet services, one geography. There are people that do one product, multiple geography. We believe that HSBC will be among the first that do multiproduct, multigeography. We are engaged with IBM on the leading edge of technology to achieve this. It will be – it is being tied – up now, being used by staff, tested by staff; it will be rolled out progressively in 2000. So, you need to identify between what's one product, one geography. If I'm using it to buy from my local supermarket, that's great. But there isn't a supermarket yet that delivers around the world. If I want a bottle of wine delivered to my daughter in Hong Kong, I don't know of a supermarket yet that I can get up on the Internet to do that. We will be able to do that in financial services. So, we are pioneering and it's exciting.

It seems to me that the Internet is good for financial services which now are a bunch of ones and zeros.

They could create a virtual bank as long as you have cash, and, you know, this is an interesting debate as to how fast . . . I mean, the technology exists to move to electronic cash, but cash is only good if it's universal, and how you move it from being 'I can transfer money to you because you're a sophisticated customer and we've both got electronic purses and we can do a transaction outside the banking system' – how far you can broaden that to the corner shop, the Coke machine, the Underground, and so forth? This is a vast technological change, it's technically feasible, technologically feasible, but is it deliverable? You know, it will be, progressively, but it will take a long, long time. So, your virtual bank, you're talking about just having a website and people putting money on it and using the Internet to move money around. Even that is an act of psychological faith by a client. We've always believed that people would be much quicker to borrow money from Internet sites – because nobody minds where they borrow from – than they will to launch their savings into cyberspace. That's where branding becomes very important. If you're talking about a real virtual bank in its literal form, then you mean electronic cash. And electronic cash . . . the technology exists for us to *transact* it here; the technology does not yet exist – although I imagine it is technically feasible – for me to *deliver* electronic cash. If I have a piece of plastic here and I want to give my daughter in Hong Kong £200 for Christmas shopping, I can't plug it into something and have it instantly transferred to her in Hong Kong yet, although the bandwidth and the telephone, you know, the lines, exist to enable that to happen.

Trust is a key issue here isn't it?

Absolutely. By having 33 billion dollars-worth of capital and a track record for having been one of the strongest financial services companies in the world. Whether you measure by market capitalization, total assets, total capital.

Another area – this is finally in branding. Some people have tried to transfer their brand in other areas into financial services; do you think that that can be done?

Yes, I think you can see evidence of that. Marks & Spencer have done it. I think the capacity to do that is undeniable. Virgin have, but you know, I think they're at the beginning of doing it. I was trying to give you somebody who'd done it and was well established. GE.

Now, one other area that we're looking at in the book is asset management, and it seems to us that this is one of the driving forces in banking services over the next however many years as countries try to confront the problem of their baby boomers ageing. There are also the opportunities of hugely growing capital markets. There's a huge crop of options there for channelling that money into those capital markets. How does HSBC, and how do you, see the group working in asset management over the years and what sorts of opportunities are there for you?

Can I just do a little definition here? Eighty-five per cent of the world's economy lies in North America, the European Union and Japan. I would estimate that less than half of the world's population holds a bank account. Five billion people – if you take China, India, Indonesia – are living in the developing world. Only 20 per cent of the people in Argentina have a bank account, only 30 per cent of the people in Brazil have a bank account, maybe 15 per cent of the people in India have a bank account. So, there is a potential for a huge demand for basic financial services in these countries, that have nothing to do with the Internet, have nothing to do with asset management, just to have put a little bit of surplus cash in a safe place instead of under the mattress. And you don't want to lose sight of that because, if you do, you miss out on one of the real growth aspects of HSBC. Why has HSBC grown at 20 per cent per annum compound for over 25 years? Because it's been providing banking services in this environment rather than in Britain, where 70 per cent of the people have a bank account and the demand for financial services is far more constrained to the level of nominal GNP, whereas the demand for financial services in Brazil has the ability to outstretch nominal GNP growth by a tremendous factor. So you need to have that backdrop.

“It is absolutely fair to say that the amount of money that is left in Western mature economies in bank accounts, is growing very slowly.”

Back to your question, asset management. What we're seeing happening progressively is that people used to keep larger amounts of money deposited in banks because they needed to keep enough money there to cover their transactional needs – be they individuals or be they companies. Progressively, as the world has moved on to different forms of payment mechanisms – credit cards, direct debits, bill payment – the amount that people keep in their bank accounts has diminished and they have assets, simultaneously freed up money, to be invested in other financial assets. Similarly, there's been a rise in disposable income and people have more surplus income to use in investments. So, it is absolutely fair to say that the amount of money that is left in Western mature economies in bank accounts, is growing very slowly. But the amount that is being invested is growing very quickly – and that's what you're really seeing in financial services today. It's a battle for the customer and the banks are saying, 'I can do your insurance, I can do your investment business for you just as well as the insurance companies or the other investment institutions', and the investment or the insurance companies say, 'I can do your banking better than the banks'. You're actually seeing a product-driven financial services industry being transformed into a customer-oriented financial services industry, where the battle is about who can win the customer's business. You've got banks trying to win insurance – call it 'bank assurance' – you've got insurance trying to win banks; call it 'Egg', and so it goes on. And the evidence is that this will grow, particularly as you see in the European Union the need to fund pensions, the emerging equity culture that exists in 'Euroland' and it will grow. Some of this will be done through pooled investments, mutual funds – 'unit trusts' as we call them here, 'mutual funds' in America. Some of it will be done through brokers, some of it will be done through banks, some of it will be done through 401K [US pension plans] or defined contribution insurance plans, but all of these vehicles point towards an increase in the demand for financial services at the investment and insurance end of the business. So, focusing on assets, I don't know . . . whether you do it through an asset, a fund management company or whether you do it through just pure delivery of these products through your bank, but the demand is rising. How individual institutions respond to the demand will be a matter of where they perceive the best way of doing it is and what they perceive to be the best way of doing it.

So does HSBC have any particular model that it favours around the world?

We have 5,500 offices around the world where we meet our customers every day. We don't believe that we should only sell our own products, because it comes back to fair dealing; we believe we should sell what's in our customers' interests. So we will distribute any investment product or insurance product, provided we have exercised strong due diligence on it and we believe it to be a fair product. And we will do that with our clients in the branches, on the telephones, over the Net, via whatever distribution channel they feel comfortable with. But the evidence at the moment suggests that people like to talk face to face about investment products and more complicated insurance products and they will only buy over the telephone, over the Net, those items which are fairly straightforward and plain vanilla; but that will change.

Do you think, then, that HSBC would ever need to buy . . . pure asset managers or pure insurance companies?

You're buying the production facility. We don't think, you know, there are different views on this, but our view is when you buy a share in HSBC you are essentially buying a share in a fantastic client list that straddles nearly all of the major geographies of wealth creation; you know, areas where wealth is being created around the world. We don't think we have to own the person that manufactures the life insurance or manufactures the unit trusts, but we think that we should vet those products and where they pass our tests, we should distribute them to our clients.

So distribution is more important than production?

Absolutely.

Do you have any strong views about how big a financial institution needs to be to be able to create a global background or whether economies of scale kick in at any point or whether it's all irrelevant? Citibank, for example, were very keen on one billion customers, is that right? That aside, I mean, what are your views on scale, does it need to be a certain size or what do you think of it?

In a service business, the most important thing is that it's manageable in terms of providing the services as close to your customers as you can. So, one of the great strengths of HSBC is that it's broken down into manageable units. We offer the template of the products and our CEO in Malaysia can . . . package them in the way that suits the customer.

You don't have a product in HSBC that's designed at the centre – one size fits all. I think tailoring your products to suit your different markets is terribly important. What you do get out of size are economies of scale on purchasing, which in terms of hard-wearing information technology, in terms of telephone communications, bandwidths – all huge potential costs for us – in terms of stationery, in terms of travel, in terms of hotel usage, all of those, unquestionably you can gain through economies of scale. So, I think size would favour people, but in the final analysis you want to treat each individual in the way they want to treated, and scale, yes, the larger the business, the more difficult it is to deliver a personal service, which is why at HSBC we believe in having the business broken down into manageable units.

That must be something to grapple with as these big companies get bigger and bigger.

Yes, you need to be able to aggregate risk very clearly, and the more capital you have, the stronger your ability to handle risks, so, to that extent, it's an advantage.

It must be difficult for an ever-growing financial services company to try to keep its eye on the ball. It must be a problem for really big financial services companies to be so big they lose touch with their customers.

Well, it's my job to make sure that part of every day I spend with a client and that we never lose the certain knowledge as we walk through the door in the morning that it's our clients that are at the heart of everything that HSBC does.

Is there anything that you're doing specifically to keep that customer focus, from breaking down?

I ask myself the question every evening on my way home – 'How many clients did you meet today?'

Another area that we're looking at is regulation. Some of these questions are designed for the regulators themselves, so it's not really appropriate, but what do you think of the idea of a global banking regulator? As we get more of these global banking and financial services companies created, what do you think about that idea?

Conceptually, HSBC wouldn't have a problem with that idea because I think it's up to the elected government and/or governments around the world to decide how it is they want to regulate financial services, and, if collectively, governments together say they want to do it with a global financial regulator, then HSBC would be entirely comfortable. But I think that we need to bear in mind that an organization like HSBC, operating in 80 countries, has 220 regulators around the world. Regulations are very much set according to a domestic political agenda. What's important to politicians about financial services in the United Kingdom isn't necessarily what's important to politicians in Malaysia. So, a global financial architecture for an organization like HSBC presupposes that 80 governments around the world have agreed that that they would rather have HSBC regulated by one international body and, presumably, less by their domestic regulators, and I think we're quite a long way from that.

One other area that we wanted to look at was, in being a global operator, do you really need to be in each part of the globe? At the moment, HSBC is obviously very strong in the UK and in Asia and in Latin America, and now in North America it's even stronger, but in Continental Europe it's not as strong as in other areas. Do you really need to be there to be a global player?

I think that if you look at the last 30 years, what you have witnessed is banks that were in the international business retreating from it. And if you go back to the Sixties, maybe then it was fashionable to think that you needed to fly the flag in as many geographies as you could. I think that that would be very far from the way HSBC sees the world. We think we need to be in countries where we can make sense of it for our shareholders and where we can make a contribution to the host economy. And one has to say that that means you're unlikely . . . you see, if global is 225 countries in the world, we're only in 80, you're not going to see, in my view, a truly global bank, but I would say that HSBC is as international as any financial institution in the world today. So we won't be in every geography, we'll only be in the geographies where, as I say, we can make sense of it to our shareholders and contribute to the host country's economy.

> “I can't see anything in the next century that says that a customer has to buy an insurance product from an insurance company, banking services from a bank, investment services from an investment institution.”

Out in the States there's a debate about whether or not banks should get together with insurers. I think you partly answered the question earlier when you talked about production and distribution, but what are your views generally on banks and insurers getting together and whether or not they can really create benefits by being together?

Well, Glass-Steagall is much more about investment banking than commercial banking and, in a sense, what you're really seeing is America having its system on the same footing as that in the UK and Germany and many other countries of the world. I think it's Japan and America that are the conspicuous examples of countries that try to draw a clear line between investment banking and commercial banking. I can't see anything in the next century that says that a customer has to buy an insurance product from an insurance company, banking services from a bank, investment services from an investment institution. I think any company such as HSBC that offers each one of those services in a competitive, good-value way will attract the business. So, I think it is perfectly possible for a customer to do all of that financial business with HSBC, provided we make certain that, as I say, we offer good products of fair value.

On that issue of being a distributor for perhaps other people's products, do you have a view about whether this should be done at arm's length or whether you need some sort of partnership arrangement with someone who is the producer?

I don't think you need a partnership arrangement. What you need is a good due diligence team that says 'These are quality products and we can sell these with confidence to HSBC's clients'. I think it's up to us to make sure that we deliver them, we don't need the producer looking over our shoulder.

Another question we've got here is this issue of risk and I think that partly this question was written in the aftermath of the LTCM issue. Is there a point where some of these global financial groups become so big that they become dangerous to the stability of the world's financial system, where one takes over and is so big that it could be dangerous for the rest?

Financial services have always been vulnerable to that – absolutely – because there is a huge interconnection between one financial institution and another. Why? Because we all have learned over the centuries that maintaining liquidity is very important for depositor confidence. And how do you maintain liquidity? You lend it in the bank. And there are many financial institutions whose largest risk exposure is to our own industry, which tells you of the interconnectivity of banks and financial institutions around the world. So, I can understand full well when the Basle Committee says it wants to revise the capital rules, but it does not want to see less capital in the financial services industry.

Do you think there's a danger that there will be fewer and fewer larger and larger groups, where this becomes a problem? Do you think you could create a risk?

The risk is always there. There is no such thing as risk-free banking. But I think it's more there in that it exists less in the cash markets and exists more in the derivative markets.

How do you think HSBC will look in, let's say, five, ten years' time, from a consumer point of view and from the investor point of view?

Naturally, I would wish that it was a well-known and well-respected name to clients around the world and that it is an investment that has delivered long-term consistent growth and value to our shareholders.

MARSHALL CARTER

Chairman and Chief Executive Officer,
State Street Corporation

INTERVIEW BY TONY MUNROE

The first section here is on demographics.

That says it all right there. See that ad we did? I would say the demographic shift in the world is a revolution that is going to impact us. A change that is going to impact us even more than the Internet. The reason being, we don't yet know what 40-year retirements are going to do. We are talking about *40*-year retirements. You're how old – 20 or . . .?

30.

OK. You entered the workforce when you were what – 22?

Yes.

I'll be 60 in a couple of months and I have been in the workforce since I was 17 or 18, I was in college and everything. You know, I could have a 30-year retirement, too. And, I think what is happening is – for the average person in the world – not people like us who make reasonable salaries – this 30- to 40-year retirement is very significant. Because it drives everything else.

Right. So, as the baby boom generation, you know, turns from savers into dis-savers, as they put it here, how does that affect competition in the asset management industry?

Well, the first thing that I hear about these baby boomers, they start to withdraw from the market and spend. And that's going to cause the market to go down. Two reasons why I disagree with that trend. First is – people don't pull it out and take it home. Then the most conservative would be to put it in a bank in CDs (Certificates of Deposit). But, then the bank uses it for things like that. Second is – your generation tends to be now viewed as a saving generation. You guys have mutual funds. You started 401Ks when you were 22 – they are going to grow. So, they're going to fill in behind that generation. So, I don't accept this view that the market is going to crash when the baby boomers start pulling it out because they are not going to pull it out all at once.

But they won't be putting in as much.

That's true. Yes. But then your generation will pick up that.

Europe is widely expected to see an explosion in the asset management industry. What factors might constrain the pace of growth – regulation, traditional saving habits and the high cost of labour. How do you see those factors weighing?

I think that the latter one is not an issue. The high cost of labour is already here in the asset management business, if you look at the salaries. Plus, the asset management business tends to be an efficient business, especially if you go to indexes. So, it doesn't take many people to manage these assets. I think the first trend that is going to impact this is that the European governments – with the exception of the UK – privatized in 1978 – their pension fund, part of it – has to get this burden of providing the retirement off their backs. Because they now have almost shrinking populations. Every German worker puts 19.2 per cent of his or her salary into the German pension system. Now, your generation in Germany is not real happy about that. So I think that's the real trend. I also think that cultural changes can be as significant in Europe as you see in places like Japan. You know, in Japan, 83 per cent of the people have some of their savings in the postal system? Well, in Japan the post office is like a savings bank, actually. Well, in Europe, the big universal banks have a phenomenal share of the savings. And mutual funds are really just getting going. So, I think the shift from countries of savers to countries of investors is as much cultural as anything else. And it is going to take some time.

> “I would say the demographic shift in the world is a revolution that is going to impact us. A change that is going to impact us even more than the Internet.”

Big banks in Europe now control the distribution network that asset management companies are seen needing to prosper. What does this imply for new entrants, particularly US firms wanting to tap that market?

I think it implies that it is going to be . . . two things in my mind that hit me right away. You can go it alone, but it might be slower, and that implies that you probably need a partner. You need to go in, you need a partner for distribution, but then the question is, OK, if you partner up with these big European universal banks for distribution, how many years does it take them before they say, 'Well, I have my own mutual fund now, I don't need you any more'? So there's a danger in partnering up. The other danger in partnering up is that you lose your brand. Which, I think, is why Fidelity tends to go it alone in places. They don't want to lose their brand.

“I don't think it would be good for the world if these financial institutions adopt the view, in their own mind, that they are too big to fail”

We'll return to branding, actually, and now we are on to regulation. Has the pace of consolidation created global giants that are too big to fail.

I hope not because we will then be in the position where maybe these companies will be like the old phone company – Ma Bell – they won't change with the times. I think the most difficult issue that we face is that you have to ask before that question. How are we going to deal with multinationals when they get in trouble? Who has jurisdiction? What is a dominant country of regulation jurisdiction? For example, we started a European Bank, and we chose the British regulators. Where do we have the headquarters? We could have chosen any of the EU countries. But I would say, I don't think it would be good for the world if these financial institutions adopt the view, in their own mind, that they are too big to fail, and that, if they get into trouble by lousy strategic decisions, somebody's going to bail them out.

Should there be a global super-regulator?

I don't think it is possible to get a global supra-regulator in place.

OK. Does the creation of the euro require a more centralized system of banking supervision?

It is too early to tell, maybe. Because I don't think one year . . . I don't think that we have had any euro-based banks that have gone belly up, gotten in trouble. The question is whether or not, when a euro-based bank gets in trouble, the country will take immediate, swift actions or will it revert back to its traditional country mode?

With the bundling of various financial services under one roof, does this increase the likelihood of conflicts of interest arising?

Well, when you say conflict of interest, do you mean a product overlap or one part of the company competing with another part?

I think both, actually. And suitability, I'm presuming if you have insurance, securities and deposit-taking all under one roof.

Are you back to pre-Glass-Steagall?

Well, yes, but we are speaking globally, I think, not just the US.

In today's world . . . for example, yesterday I had lunch with the senior relationship officer in charge of relationship banking for Citigroup. And, Citigroup is one of our top two dozen customers. They are also one of our top competitors. They are also one of our top counterparties. In today's financial services world, everybody is a competitor, a counterparty and a customer with each other, and the most sophisticated companies have no trouble dealing with that. For example, we process mutual funds for other large investment managers.

At the same time, our 401K [pension plans] salesforce has been going head-to-head somewhere out in the Midwest for some 401Ks for some business. At the same time, our FX [foreign exchange] trading desks are probably using each other as a counterparty on some $200 million dollar deal. So, sophisticated companies recognize that, with a level playing field in financial services, these things will happen. In the nine years that I have been CEO here, I've only had one customer who I almost had to say, 'If you are uncomfortable with us being your customer, counterparty and competitor, then, please take your business somewhere else.' Now, they didn't actually have to do that, but you know, some day you might have to.

All right. Has the intense, competitive nature of financial services rendered many institutions less fit to cope with the future economic downturn. In other words, how healthy are today's balance sheets, do you think?

Now, I don't have a good sense for that, because of the industries – insurance, banking, broker–dealer, investment managers are so different. It seems to me like the insurance companies are in pretty good shape. The banks are in pretty good shape, I guess. I still think that rather than ask that question about the balance sheet, I think the more important question is if you take a major financial institution, what is the composition of the revenue stream and the profits between highly volatile sources, and non-volatile sources? So, if you look at our earning stream, you will see a very high percentage of fee income which tends to be annuity-like, and you'll see maybe 15 per cent highly volatile sources – like securities lending and FX.

Now, if I looked at a financial services company and I saw that 60 per cent of their revenue every year came from what I would consider to be highly volatile sources, that, to me, may be more important, when you consider a downturn in the global economy, than their actual balance sheet strength.

OK. All right. Branding. Does achieving a brand name mean being all things to all people or are their niche markets where one can carve out profitable opportunities? And I'm sure you have an opinion on it.

Needless to say, we agree with number two, because that's what we are. I think that there needs to be a term that doesn't describe niche as small. The problem is 'niche' carries with it the connotation of small. Because you describe us – we have $6 trillion in custody. We have $667 billion of assets under management. So, basically, we control here $6.6, $6.7 trillion. Total market cap of the 100 or so stock markets in the world that you can invest in is about $50 trillion.

So, passing through this place every day is about 12 per cent of the world's wealth. And I don't think you would call us a niche player – I think you would call us a very . . . an institution that's very focused on what they do well, which is manage assets and service assets.

All right. What do traditional financial service providers need to do to combat competition from outside the industry or is that an issue even?

I think that is an issue only in certain areas. We carry a certain amount of fiduciary risk which requires us to have a capital base. And, we don't see many of these dot.coms or Microsoft-type companies that are on-line. They might be able to be our competitor in providing information technology-based services, but we don't see them wanting the fiduciary risk. I mean you know enough about custody – you know about corporate actions, right? And how corporate actions get executed and all? And, if you miss one, you have to pay for that out of your pocket?

Right.

Yes. I mean I can point to cases where, let's say, you have three portfolios that have a large number of stock warrants. And, for one reason or another, you execute the warrants in two portfolios and you don't in the third. And when the customer finds out about it the next day, you have to go on the open market and you can buy the stock that you should have gotten through the warrant. And there's sure to be a $50 difference in price. You have to make that up out of your pocket. Just like loan losses, in commercial banks. Well, we don't see a lot of the non-financially based companies that want to assume that risk. Nor do we see the customers that want to sign up with them, and not be covered by that risk. Because, you can bet, if we make a mistake on a corporate action for a big mutual fund, they are not going to split it with us.

Yes, we understand.

We didn't drop the ball, *you* guys dropped the ball, [laughter] you know?

How much is size linked to branding?

I think size is important – no, size and multiplicity of products. Size and a multitude of products are important for branding. And I would use us as an example. Until a few years ago, we were sort of name-challenged, for lack of a better term. So, for example, I go to Germany and make a call on an enormous German manufacturing company. I meet the treasurer, and then I work for half a day with the pension manager. And the pension manager wants to get his master trust serviced. So, he puts together the package for this chief financial officer, and the four finalists are Chase, Bankers Trust, UBS and State Street. Now, the pension manager clearly knows about State Street because he reads *Plan Sponsor*, he reads *The Economist*, he reads *Global Custodian*. And he looks at the Reuters stuff and you guys do a pretty good job of covering custodians, but the treasurer and the CFO don't know State Street. So they say, 'Who is this little Massachusetts bank? And why do they only do this focused business?' Most of the questions that I get when I go overseas are . . . in the world of universal banks we are a real anomaly. A real anomaly. And they always ask us, 'How can you be so successful – 22 years of double-digit earnings per share with only your limited product set?' Our answer is that we know how to do what we do very well. And we don't do things that we don't know how to do and don't do well. So that's not a niche player any more – that is a focus player.

“We are a real anomaly. And they always ask us, 'How can you be so successful – 22 years of double-digit earnings per share with only your limited product set?' Our answer is that we know how to do what we do very well. That's not a niche player any more – that is a focus player.”

All right. Technology in e-commerce. What is the future role of information in global banks with big distribution networks and electronic transaction systems. Could you develop proprietary information on transactions that would be used to generate information products?

OK. What sorts of products?

Information about portfolios, foreign exchange, flow of foreign exchange around the world.

I think it can, but there is going to be a privacy issue, which is coming up big in this country, which may or may not come up outside the United States. And the privacy issue is – if one of these new financial services companies owns an insurance company, credit cards, bank, mutual fund, healthcare processor, used cars, leases – how much exchange of facts that you make so much a month, have a 7-year-old Dodge Dart, you know, I mean, don't have any life insurance . . . I mean, the stuff you filled out for your HMO [Health maintenance organisation], that they're processing. The real question is, are these guys going to barrage you with mail, or a phone call at dinnertime?

Right, it's at dinnertime. The answer is 'Yes'. Probably.

Yes, but in this country, there's starting to be an effort within the States – the individual States – because the federal finance services legislation . . . I don't think that they address it. Didn't they, like, sort of step aside on this one?

Yes.

At the very end, they, like, punted on this one. Now, you know, this has always been true. I think the interesting thing is the way that this has been taking a turn. I worked for a big money centre bank in New York and the big money centre banks and the big financial services institutions tend to be collections of product companies, so, when I was in New York City, a customer named Marsh Carter bought products from seven companies. There were seven Marsh Carters in the books and records of this big conglomerate. I then went for three years to work in a very small regional bank in upstate New York. Now, this bank had a customer indicative file, where they recorded all of the products that a customer used. So, in this bank there was *one* customer named Carter who used nine products. And that's what we do here. We have a tremendous cross-sell ratio. But, so this concept of cross-selling in the community and small regional banks has always been there. I don't know – where did you grow up?

In DC.

“People think when they talk cross-selling, people think that you are talking about Citigroup . . . The small banks do it because their customer-indicative file is your account officer. So you had like a walking database as opposed to a client database that people say that they are trying to exploit.”

Who did you bank with – Riggs? Growing up? Or where did your folks bank?

Riggs initially, and then American Security.

American Security.

Riggs is the main one.

Yes, but I'll bet your folks did everything at Riggs in those days – in the Fifties and Sixties?

Well, it was the Seventies and Eighties – Sixties, Seventies, and Eighties.

Yes.

I would presume so. I don't know to be honest with you.

Smaller banks have always done this. In fact, I'm almost wondering why [a side question to Gregg Ahearn of State Street] the ABA [American Bankers' Association] and the SIA [Securities Industry Association] don't look at this. Why don't they draw a parallel to the small, retail community banks?

Because people think when they talk cross-selling, people think that you are talking about Citigroup, not Riggs, or Cambridgeport Bank, or something.

Do you live in Cambridge?

No, I live on Beacon Hill. but I am pulling out a small bank.

No, no, I know, because I live in Cambridge. But that's exactly right. Cambridgeport has always provided – my wife banks at Cambridge Trust. They can do just about everything for her.

Greg Ahearn: Great little bank too.

Yes.

Greg Ahearn: You've got the small banks in the bottom, and of course, but your wife will get dragged into it because of the big ones, and up here – they will overwhelm people with trades and all.

Well, you know how the small banks do it? The small banks do it because their customer-indicative file is your account officer. That's how we did it at upstate New York – a $3 billion dollar bank with 140 branches. Those branch offices had handled a company that made ballpoint pens over in Buffalo. *They* did – they knew what his banking needs were and they tried to provide them. So you had like a walking database as opposed to a client database that people say that they are trying to exploit.

Yes. I remember when I was at the Herald *I did a story on Citizens when they started selling mutual funds – but they have for a while. Citizens, here in town. And the biggest, most – I guess lucrative – they got the most mutual fund sales in branches in sort of low to moderate-income neighbourhoods. And I think it was because people didn't have relationships with anyone else. Their only present relationship was with a bank. They didn't have necessarily a 401K with Fidelity or anybody else.*

And they might have been distrustful of personal financial advisers.

Yes.

Plus, in that particular neighbourhood, I'll bet that you ran square into the bug-a-boo of banks when they started selling mutual funds, which was that the average person thought they were getting an FDIC-insured item.

Well, that certainly came up. Yes. All right. What is the future of traditional exchanges? Like, the NYSE?

Well, my own personal view is that the floor exchanges will not disappear in my lifetime. And, as I said, I'll be 60 by the time this book comes out. But, it might in your lifetime. I still think that there's a strong market nature to what we do. Although Nasdaq has certainly proved that you don't need a trading floor. And, countries like India are going on a Nasdaq-type model, so you certainly can do it. I think that these alternative trading networks, these exchanges, are clearly going to be around, the wave of the future. But I think it is going to be very difficult to give up the old floor trade, but, what may happen is the floor trader that represents the firm – it's so electronic now. You know the little things you see the UPS guy carrying?

Yes.

They may be – what you may have instead of a geographically diversified linked market, you'll have a geographically focused market, but people will still be operating electronically in that market. That's really what you have at the Boston Stock Exchange now. You walk over to the Boston Stock Exchange and what you see is – not like a trading floor, trading like in New York – but everybody sitting at their terminals, but in a floor environment. And there is no reason why that terminal, by the time another ten years goes by, has not got the same amount of computing power they had in the early space ships. The early space capsules. Just like the UPS guy has. Or, when you go into Staples and the guys are doing inventory control . . . That's incredible technology.

Will the new ECNs – these new networks – have sufficient liquidity, do you think, to displace traditional exchanges?

I would say, right now they don't. I think the question is going to have to be determined as to whether they can link into liquidity pools through the people that own them or that have partial ownership. I think that is a big question that has got to be decided. The good example of this is the one ECN [electronic communications networks] that all the different guys own. Goldman Sachs – and somebody I can't think of the name of – Archipelago – is that one of those?

Yes.

That's a good example. And I don't think that you find out the answer to that question, until you have a 20 per cent market correction.

OK. Do you think we'll see consolidation among these ECNs?

Yes, just like everything else, sure.

On-line consumer banking. What is the future in the US, Europe and Asia? Are there cultural, regulatory and legal obstacles to the proliferation of such services?

Of course, but I'll have to caveat my answer that we do no retail banking any more. I would say that I am a reasonably computer-astute individual. I don't think it is going to make a big splash in America – and it is pretty popular now – until all of this stuff comes across a single pipe into your house and into your TV. You can sit in front of your TV with your clicker and bring it up and do it a lot easier than you can do it now. I am still waiting for the chequeless society. [Laughter] And, in fact, the Europeans are actually way ahead of the US on the chequeless society and using euro-cards and things like that.

Electronic deposits and all that?

All that stuff, yes. And not even having to worry about paying your utility bill and things like that. But, for some reason, and, I guess, I wonder if it – if you look at the second order, or the second or third or fourth order – the reason why people in America write cheques, I think it is probably linked to the IRS – they still demand proof. And proof of charitable contributions is a letter or a cancelled cheque or something like that.

That's interesting. OK, I think we are going to talk about risk now. What are the lessons learned from the global crises – 1997 and 1998? And have there been measures taken to tighten the monitoring activities of firms like Long-Term Capital Management and their relationships with banks?

Well, first, from 1988 – after the crash of 1987 until 1995, I was the Co-Chairman of the US working committee in the Group of Thirty. Which went from same-day funds to T plus Three [The time from when a trade occurs to when it is settled; 3 = days]. And I think the success of the efforts and securities processing by the Securities Industry Association, G-30, DTC [The Depository Trust Company], everybody, has been that, during this crisis of 1997 and 1998, there was not a single country that had the kind of problems processing the flows of capital and securities that we had in 1987 when you had 40 per cent fail rates. And the countries that did have problems, like Malaysia, I mean they, like, sort of changed the rules. Right there, to curb the off-shore investments. So, it was really a different issue. That's – so that is lesson number one. Lesson number one is we have made tremendous strides in freeing up the flow of capital and securities around the world – electronically. Number Two – the big shock to major shareholders of Long-Term Capital Management was the multiple places in their company that had exposure to LTCM and didn't know it. Now, if you go back and look at them – I won't mention any names. So, for example, you had one big company that had a clearly owned part of it. They had invested in it. Then they had put part of their retirement fund in it. Then they had put some of their private clients in it. And then the trading floor was tracking their securities, so that they were doing some of the same kind of trades. So, I think the big shock that hit me was nobody had a single, consolidated, massive, risk-management system that portrayed all the risk from a customer. And this is, like, the opposite of a customer-indicative file. This would be a customer risk profile. Which is where you say to yourself, 'Show me the 17 ways – bring up Company X-Y-Z, located in Australia, and show me across my entire global organization – every place where we plug in a user.'

Right. Every point of exposure.

That's what you've got to have. And we're building one of those – we have had one of those for a few years – but it is mostly for the top several hundred clients, where you have major risk. It is not for the $10 million dollar pension fund.

All right. Do regulators have adequate means to measure risk in financial institutions? Is there the need for a global body that monitors risk?

I don't think that there is a need for a global body. I think there's a need for the Federal Reserve Banks – for the federal, for the central banks in each country – and the central securities and exchange commissions, and the market apparatus to continue talking and sharing information. But I don't see where the creation of a giant bureaucracy, 'Regulator in the Sky,' or agency is going to – I mean we already have the BIS anyway – Bank for International Settlement – so they – maybe their role could be expanded. I think that the – I don't know the answer. I don't know the answer to the question – do the regulators get enough free-flow of information that they don't have to go out and ask to monitor risk? I guarantee, though, if the Federal Reserve Bank, or the SEC [Securities and Exchange Commission] felt like they weren't getting enough, they would certainly change. For example, I will give you an example of how they do change. As mutual funds have grown tremendously in the last ten years, the Federal Reserve Bank has asked major processors like us for different kinds of periodic reports on size and distribution pattern and all. So, when they realize they don't have enough information, they go out and get it.

OK. Is the assumption of greater risk by individuals in managing their futures a positive or a negative development for the health of the global financial system? Very timely.

Yes, I think it is a positive because it will feed more capital into the system. But this is where you really run into the culture of savers versus investors and that is going to be a country-by-country thing. You know, if a country has a reputation of inefficient or insufficient regulation in their securities industry and stock markets – so that there have been big scandals . . . Then they are going to have trouble shifting people away from traditional savings. For example, in this country, since 1940, in the 1940s Act – I think with the exception of Bernie Cornfeld, which was the 1960s or the 1970s – we haven't had a single major scandal in the mutual fund industry. So the 1940 Bill – the SEC Act of 1940 – and its stability and people's faith in our securities industry – certainly must have helped these last few years. And American companies are very transparent in their earnings and their proxies. We don't see that in all the countries that you can invest in.

Right. Right. But in terms of just speaking of the assumption of risk by individuals, I mean, there's not so much a risk of fraud so much as just market volatility.

Yes. And once you invest outside your own country, you have foreign exchange volatility. We see in 401Ks that Americans are very conservative. In their investment pattern, and women are even more conservative than men.

Despite this dot.com bubble that people talk about?

Yes. But did you see – it was really interesting. When did the market dip? Three months ago? Three or four months ago. Did you see where the money flowed out of the dot.com info-tech into the traditional GEs, General Motors and people like that? That surprised me. That *really* surprised me.

Why did it surprise you?

Because here people are shifting out of the future into the smokestack industries. And you wonder, well, what are they thinking about? You know, you go back . . . when was the latest hit? Because it was written up . . .

It was in the third quarter.

And so the question is, you look at this pattern and – I don't even know how much it was, but it would have to be a couple of hundred billion for the *Journal* and all – and then the question is, 'OK, why did people do that? What was their thinking pattern of going back to smokestack America, from dot.com America?' That would be a pretty catchy little story.

Yes. All right. Consolidation again. Are there limits to the trend towards consolidation, in terms of efficiency and economies of scale? And, does technology lead to more efficient ways of servicing financial needs and thereby reduce the scope of mammoth organizations?

Yes, I think that the answer to that question is 'Yes', definitely. Technology can prevent the lack of coordination, lack of customer focus that you would get, say, ten years ago. Where people from one business unit in a big company would call on the same customer without knowing that the other guys were there. But, I would say that the biggest is the co-equal partner with information technology, to do that is tough management. Management has to make sure that the people from the insurance subsidiary don't go visit X-Y-Z without checking with some central source, you know. So that everybody knows – and that management relates to rules of the road – how you deal with customers from multiple-product companies and, second, how you communicate that.

Is there a point at which economies of scale are no longer economies? Where they are too big to really be able to be managed efficiently or does technology mitigate that?

Well, technology helps that. But, I think there is a point where you – I'd probably have to break the units into faster-moving more market-focused units. For example, for us, it would be at six trillion – we are still comfortable that we can process a lot of things centrally. At nine trillion – we may say to ourselves, 'OK, we are going to have three processing organizations.' You know, Europe, Middle East, Africa, North and South America, Asia. And we'll bridge across them for those customers that are located in more than one spot. Today, we don't need to do that. But, we certainly couldn't do that without technology in the future.

All right. Having all of one's financial needs served by one organization seems to be the strategic goal of certain financial institutions. From the customer's standpoint, what are the perceived benefits and drawbacks of such an arrangement?

Well, the perceived benefits are, of course, you are only divulging all your information to one source. And one source should be able to meet your needs. The risk, of course, is if that company gets in trouble, you have all your eggs in one basket. That's the risk.

OK. Are there competition issues that might arise from further consolidation – from a regulatory perspective, what are the systemic risk implications of larger international institutions?

Yeah, I think there probably are some sorts of systemic risks. Because one player could have – one player that gets in trouble could have a much great impact on the markets of the world. And to the extent that there are fewer of these big players, you get less of an ability to maybe bail them out. I think there is also – there could be an anti-trust issue in this country.

The euro. How rapid is consolidation likely to be in Europe, given the euro's introduction?

Boy, I don't know. As I say, we are a year into it and a lot of things happened that we didn't think would happen – like parity with the dollar. That was a big surprise to me. And it even dipped below the dollar a few times. We certainly don't think we've seen the start of some massive shift. I think what we've seen is people doing like we do, which is OK – how do we attack the top 500 corporations in Europe as a whole – forget about our structural needs. Country – let's go for the . . .

Treat it as one place?

Yes. Treat it, treat Euroland as one place. Right.

OK. With regard to mergers within Europe.

I think you are going to see those. But, I don't see a trend yet because, don't forget, I think some of these institutions still operate under their country regulations. And we don't see that much change.

So, what are the obstacles to European cross-border mergers, and how important is the role of national authorities and central banks over there?

I think, in the next five to ten years, the role of the national authorities and central banks is still going to be very strong. And there's not a – I also am not convinced that all countries view the European Commission the same way, too. I think the big test will come when one or two countries allow their ratios and their financial status to drop below the criteria that got them in the euro in the first place. Then the question is, 'Are they going to change the criteria? Are they going to make a special case? Are they going to throw them out?' I don't see them throwing them out.

It's a big difference too whether it is Germany or Portugal.

[Laughter] Right. That is exactly right, yes. How many 800-pound gorillas can you have in the cage. I would agree with you on that, yes. I think it is just too early to tell.

All right. Well, that's it – if there is anything else that you would like to add?

No, I think – no, I'll tell you what I do think is the big issue is pension reform. Pensions, because of the ageing population. The pressures on the ageing population go head-to-head with pension reform. And, you know, pension reform provides a great source of investment capital for countries. It makes the securities markets rise and it'll bolster economic growth. So, we think that pension reform will go hand-in-hand in this next 20 years.

ANGEL CORCOSTEGUI

Chief Executive
Banco Santander Central Hispano (BSCH)

INTERVIEW BY LIZ O'LEARY

Are there limits to the trend towards consolidation in terms of efficiencies and economies of scale?

It is true that there is a limit to consolidation advantages in terms of economies of scale, but size is not just important for achieving lower costs through economies of scale. It is also necessary to enable risk diversification, improve service quality to a more and more global clientele and attract the best human resources.

We must remember that European banks are still behind US firms in size and profitability, due mainly to the intensive bank sector concentration undergone over recent years in North America. From Europe we are competing with the large US banks for global clients, a segment proliferating as a result of globalization and consolidation in industrial sectors. We are also competing with US investment banks in the capital markets, so we must acquire greater management capability here, as our companies' search for finance is switching towards the markets. These are all reasons to think there is still plenty of room for financial sector consolidation in Europe.

Could technology lead to more efficient ways of servicing financial needs and thereby reduce the scope for mammoth organizations?

There is no doubt that technological development is one of the main motors of change in the financial system. In our sector, technology is

> "Technology, far from representing a threat to the leading banks, is an instrument which, if exploited well, can boost their efficiency and competitivity even more."

allowing new competitors all over the world to rapidly develop numerous e-businesses to exploit the rapid growth of potential customers and the low per-transaction cost. However, technology is an even greater source of opportunity for the large banks, who already have an immense client base and brand image the new competitors do not possess and could take years to acquire. All e-business is a volumes not margins business, and volume is determined by the number of clients. As such, technology application in firms starting out with a wide client base offers competitive advantages that are hard to beat. Hence, technology, far from representing a threat to the leading banks, is an instrument which, if exploited well, can boost their efficiency and competitivity even more.

Having all of one's financial needs served by one organization seems to be the strategic goal of certain financial institutions. From a customer standpoint, what are the perceived benefits and drawbacks of such an arrangement?

Mergers in the financial sector are not limited to banks, but, rather, seek to create large financial groups active in retail banking, insurance, asset management, pension funds, etc. Multiproduct integration aims to offer a global response to all the customers' financial needs through creation of large 'financial service supermarkets'.

This strategy enables substantial cost savings and efficiency gains, which undoubtedly benefit consumers. The groups' greater size will increase their ability to offer cheaper products and services and invest in new services or improve existing ones, raising customer satisfaction. However, along with a wide range of products, it is crucial to offer customers global and very personalized advice. In an ever more complex and opportunity-filled financial world, consumers will value the convenience of retaining one or a few advisers offering global solutions to their multiple specific requirements.

Are there competition issues that might arise from further consolidation?

The consolidation taking place in the banking industry is a strategic response to a business background demanding greater competiveness and efficiency. Banks are seeking greater size precisely to compete better in a market transformed by globalization, the demographic transformation and the technology revolution.

Through consolidation, competition increases in the first division, where more and more large groups are present. If we look at the world bank ranking by assets, we find that the five leading firms are financial groups created from 1998 and 1999 mergers, and they are, on average, four times as big as the top five entities just ten years ago. These banks are already competing on a global, not national level.

These trends to consolidation and internationalization are also stimulating competition between smaller firms, which must better defend their traditional market niches, whether geographic, sectorial or in certain products. The increase in competition is particularly clear in EMU [European Monetary Union], where all financial firms now compete with the region's over 9000 banks. This increasing competition at all levels demands efficiency gains by banks that clearly benefit consumers.

“The five leading firms are financial groups created from 1998 and 1999 mergers, and they are, on average, four times as big as the top five entities just ten years ago. These banks are already competing on a global, not national level.”

It is worth mentioning the case of the United States, where bank consolidation has not prejudiced private clients of financial services. On the contrary, competition has notably improved consumers' finance terms.

From a regulatory perspective, what are the systemic risk implications of larger international institutions?

The financial system's transformation demands, without doubt, a response in terms of regulation and supervision. At present, regulation is based on a clear separation of financial activities (save in the UK, perhaps) and, on a domestic approach, whereas the institutions are more and more global and complex. Furthermore, deregulation of the international financial industry has boosted the trend towards disintermediation, tightening the connection between banking business and the capital markets.

These changes alter the nature of risks in the international financial system and make regulatory and supervisory reform necessary in order to offer a sufficient guarantee in the new context. This has been recognized by the regulators themselves, who propose a review of the 1988 Basle Accord, the main basis for international financial regulation.

As this proposal states, apart from better integration and internationalization of supervision, the reform should take into account the chance of advancing towards greater bank auto-regulation, given two fundamental factors: the greater discipline demanded by ever more efficient and competitive markets and the growing development of highly sophisticated research and risk control systems in the banks themselves.

How rapid is consolidation likely to be in Europe given the euro's introduction?

Consolidation in the European bank sector is proving fast and intense. The euro pushes our sector to remodel itself in European terms, as it has eliminated national currencies as a barrier between domestic markets. For this reason, the banks first seek size in order to compete on a European level.

There has been continuous news of bank mergers since the beginning of the year. Indeed, we may say that we began the process when we announced the merger of Banco Santander and Banco Central Hispano just a fortnight after the launch of EMU. Some deals have not worked out, but it is true that the sector is in the full throes of transformation. Probably, by the time euro notes and coins arrive, we will have a significantly different European banking map than the one we know today.

In BSCH, we are committed to this process of a financial Europe. We want to be a leading bank in the Europe of the euro, and this is where we are dedicating our efforts and energies.

What are the obstacles to European cross-border mergers?

The road to the consolidation of an integrated European bank sector is not free of obstacles. There are technical barriers, such as the different tax, accounting, good management and supervisory systems. But these technical barriers will be gradually resolved as European bank consolidation advances.

None the less, apart from the technical barriers, creation of a European banking industry is being hampered by some national authorities' insistence on championing the domestic nature of their financial sectors.

This political reticence is delaying creation of pan-European firms capable of efficiently producing and marketing financial products throughout the European market. Transnational consolidation is the natural tendency of banking in an integrated monetary area. Indeed, this is the experience of USA, where elimination of the restrictions on inter-State bank mergers started at the end of the 1980s gave way to an unstoppable process of mergers and acquisitions.

But EMU furthermore offers the European financial system the chance to compete with the North Americans on a global scale. For this to occur, it is necessary to create European leading banks that are sufficiently large and competitive.

In short, protectionist attitudes only hamper the process of consolidation in European banking, which is not just a natural response to the new size of the market, but would also raise the financial sector's efficiency and its international competitiveness.

How important is the role of national authorities and central banks?

National authorities and central banks have an essential role to play in the European financial system's integration. Seeing that the process is unstoppable and knowing the advantages integration holds for firms' competitiveness and for their customers, the authorities' aim should be to facilitate full exploitation of the opportunities opened up by monetary union.

In general, what is needed is that all the authorities, institutions and the private sector of member countries wake up to the new realities of the European market. In this sense, the responsibility of national and European authorities is to ensure their companies and citizens know and benefit to the full from the opportunities offered by the new market.

ANDREW CROCKETT

General Manager, BIS
(Bank for International Settlement)

INTERVIEW BY ALICE RATCLIFFE

Given consolidation in the financial industry, have institutions been created that are too big to fail?

It has always been the case that the difficulties of large financial institutions pose public policy issues and, in some cases, necessitate some kind of public intervention. Presumably, as more institutions get larger and more complex, the public policy issues that are raised by those difficulties themselves become more complex. That doesn't mean to say that a large institution, just because it is large, is going to be protected. It can fail in different ways: it can be merged or it can, in certain circumstances, be wound down through official action. The owners of the institution are always liable to lose their money and the managers their positions. No institution is guaranteed to survive in its existing form if, through bad management, it makes losses.

We have got to be very careful about how we deal with large institutions. It is a question of striking a balance between protecting the system and avoiding moral hazard that protects people from the consequences of their own actions.

Would that make for a more pre-emptive type of intervention on the part of regulators?

I think regulators have been moving in the direction of more pre-emptive action. It is always better to close an institution when it still has positive net worth, because the liquidation of a financial institution, by its nature, involves losses. You find yourself having to sell non-marketable assets, and you sell them for below book value. So, if you can deal with the situation while there is still value left in the institution – a positive net worth – then you will be able to do it without causing a crisis. Of course, on the other hand, in many jurisdictions there may be legal questions of the ability of outsiders to wind up an institution that still has positive value.

How much of the burden is the private sector to bear?

It is always best to avoid, if you can, the use of public money because, if public money is used, the burden falls on taxpayers, and you are setting officials' judgements against the market. But what can, and does, happen is that other institutions in the private sector that might be complementary with the institution in difficulty may be willing to take it over. So it is better to do it that way. But there have been occasions in the past in which some public involvement was unavoidable. In the case of the United States, the Federal Deposit Insurance Corporation will use money to induce a takeover, if that is a cheaper outcome than simply paying off the depositors.

Has the balance shifted more towards favouring private-sector rescues?

I think the balance of opinion is moving against using public funds, and making the market face up to the consequences of its own bad decisions. That doesn't mean to say that public policy issues are not involved. They obviously are when you have an institution that is so large and complex that its operations, or its failure, would affect a large number of other institutions. But, the management of that situation is not a simple on-off, we-rescue-it-or-we-don't – there are different kinds of actions that can be undertaken.

Are regulators going to be more interventionist?

I don't think of it as being more interventionist. A number of regulators have been looking at the issue of what to do when the capital of regulated institutions falls below the prescribed minimum. And there is, it seems to me, a good case for regulatory intervention at an early stage. You may call that more interventionist, but it avoids a situation arising where an institution is likely to fail with losses that are spread beyond the losses of shareholders and managers.

Which areas will receive more attention in the future?

Regulators will increasingly be paying attention to the qualitative aspects of risk management, and not simply quantitative measures of capital or leverage. Qualitative aspects refer to the quality of senior management's understanding of the nature of risk, what impact it can have on a bank's balance sheet, and how they can guard against it. This includes internal systems of control. In the future, supervision will become less a quantitative exercise of adding up certain elements of the liability and asset sides of the balance sheet, and comparing their size. It will become a much more analytical and qualitative exercise of trying to assess how well a bank is protected against unexpected events, how well its risks are hedged, how well they are priced, how well they are traded, and so on.

What about the individual activities within banks? Is there any particular one of particular concern?

Credit risk is the largest source of risk in a bank's balance sheet, and where the problems usually come from. We know that, in the past, banks have gotten into difficulties through hidden concentrations of risk. What that shows us is, it is no good simply asking, 'Does a bank have more than X per cent of its capital lent to an individual customer?' If customers are in the same business, they may be subject to the same external shocks, and this leads to what is sometimes called a hidden concentration of risk. Supervisors will increasingly look at the vulnerability of a bank to a risk factor, rather than to an individual counterparty.

So, we don't ask how much money is lent to borrower A or borrower B. We ask how much money is exposed in the event that the economy slows down or in the event that interest rates go up significantly or the economy of a particular geographic region gets into difficulties. That means taking risk factors and trying to measure and estimate how the impact affects vulnerability.

Is there any need for a supra-regulator?

It is correct to talk about cooperation, but it is wrong to think that there would be an easy solution through the creation of a supra-national regulatory body. Whether you like it or not, the world is organized according to sovereign states. Their parliaments have got responsibilities, which include regulation. They will not easily cede those to a supra-national body. So, I don't see this happening very quickly. And it is not, in my opinion, in all cases, desirable. There are certain advantages in economies of scale, but there are also disadvantages. If you give a single regulator all-encompassing powers, there is the risk of over-regulation, because regulators are driven by their own incentive structure. Not only do we have geographical segmentation of regulatory jurisdictions, we will also have market segmentation for some time to come, between the insurance sector, the securities sector and the banking sector.

The difficult and delicate public policy objective is to find the right degree of regulation – on the one hand not too little, but also not too much. The existence of different regulatory regimes offers one protection against over-regulation.

Through international cooperation, different regulators try to reach agreement on minimum standards that will be applied everywhere, and on what constitutes appropriate information sharing. We are likely to move ahead for the foreseeable future by intensifying cooperation amongst independent regulatory bodies, all with a growing awareness of the importance of adequate minimum regulation throughout the world.

We see this process at work in the creation of international standard-setting bodies. These include the Basle Committee,[1] IOSCO,[2] and the International Association of Insurance Supervisors (IAIS). Those are all useful developments, and need to be encouraged. There is even a forum, called the Joint Forum,[3] for cooperation between them. There is also the Financial Stability Forum,[4] which has the overarching responsibility to coordinate the different standard-setting bodies, central banks, finance ministries and broader international organizations like the International Monetary Fund (IMF) and the World Bank.

“The difficult and delicate public policy objective is to find the right degree of regulation – on the one hand not too little, but also not too much. The existence of different regulatory regimes offers one protection against over-regulation.”

Do you see, at least in the euro countries, that the geographic boundaries are breaking down?

I think this is taking place, but as a deepening of the European Union legislation rather than because of Euroland *per se*. That seems to me a natural development out of the strategy of deepening the European Union, harmonizing regulation and developing a single market. But it is more a reflection of the objectives, goals and future of the European Union than it is a precursor of what is going to happen worldwide.

What do you personally think was learned from the crises of 1998?

The lessons will continue to be drawn and developed, and probably adapted in the light of future crises. Probably all we can say now – probably all we can ever say – is that we only have interim answers.

There are several lessons, which can be divided between those that are lessons about prevention and those that are lessons about management of crises. With respect to prevention, you need to have strong macroeconomic policies and those need to include an exchange rate regime that is consistent with the degree of flexibility or rigidity in domestic economy. We always knew this, but it has been relearned. In practice, what that means is countries will have to be willing to have more flexible exchange rates than they had, if they don't have highly flexible domestic economies.

We have also learned that weaknesses in the domestic financial system can compound difficulties that arise as a result of currency crises or macroeconomic weaknesses to a much greater extent than we thought was possible before. Moreover, it can come through contagion. So you need to find ways of strengthening domestic financial systems. In some senses this is the core lesson. And you see it being learned in the emphasis that the IMF now places on financial system soundness as part and parcel of its overarching surveillance activities.

We also have learned that financial system soundness is a very broad concept. It is not just a question of pumping some capital into the banks. You have got to have a whole set of prudential standards and best practice codes, and a means to encourage countries to pursue them. You need a way to discipline those that don't pursue them, and so on.

“We have learned that weaknesses in the domestic financial system can compound difficulties that arise as a result of currency crises or macroeconomic weaknesses to a much greater extent than we thought was possible before.”

On the crisis management side, I am not sure the lesson has been learned yet. An issue that we know is important is appropriately sharing responsibilities between the public and private sector.

This means neither simply using the public sector to make up the funding gap caused when the private sector withdraws credits to countries, nor, on the other hand, using compulsory methods to force a private-sector participation when it doesn't want to participate. That is very difficult to do. We aren't there yet. I think that is going to be the key issue: finding better balance between public and private roles and defining those roles in a more complementary and better way than in the past.

Should banks be allowed to sit at the table with regulators if they are asked to share the burden?

Yes and no. There is definitely a willingness to hear the views of the private sector and take into account what it thinks will be most acceptable to markets, what will least interfere with the effective working of the market mechanism and to discuss approaches ahead of time. Maybe there has been an inadequate degree of discussion of that in the past. I think perhaps there has. And I hope that will be corrected.

All of us in the public sector want to learn what can be learned from practitioners in the private sector. But the private sector shouldn't join in decisions about how the public sector should use its money and how much it should leave to be done by the private sector. The public sector has to do certain things by itself. I don't think you can have co-responsibility in the use of public funds.

Yet, the BIS hosts meetings with representatives from private-sector banks.

Occasionally. We have been doing it for a number of years. In fact, ever since I came here.[5] It doesn't happen very frequently, but from time to time. We find it very useful as a means of enhancing understanding. And they are unique in that people feel they can talk reasonably frankly and freely. So, I think they have been valuable. We will probably go on having them, but, I don't like it if those are thought to be crisis meetings or meetings to discuss a particular agenda.

Do you see conflicts of interest arising from bancassurance?

Bancassurance has been a hot topic amongst regulators, with different approaches being pursued. We are seeing the boundaries coming down in the industry. Most regulators would accept that, although insurance and banking are different activities, the risk profile in both can be managed in such a way that the risks don't look very much different. The risks, when you first take them on to the books, are quite different. But use of derivatives can transform the activities.

The boundaries will gradually get more and more blurred. Yet they are very different industries, with different accounting principles. You

“We on the regulatory side will aim to make sure supervisory and prudential rules are geared towards drawing a line beyond which competition becomes imprudent behaviour.”

cannot look at a consolidated balance sheet of a bank and insurance company and easily understand it. It is a much more difficult exercise to look at a bancassurance company, rather than to look at two separate companies that come under one consolidated enterprise. That will be the challenge, to understand whether a combined bancassurance entity is hedging risks and improving the security of the operation or doubling up the risks by taking ones that are not so well understood.

Is competition between banks eroding their balance sheets?

In general, we like competition in the economy, because it produces greater service to the consumer. But on the financial side, competition driven by the need to improve returns for shareholders can sometimes induce greater risks to be taken. It is all right to take risks if you know the risks you are taking and they are properly priced and understood by shareholders and counterparties, but, of course, the risks are not always fully understood. There are cases where competition is driving financial institutions to take unjustified risks. We have seen occasions where spreads have become very low, where protective covenants in financial contracts have been let go, because competitive forces have tilted the balance in favour of the borrower, and against the lender. We on the regulatory side will aim to make sure supervisory and prudential rules are geared towards drawing a line beyond which competition becomes imprudent behaviour, and making sure that banks and other financial institutions stop short of that line. That is not something you can define in a very easy way or quantitative sense. It has to be done by sensitive supervision of the more qualitative type.

What about extending credit backed by securities? Is that an area where competition might lead to imprudent behaviour?

I think it is an area to be looked at. What an institution needs to know is ‘Am I protected against a movement in the market?’

Generally this is of concern when a market is going down, but a rising market can also increase risk. As we saw in the gold industry, certain gold producers turned out to be adversely affected by a rise in the gold price, because they were short sellers.

And what is the danger when equity values have risen every year?

Japanese firms in the late 1980s wrote contracts with guaranteed returns of 5 or 6 per cent. Now, if you were extrapolating the previous 20 years in the Japanese stock market, it was a safe bet, but we know now, of course, the Japanese stock market is not carrying on at 5 per cent a year. So, those contracts are actually very expensive to the issuing company.

You have to make sure that the issuers understand the nature of the risks they are running – hopefully, their customers do, too – and be prepared in cases where you think risks have been inadequately reflected in the firms' activities.

What about credit risk models? Do banks need to take a hard look at their own models in such cases?

I am sure they look at their own models. But regulators also have a responsibility, where banks are being driven by their models, to take a second look and say if the model being used is adequately robust, and not just a model that tells you, 'Everything will be all right in the future, because it was all right in the past.'

Even in the big banks, the models have been developed on the basis of relationships observed to have held in the past. There is a need for imagination to be exercised and to say, 'Let's not look at what has happened in the past as a guide to the future, but let's imagine how the future could be different from the past, in ways that would pose dangers and risks, and then to manage or adapt the models to take account of that.'

NOTES

1 The Basel Committee on Banking Supervision was established in 1975 by the central bank governors of the group of ten countries (Belgium, Britain, Canada, France, Germany, Italy, Japan, the Netherlands, Sweden, and the United States, as well as Switzerland as the eleventh country). It was set up in response to failure, or near-failure, of banks in different countries in 1973 and 1974. The Committee usually meets at the BIS, where it is headquartered with a permanent Secretariat. It is best known for the Basel Accord, which sets forth standards on the capital banks set aside to cover risks.

2 IOSCO stands for International Organization of Securities Commissions (IOSCO).

3 The Joint Forum on Financial Conglomerates comprises the Basel Committee, IOSCO and the International Association of Insurance Supervisors.

4 Andrew Crockett is the President of the Financial Stability Forum, set up by the group of seven countries (Britain, Canada, France, Germany, Italy, Japan and the United States) at the urging of former Bundesbank President Hans Tietmeyer in the spring of 1999 following a series of crises in the global financial system.

5 Crockett, who began his career at the Bank of England and then served roughly two decades at the International Monetary Fund, took up his current post at the BIS in 1994.

HOWARD DAVIES

Chairman, Financial Services Authority (FSA), UK

INTERVIEW BY JOE ORTIZ

Has the pace of industry consolidation created global giants that are too big to fail? And, if so, what are the likely consequences for the behaviour and activities of such institutions?

Well, we don't believe that it is sensible to talk about institutions that are too big to fail because that implies that there is some kind of official backing for them and that, in turn, reduces their willingness to control their own risks. And, therefore, we systematically decline to identify that there are any institutions of this kind.

It is clear, however, that there are institutions whose failure would create systemic risk and that is why you have a lender of last resort able to provide liquidity to the market when necessary. But I think it's important to recognize that that might not necessarily be support which would do a lot for the institution which failed. It might be, and indeed might more often be likely to be, support that would help institutions that have not failed.

Nor, indeed, and I think this even more important, would lender of last resort support, available from the Bank of England or whoever, do anything for the shareholders of an institution that has failed. As soon as an institution comes in here and says, 'Look, we've failed and is there any possibility of official support?', then its shareholders have left their money outside the door. Therefore, from a shareholder point of view, it's very important that people understand that there is no institution that is called too big to fail.

Now, as a practical matter, industry consolidation both domestically and internationally has created institutions which are very large and very complex and that are very challenging to regulate effectively.

Domestically, we think the best answer to that is a single regulator, so that in the case of, say, Lloyds TSB or HSBC, at least there is one regulator that can get its hands around the totality of the risk taken by that institution and that accepts the responsibility for consolidated supervision and regulation of the institution. It doesn't solve all problems, but at least it gives you a better chance of having a vision of what the institution is doing overall.

“It's very important that people understand that there is no institution that is called too big to fail.”

Internationally, obviously things are more complicated. We believe that it's very important that there should be consolidated supervision of these major institutions and that the lead supervisor in the relevant jurisdiction should take responsibility for it, with good relationships and good information sharing systems with the supervisor in the 'home state', if you like.

So, we take responsibility for HSBC and we talk to the Indonesians and the Indians and the Chinese, wherever they are strong, and, similarly, the Fed takes responsibility for Citibank and we relate to them.

There is a network of regulators which allows you a reasonable understanding of what these huge groups are doing, but I don't want to sound too complacent about that because actually it is very hard to do and requires constant maintenance of those links in order to ensure that the regulators are up to speed with developments in the market and that's the biggest challenge we face, really.

In reality, what we do for institutions for whom we are the consolidated regulator is to look around the world and find the areas of activity where the institution could put at risk, typically, and as a rule of thumb, 5 per cent of its capital. If 5 per cent is riding on its management in that area, then that is of interest to us.

Does the complexity and systemic risk inherent in today's markets make the need for a super-global regulator more urgent? What are the arguments against such a development?

Well, you've got to decide what you mean by a super-global regulator. Do you mean a regulator which could act to require an institution to hold more capital, get rid of its chairman or whatever we might think appropriate or do you mean a global set of rules and procedures and good practices of regulation?

On the first, I think it's inconceivable for the foreseeable future that countries would be ready to hand over control of their financial institutions to a global regulator. There is no legal basis for that and I don't think we are anywhere close to it, frankly.

In the case of common rules, there currently are some sets of rules: for banking by the Basle Committee; for securities trading by IOSCO; and for insurance regulation by the IAIS. And those are voluntary rules and codes of practice except, in the case of banking, if you don't meet the Basle capital standards, then you shouldn't be able to operate cross-border and we certainly wouldn't have any bank here which didn't meet the Basle minimum for capital.

So, to that extent, there is enforcement, as long as you can believe the accounts they produce in the country where they are.

At the moment, there is a big debate internationally on the implementation of regulatory standards across the world and my own view is that not enough is done to police that implementation. The IMF is starting to do it by starting to introduce financial sector assessment programmes as part of its Article Four assessment of whether or not people are eligible for IMF or World Bank support. They have done that in South Africa, in Lebanon and India and they are making recommendations as to how they can improve their financial supervision in order to meet these global standards. My own view is that this is the right way to go.

How does the current system fall down?

At the moment, in banking, there are the Basle core principles of banking supervision. All countries, as far as I am aware, say, 'Oh yes, we plan to meet the Basle standards.' Actually some acknowledge openly that they haven't yet done so. China, for example, is very straightforward about it.

If, however, you look at the Asian crisis of 1997/98, you discover that some countries that said they had met the Basle principles clearly, in the light of events, hadn't. First of all, their accounting was wrong so that there were a lot of bad debts in the banks that were not recognized. They also had a lot of connected lending – banks were lending to companies in the same group and borrowing from companies in the same group and regarding that as external capital which it isn't. There were large exposures – some banks had lent 50 per cent of their balance sheet to one large borrower or perhaps a related borrower and that that had not been properly accounted for. So some of the reported figures for banks' capital in these countries were clearly, in retrospect, wrong. It was not proper risk capital. That's why the issue has become of greater interest to people. People realized that it wasn't good enough for countries just to say they had met the standards because when the shit hit the fan, they hadn't.

“A firmly regulated financial system is just as important as a sound fiscal position because if the economy takes a dive, if your financial system is unsound, what could have been just a market correction turns into a wholesale collapse.”

What lessons have been learnt from the Asian turmoil?

The key one has been that there needs to be some external discipline on financial systems around the world and there needs to be some better kind of enforcement or, at least, exposure of the quality of financial regulation and that the quality of financial regulation is as important an aspect of the viability of a country and the sensible nature of its policies as its fiscal position.

The IMF, when looking at its lending programmes, was very, very sharp on the fiscal positions and, indeed, some of the countries in Asia had quite good fiscal positions, but what they didn't look at was the health of their banking systems and they found that the banking systems were very heavily exposed, there were huge uncovered currency risks and that these things were allowed to go on because there was not effective independent financial regulation. So, from my point of view, the key lesson has been that a firmly regulated financial system is just as important as a sound fiscal position because if the economy takes a dive, then, if your financial system is unsound, then what could have been just a market correction turns into a wholesale collapse.

Could conflicts of interest arise from the bundling of various financial services under one roof – insurance, securities trading, deposit taking, lending?

I'm not sure that I would describe them as conflicts of interest exactly, because I think the interest of an institution's shareholders is to stay in business and make money out of all the things that it does.

What it does create is some interesting interaction of risks because what you need to do as a supervisor – and, indeed, if you are running one of these consolidated institutions – is to look at the interaction of risks on the insurance book, the securities book and the banking book.

Now, there can be circumstances in which they partially offset each other and the overall robustness of the institution can be better. On the other hand, there could be circumstances where the risks accumulate. Therefore, when you look at the overall capital that has to be held, you have to look at the interaction of the different risks being run by the institution in the different parts of the operation and that is the key task.

Are financial institutions good at doing that?

Well, the technology of doing so is relatively young. Until 1999, in the US, it hasn't been possible to hold a bank and an insurance company in the same holding company. In many cases, in the financial markets, you would look to the US and see how it worked there. You can't do that, but there have been bancassurance models in Europe and now we have them here – Lloyds TSB and Scottish Widows, for example – but I think the honest answer is that it's early days, quite frankly. So there isn't a long record of large financial institutions with both banking and insurance businesses in them you can look at. There's a lot of learning to do.

How healthy do you think balance sheets are in the financial services industry? Does the intense competitive nature of the business mean that some institutions will be less able to cope in the next downturn?

If you look at banks in the UK, they are very well capitalized at the present time; they have been very profitable for some years. That's because they have typically lived with a rather volatile economic environment and have made good money four years out of five and lost a lot in the fifth year. Recently, we haven't had a bad year – 1991/92 was really the last bad year – so, our banks are very profitable at the moment. There are all kinds of new competitive pressures on them, like the Internet and new entrants, but at the moment their balance sheets are very strong and are typically well capitalized – almost all hold appreciably more capital than we require – and so capitalization of the banking system is not at the moment something we are anxious about.

I'd say that our banking system has a reasonable degree of prudence – an ability to cope with a downturn. It depends what kind of recession you've got. Clearly some recessions would test the banking system, but the sort of downturns we've had in the past two decades would cause a big hole in the profit and loss account but would not, in my view, put their viability at risk.

On the insurance side, general insurance profitability is relatively weak. On the life side, the business is strong, but the balance sheets in the life funds of some of our companies have been hit by provisions against pensions misselling in particular, to the extent that some of them have not got the kind of free capital they used to have.

Overall, however, that's not something that causes us high anxiety, but you will see that there has been some consolidation, especially among smaller-sized companies, partly driven by the fact that their capital position has not been strong enough to take on a lot of new business. We have been a long way away from anything that would constitute a failure but there has been some pressure to consolidate.

Does the creation of the euro require a more centralized system of banking supervision?

Not in itself. The important issue is the creation of a single market in financial services rather than the introduction of the euro. The issue is that if you have European banks operating across borders, as they now can do, what does that mean for banking supervision?

In principle, the existing structure is adequate, in that there is a home/host structure whereby the home supervisor, wherever the parent is, is responsible for overall supervision, while the host, wherever the bank operates, is responsible for making sure that it operates according to local rules. But, for example, we have here first-e, which is a French bank. I'm not responsible for its capital soundness, the French are. It operates in my market because it's authorized by the French.

And so, in principle, this structure is fine, but the stimulus of the euro will produce more cross-border activity and I think there is a need for more intensified collaboration in Europe. We have to make sure that we each understand the risks being taken in our markets by these big consolidated institutions.

So, I would expect to see an enhancement of cooperation in Europe among banking supervisors, but I'm not sure that we are close to a single regulator, for the reasons I advanced earlier. But, maybe one day, we will get to that stage in Europe because the issues in Europe are different than in the rest of the world, in the sense that in Europe we do agree to share sovereignty some time when it is necessary to do so.

How does the system cope with mergers?

If banks merge, someone *has* to be responsible for the consolidated supervision and the overall soundness of the institution. That flows out of the post-BCCI directive where BCCI was, technically speaking, an unsuperviseable institution. It wasn't anywhere – it was owned in Abu Dhabi, had a registered office in Luxembourg and most of its management was in London, but nobody was prepared to say that it was their bank. That was a flaw in the system and, since then, every bank has to be somewhere and be supervised by someone. If two banks merge, even if it's a merger of equals, they would have to decide where they were based and which supervisor would be responsible for the overall balance sheet. Those issues do arise from time to time, but we do insist that the banks decide. They have to.

What are the implications for supervision of Internet banking and trading?

In general, many of the same principles apply on the Internet that apply for investors elsewhere. People offering advice have to be authorized just in the same way.

As far as policing is concerned, in many respects, the Internet is easier to police than other forms, in the sense that I have no idea what is going through people's letter boxes, but, on the Internet, in principle, we can access it and it's a public medium. The other good thing about it is that it creates an automatic audit trail, and many regulatory disputes are about 'What the bloke said, did he promise you this or did he not?' So that can be easier on the Internet because, typically, the punter has all the information on his hard disk.

The most important issue in relation to the Internet is one of jurisdiction, i.e. where is the website? We would say that if you want to be advertising investments in the UK, then you must be authorized by us, and that's the same if you are physically here or you are somewhere else, targetting your offerings at UK consumers.

We have a set of commonsense tests which are the same as the SEC uses.

If the site is only in Greek and you can only access it via a direct debit from your drachma bank account, then the chances are it's not really being targetted at the UK.

If they are doing business here, we'll say to them, 'You need to be authorized here. If you are not, then please know that you are committing an offence.' Of course, the prosecution of that cannot be straightforward if they do not have a physical presence here, so we would then go to the other regulators, if we know where that presence is, and say they have to be told they are not allowed to do this.

They will typically respond to that because they don't want to have their firms advertising illegally, just as, in the same way, we would say to our firms, 'It's a matter of interest to us if you are breaching regulations [in another country] because it shows that your are not really a very trustworthy firm.' So we would take action and we have in our principles the idea that a good firm should obey the regulations wherever it is doing business.

All of this sounds very fine and dandy, but, none the less, there may be websites, and, indeed, there *are* websites, that are put up in offshore centres that are not interested in being regulated by anybody, and in those cases there is nothing we can do to help people, I'm afraid. But then fools have always been able to be parted from their money and if people send wires to some obscure bank which is unauthorized then their money is at risk. History is littered with examples of people sending money in response to brown envelopes to totally unauthorized, firms, so there's nothing new.

There are problems for regulators, but, in the future – and we are not far from this – we will have on our own website a list of all authorized institutions. It will be easier than it has been in the past for people to check and we will be encouraging businesses to have a hyperlink from their site.

We will have to do a lot more consumer education and that will be a test for us, but, in principle, many of the same arguments apply to Internet selling that have always applied.

How can risk be measured in diverse financial companies, should risk management be more centralized?

We don't want to be to prescriptive – it depends on how the rest of the business is run. If you have a loose confederation of financial services businesses that happen to be part of a single holding company structure and the business decisions are taken by the relevant CEOs of those businesses, then you would want your risk management decisions to be taken alongside where the business decisions are being taken. You would need some group consolidation, but not the kind that stopped each business relating to its own risk.

> “The LTCM risk model told them that the loss they incurred on one day at the end of August 1998 should have occurred once every 80 trillion years. It happened again the following week.”

Risk management should be part of the firm's strategy because the question of a firm's risk appetite is really a fundamental one to its strategy. They have to ask themselves how much risk they want to take, how volatile their income stream is going to be and how that will relate to the type of returns they are able to achieve.

Are firms too dependent on quantitative models and lacking in qualitative judgement?

Some are. We do find cases of institutions where risk models are treated too reverentially and we always recommend they should be stress tested for scenarios that management determines – events that could happen – and then impose them on your risk capital.

A good example of this is the case of LTCM where their risk model told them that the loss they incurred on one day at the end of August 1998 was a loss that only should have occurred once every 80 trillion years. Then it happened again the following week. Either they were very unlucky people or there was something slightly wrong with their risk model. What happened was that they didn't say to it, 'What if the fundamental relationships are turned on their heads for a while? What if the spread between emerging market bonds over US Treasuries was to widen hugely after some event? After all, it was not a completely improbable event.

The model was only working on *past* data, so, we say, that, in addition to back testing, you have to do stress testing and that it must be judgemental because the stress testing doesn't come out of a black box.

ROGER FERGUSON

Vice-Chairman, Federal Reserve Board

INTERVIEW BY ANDREW CLARK AND KNUT ENGELMANN

If I could start with a very broad question, what do you see as being some of the key challenges that will face banks and bankers in the twenty-first century and how are these likely to affect the direction and evolution of bank supervision, both in the United States and globally?

It *is* a broad question, but I think it's the right place to start.

I think the challenges that are going to face banks and bankers will come in two or three different forms.

The first challenge is to make the basic strategic decisions. Particularly in the United States, but more broadly, I think, around the world – as we see what we describe as financial modernization going forward – bankers will be forced to decide what kind of institution they want to be. We already see a number of different approaches emerging.

There are some that have decided that they really want to take advantage of a range of opportunities and do a bit of everything on a global scale. So you have the Citibank model – they're going to do retail banking, wholesale banking, what one would think of as investment banking, private banking, operations, etc., etc., and include in that securities work and insurance. That's one model.

The other model is – taken again in a US context – a bank like State Street. It is a bank, and will remain a bank, but clearly is doing a very narrow sliver of what a bank might do. There are other banks that fall in to that category, too.

So, I think one of the first challenges is to figure out where you want to be in terms of this whole spectrum of activities. How broad do you want to be or how narrow do you want to be?

Related to that, obviously, is geographic growth. If you want to compete effectively on all three of the major developed continents at this stage – or, if you include Australia, potentially four places – one can see where banking is quite attractive. And if you go into Latin America, that's five. Do you want to cover the globe, following your clients if they are global or creating clients in each pocket? Are you prepared to really focus in narrowly and defend a geographic niche against all comers, but cover that niche fully? So, there is that range of strategic questions – that have to do with who you are, what you do and where you do it.

I think there is another a very important challenge ahead for bankers, which has to do with the fact that – almost regardless of how you do this business – there is the challenge of effective risk mitigation and risk intermediation. So, the second question becomes, how do you keep your risk-management skills honed enough to deal with a world of high-tech finance? Because, I think, in each one of these areas – be it consumer credit cards, autolending, fancy underwriting of hot IPOs, whatever it may be – the nature of the risk is changing. It's changing because the products and services are being more technologically enabled and so institutions are capable of slicing risk more thinly – they're creating layers of risk, they're doing credit enhancement – but all of that means that the ability to recognize risk, measure risk, manage risk, offset risk, the entire world of risk control is going to become an even greater challenge for institutions.

The third challenge, obviously, is defining who your competitors are. In some areas, your competitors are no longer financial institutions or potentially might not be financial institutions.

I guess the fourth [challenge] is that, ultimately, financial services – particularly banking, but others as well – is a trust-based business and an institution has to understand how to maintain the trust of customers, counterparties and, to some extent, the market, while also squeezing the last bit of revenue out of opportunity. One of the issues that obviously comes into play as part of the debate here in the United States about financial modernization is the ability of institutions to use the information they gather about their customers in ways that, perhaps, their customers may not have envisioned it being used – sharing information among affiliates, sharing information with outsiders. The underlying model, particularly in the strategy of broadening participation, is that there is room for cross-marketing and cross-selling. Well, that presumes using information and that, I think, raises in the minds of many people a number of concerns with respect to privacy and trust.

The same thing is true with respect to counterparties. We saw in the LTCM case that there's a great deal of trust that LTCM's counterparties had *vis-à-vis* that institution for a variety of reasons, including the record of great success that it had amassed, the individuals involved, the general understanding, but not specific understanding, of the strategies that were involved. The managers of LTCM were taken, many times, at their word. So, is that trust going to continue to exist, having seen that – in a world of high-tech finance that moves pretty quickly – you need to have something more than just simply the word of your counterparty?

The final thing that I see as a challenge is that, almost regardless of which strategy one chooses, because of technology and because of the ability to use information very quickly and analyze it and act upon it, we have a global financial services world. It's global in a couple of ways. One is finance itself is global; there are now in the industrial economies and transitional economies about $510 billion worth of current account deficits that have to be financed annually, which means $510 billion more or less, just for the US, Europe, transitional economies, flows across borders. That gets done, generally, quite efficiently. However, we've discovered from the Russian problem that a meltdown in one small, apparently insignificant part of that world can end up having potential implications with respect to the health of institutions someplace else that may not have been directly exposed – or even indirectly exposed – to the country that originated the problem.

So, you can see, there are several different things – who you're going to be, who you're going to serve, how you're going to deal with the risk that emerges, thinking about this in a global context, recognizing that you're in a trust-based business. All, if anything, taking a tough business – banking – with relatively thin margins – and making it tougher.

Now, the second part of your question was, what are the implications for regulation? I think the implications fall into two or three categories.

The first implication is that regulators and supervisors have to build skills. Supervisors, in particular, have to build a new set of skills to deal with this broad range of institutions. That, I think, is going to mean deeper specialization. We're probably moving away from the general bank examiner model. We're obviously going to have to build skills in areas of technology, for example, which had not been key historically, though obviously always important. That's one

The second is that regulators are going to have to recognize that, in some places, they are going to be catching up with the fast-moving market and we're going to have to be able to do that much more quickly. We're going to have to be able to learn how to spot risks before they become crises. In a world in which accidents happen, if you're part of the police force, there are two ways to deal with your role. One is you try to set up the rules as quickly as you can and organize things so as to minimize the likelihood and scale of accidents. The second is you act very quickly when you see the accidents emerging. You've got to able to, in a world where – to continue the analogy – the traffic patterns are changing pretty quickly, oversee all this relatively quickly, process the incoming information quickly and come up with new sets of regulations that will preclude as many accidents as possible. Being preventive, but figuring out how to be preventive in a world that is changing very, very quickly.

An obvious example now is the world of Internet banking, which opens up a full panoply of ways for institutions to interact with each other and individuals. Can any regulator claim that he or she can see the future of Internet banking clearly enough to know what risks we have to guard against now, without simultaneously creating a stifling envelope of regulation that stops innovation? So, getting that balance of being pre-emptive without stifling innovation is, I think, the second challenge for regulators.

Part of the way out of this dilemma or challenge for regulators of having both skills, and having to be forward-looking without being stifling is the third part of my answer, which is understanding how to use market information.

We need to encourage more transparency, so that the markets can see into these opaque institutions a little better, understand the risks they are taking, price their publicly traded bonds and equities reflecting that underlying risk and then the regulators need to be able to interpret the signals the market is giving because, I think, one of the best aids that regulators can have when we're running fast in a world that's running even faster is letting the natural regulatory market forces work. When all is said and done, human regulators are very good, but the market is still the best regulator. Therefore, we need to understand how to enhance the ability of the market to work by encouraging transparency and we need to improve our skills at reading the market signals that come back.

If I could come back to the risks that you talked about earlier, which you said were changing very fast with new technology and products. Would you find it fair to say that the risks inherent in banking now are not only different but also greater than they have been in the past?

I think the risks are certainly different. Whether or not the new risk in the system is greater is hard to say because, certainly, the ability to take risks has gone up, but then the risk-management skills have gone up as well. The same IT that allows for the introduction of riskier products and services allows for us to understand that risk. We also have a world of financial engineering in which layers of risk get disagreggated and sent off to the individuals who can best bear the risk. We have risk-enhancement technologies. So, it's really hard for me to say that the net risk has gone up. I can see, in some sense, that the gross risk, if you will, has gone up, perhaps, but so have the risk-management tools. Frankly, so has our understanding, so has our experience. So, while I am saying that the world is riskier – in the sense of things moving more quickly, new products and services – let's not underestimate the risk-management skills that have evolved as well.

That would include both regulators and the private sector?

Including regulators, including the institutions themselves. The first group of people that have an obvious interest in managing this well are the individuals who are employed by that organization. So, those skills have gone up. Hopefully, with market analysts, for example, the ability of the market to understand the risk of institutions has gone up. As we push toward transparency, that'll better, I think, our ability. So, I'm saying it's a little bit of an action–reaction relationship here and it's not surprising. Because any financial system is relatively subject to accidents, I think what one sees is a natural tendency to offset. Risk goes up here, risk-management skills go up there. We learn something, we adjust, so I think that's really what's happened here. While the nature of the risk has changed, I think the offsetting side of this has also strengthened a little bit.

One of the reasons I think that's true is, if you look back through the course of history, if you look at the US in the 1800s or Argentina or Australia, they also, when they were developing economies, were subject to all sorts of problems. Then what happened was markets got smarter, new institutions came into play, so we ended up allowing risks to be borne without necessarily suffering the bad results because the risk-mitigating factors, the shock absorbers, also got a little stronger. That's what I think we are seeing here, the risks going up, the risk shock absorbers going up.

Even if institutions themselves have gotten better at managing these risks, has it become harder for regulators, given the increasing size and complexity of those institutions, to gain insight into them and to keep up with what they themselves are doing in terms of risk modelling?

I think your question contains a bit of the answer. As institutions become larger and more complex, doing supervision the old-fashioned way certainly becomes a challenge. It is no longer sufficient, but I think in some ways it's still necessary, to go and look at files of loan documentation. You need to do some of that, so you're not going to lose that approach that served us, generally speaking, well in the Sixties and Seventies and Eighties. However, you need to add more to that – layer on to that an understanding of risk management techniques so that you get a much more risk-focused approach to supervision.

The other thing that we should say here goes back to my first answer. The world gets very excited about the Citigroup experiment, or, at one point, I guess, the Deutsche–Dresdner linkage. We get very, very excited about the big, the new. Recognize, at least in the US, the vast majority of our institutions are still small institutions, where many of the old techniques still work. I can't make the same statement about the rest of the world, because the nature of their institutions is different, but, here, we will continue for a long time to have this tier of very large, sophisticated global players, but also thousands of community banks and local banks and small and regional banks. So, we shouldn't let all our focus go in one direction, because we at least have the obligation to manage or work in an environment that's got both ends of the spectrum.

I think some of your colleagues have talked in the past about the Fed taking steps in the direction of actually bifurcating supervisory activities as appropriate to those different constituencies. Can you tell us anything about the experience you've had with putting in specialized examination teams at the larger, complex banking organizations?

It's still quite new, and in that sense it is too early to say much about the experience. I will say a couple of things. A number of the managers of larger institutions recognize the value of this approach. They like to have a strong sense that their examiners are as sophisticated as the people they are examining, which is helpful. I think the move toward a more risk-based supervision – where we are asking questions about how they do risk management as opposed to looking through each loan document – is now, generally speaking, well regarded. I think they're coming to understand that risk-based supervision means much more interaction, greater information sharing, so, I think, we're all learning that there are some benefits to doing this. I hope, in some ways, the regulatory burden will go down, but it will require a change on the part of both regulators and bankers as we all learn how this new world of more risk-focused supervision is going to work.

Turning to the cooperative measures international bank supervisors are taking to try to get a better grip on risk in the global financial system, the work of the Basel Committee has been a particular focus of attention in several areas. In the area of capital standards, there seems to be a lively debate developing around the merits of tying regulatory capital requirements to either banks' internal risk ratings of borrowers or external credit agency evaluations or some combination of both. In your view, is the use of internal ratings systems ever likely to be practical, given that their sophistication and application can vary widely from bank to bank and country to country?

Well, I think it already is practical for some institutions. I think it is quite practical in the market book, if you will, where that risk modelling has taken place for many, many years, not just in banking but outside of banking. Where people understand the risks that are two standard deviations out, they understand the importance of doing stress testing. I think it will emerge as the art and the science of risk modelling emerges in other areas. So, I am optimistic that there will be a portion of examination or super-vision that can depend on the result of internal risk ratings. Having said that, let me emphasize that it's only a portion. We know a couple of things. One is we know that models – even the most well-developed models – are, by definition, backward-looking. We know that they build in coefficients and relationships that have historically been the norm, but we also know that, as we saw in the LTCM and Russian crises, once in a while, improbable outcomes actually can, because of external shocks, occur and so we've got to be mindful not to put too much of the supervisory weight on risk modelling because models, by definition, are imperfect. So the other supervisory approaches, as well as market discipline, come into play.

If those techniques still need development – and that appears to be something that is still in the future – what is the stopgap – relying on external ratings agencies in the interim?

Well, I wouldn't describe it as 'in the interim'. What I'm suggesting is, if you think about this as layers, where you layer on to the internal risk rating, which is not yet perfect but works well in some places, when you do layer on to it some updated versions of supervision and, yes, you do layer on to it this rating agency approach. It's described as three pillars and I think it's legitimately described that way, because you're not relying solely on any one of them, but all three of them working together can create what is, ultimately, a stable structure. So, even after all this debate and discussion about external rating agencies, I think having that information is still useful. You don't overplay it, you don't want to give a sense that the rating agencies are doing all of your job, but, on the other hand, if rating agencies are doing their jobs well – talking to management, filtering all that information through their models and their experience and coming out with a letter or number – that is useful information. Rating agency input is an important piece of market-type information that I think should be considered when institutions begin to think about the capital that's required to support their activities. So, I think, if you weight it properly, it always plays a role. It would be foolish not to take advantage of the range of information that's available.

'We will take information where we can find it', then?

I think that's legitimate – if it comes from a legitimate source, obviously. I think it's better to use information if it has independent value, as opposed to ignoring it. If this is an added piece of information that has value that is greater than its destructive value – I guess a lawyer would describe it as probative value is greater than prejudical value – then you put it in. That's the way that I would think about it – but you also recognize that it's one datum, not *all* of the data.

Sticking to one particular section of the Basel proposals, the idea of an explicit capital charge to cover potential losses arising out of operational risk. Aside from the headline-grabbing operational failures, like Barings, are banks' day-to-day risks of doing business generally on the rise with the rise in technology and the rise in market complexity, and how advanced are US banks in terms of managing those risks, generally?

I'll give you the same answer I always give on this question. Yes, the new technologies allow for new risks to be taken on. On the other hand, the risk-mitigation tools also are greater. I think where we are on operational risk, in general, is an understanding that it is important and has always been important, and the question is how do you take that into consideration. It may be one of those areas in which bank management may be fairly good at tracking operational risk and putting people in charge who know how to manage it, because it's very much a management challenge. Then the question of how it plays into the capital is a very different question, so I, at least, would like to separate those two.

The first challenge is to get the right level of management attention on operational risk, a level of attention that is at least as high as the attention on credit risk and market risk and interest risk. Then, once the management discipline comes along, I think we can understand the capital implications. There is obviously a debate, to which I don't have the answer, whether or not there should just be an add-on capital charge for all of the operational risk. Some people feel strongly that is the right answer and there are some people who don't. I must admit, I would much prefer to stake my intellectual and regulatory and supervisory energy on getting management's attention on these risks and then ask, once management is properly focused, 'How would you best go about managing operational risks?' Again, I go back to the first point I made. Regulators have a great interest in trying to create a regulatory structure that optimizes the amount of risk in the system. Each institution's managers and shareholders and bondholders have an even higher interest from an institutional standpoint and, I think, what we need to do is leverage that as much as we can.

I think we've already dealt with enhanced supervisory review, which is the second pillar of the Basel proposals. On the third pillar, market discipline, which is something that has been very strongly emphasized by the Federal Reserve, how do you balance the interest of promoting the clearest possible disclosure by banks into the public domain with the interest that everybody has in protecting proprietary information?

I think we never envisioned crossing that line, having propietary information becoming public information. I think what we're much more interested in is having management approaches, management tools and management evaluations being shared appropriately, if it is not crossing the line. We don't want to put a bank or an institution at a competitive disadvantage through disclosure. I think, therefore, one of the things that's very important is to have a dialogue with leading members of the industry to understand their sense of what can be disclosed and which things really have a competitive significance that outweighs the benefit to the system. Where that balance is going to come, I don't know. Now, we should also be clear that – even once you get to the right balance and once we start to have more institutions disclosing a bit more information at the right level – some institutions may find that the markets like what they hear and some may find they don't. So, disclosure is not necessarily going to mean that every institution is going to be judged to be better than it's currently judged – some will be better, some will be worse – but that's just one of the challenges of all this. By the way, while we're pushing for this, I think you'll find that institutional investors – perhaps individual investors to some extent, perhaps other counterparties – expect more and more disclosure anyway. So, we are perhaps a catalyst of conversation, but I don't think, when all is said and done, that we will be alone in pushing for greater public disclosure.

One related idea is that of making banks issue subordinated debt to act as a market signal as to their perceived risk profiles. How is that idea advancing since it began to be studied at the Fed?

Well, I think you know how it's advancing when you ask the question. The answer is it's being studied and I don't want to presume the answers to the study. I have said some generally favourable things about the concept, but the issue now is not so much the concept, but the detail.

Coming back to the US and some of the issues that have been prominent here. When Gramm-Leach-Billey passed last year, there were some predictions that there would be a wave of mergers following quite closely on its heels. While that hasn't happened yet, do you expect to see much further consolidation in the US financial industry down the road?

I think most people who've thought about the structure of the US industry have, for a long time, expected to see further consolidation and we've seen part of this consolidation. I'd have to check the numbers, but we've gone down from around 10,000 institutions to around 7,000 or thereabouts, so there has been consolidation. The answer to further is, 'Yes, probably further.' I will say, as I said earlier, I don't think the US will reach a stage where we have a small handful, or two handfuls, of universal banks covering the nation. There's still room for very vibrant community banks and regional banks. Their comparitive advantages have to do with their ability to understand the needs of their customers and to serve them in a way that is more, if you will, 'high touch'. I think large institutions will have some advantages of scale and the ability to invest in technologies, so that's the way I see the US market evolving.

Now, your question, implicity, was also whether the new law is going to speed up or slow down consolidation. This is going to sound funny, but, in some sense, I don't think the new law is going to change much one way or the other. I think what the new law does is not change the economic or business motivations, but makes it clearer where the boundaries are. So, within that set of boundaries, business leaders, managers of institutions, still have to make the basic business decisions. It goes back to the first point, which is it's not clear that there's only one business model that's going to be profitable. There are a number of models that are going to be profitable and people will end up being surprised at how many permutations and variations of financial service delivery are going to exist in this country. So I'm not surprised not to see a huge wave of mergers, or of merger proposals, because it's a very serious decision. Institutions know that not every merger works out well; they know that sometimes a poorly executed merger leads to an unwanted takeover a few years down the road, it leads to managers losing their jobs, shareholders losing value. So I think business leaders are wise to look at this and say 'That's interesting in terms of options, but, in some sense, the fundamental business dynamics haven't changed and we are making fundamental business decisions.'

Is that, in your opinion, what the people who are applying for Financial Holding Company status [which allows companies to take advantage of the new law] now are doing, they're keeping their options open?

That's my sense of it. As you know, we've approved about 150 or so of these applications and my sense is that many of them are keeping their options open, they want to be in a position to move quickly if their strategy and market opportunities suggest a quick movement is available. I think there may be some, frankly, who just want to be able to say they have become FHCs, but there are several motivations and I assume most of them are good motivations.

You spoke earlier about how a lot of attention focuses on the largest conglomerations. The issue that's most often mentioned in connection with that is possible systemic risk in the event of a failure of one of those institutions. How are regulators addressing that and what is your feeling on the argument that we may be creating giants that are 'too big to fail'?

Well, I think, in the US, we understand a couple of things. One is we've got a number of laws that put a real limitation on our ability to go in and save an institution, so that the concept of being too big to fail is a genie that Congress has tried to keep in the bottle.

Second, I think it is important to recognize that one of the reasons to focus on, as we have, upgrading supervision and regulation, is that, while we know we cannot stop all institutions from failing, we can at least make sure that the market is providing discipline, we're providing discipline, shareholders are providing discipline, etc., etc. None of that is going to preclude another failure, and I'd never leave that impression, but I think one of the methods to avoid the problem that you've alluded to is to have other forms of discipline to try to rein in inappropriate risk taking, or, more positively, to encourage the appropriate forms of risk management, risk mitigation.

The third point is that we've seen that large institutions in the United States *have* failed and our job is to make sure that, if that occurs, that failure does not lead to systemic risk. We are not the guarantors of every institution's health, we are attempting to make sure that we do not have an unnecessary spillover to systemic risk.

Finally, one should recognize that one of the roles we have as regulators is to try to ringfence – to fence in – the areas where there is a public subsidy, so that managers know that, at a certain point, they're not using public money as the ultimate backstop, but using shareholders' money. So, hopefully, one of the benefits of the kind of holding company structure, plus Section 23A and 23B and other things that were put into place, will be to allow that market discipline to work and manage down, again, some of the risks taken by the largest institutions where this issue of 'too big to fail' may come into play.

The ringfencing of public subsidies was a major component of debate around the Gramm-Leach-Bliley bill in terms of structural issues relating to merchant banking activities. That was largely deferred rather than settled?

Some things were deferred, including the whole merchant banking thing, which is off the table for operating subsidiaries for at least five years. I think that is appropriate. One of the things that I think we learned when the Federal Reserve first started giving institutions that we supervise the chance to undertake new kinds of activities in the underwriting area, we encouraged them to be in Section 20s [holding company affiliates]. Over time, institutions got more experienced managing them, we got more experienced regulating them. We allowed the amount of income that could come from Section 20s to gradually rise and I think that ends up being a very good model. As merchant banking on a large scale is new, at least here in the US, and as we know that there are some new risks, and hopefully some new risk-management skills, it's quite important, I think, to allow some of these activities to unfold more slowly so that everyone can learn from them.

One more question on merchant banking, specifically. The Fed has proposed to require banks to set aside more capital to cover the risks of their equity investments. Is that a sign of worry that the recent venture capital boom may have been leading some banks into injudicious investments?

The concept of having a little extra capital with respect to merchant banking reflects a couple of things. One is recognition that this is a high-return activity – that it has both components. Second, we know that we are fortunately experiencing now a record boom and, often, good economic times can mask bad judgements that may eventually become clearer as economic growth slows down. The third thing that drove me – at least, in thinking about this capital – was that our staff did a large number of interviews and discovered that, in many institutions, the economic capital for these merchant banking activities was about 50 per cent, sometimes much higher.

I note in that regard that, after we went public with this concept of a 50 per cent capital charge, at least one institution, Standard & Poors, that looks at banks, indicated publicly that they thought 50 per cent was about right for mature merchant banking, but they would think that 100 per cent capital might be right for immature, new merchant banking activities. So, there's at least one institution, that is presumably insightful, that thinks it's reasonable.

Having said all that, we need to hear what the market thinks, we have to be open to comment that comes forward. I don't think it's an unreasonable place to start, given the facts that we know, but obviously this is an area where we're all learning together and so the comments will matter a great deal.

Some in the industry have worried that this might curtail some of the private equity flows that have been a major driver of the economy. You seem to be saying that there is space already for banks to continue these investments?

As far as we can tell, there's plenty of space for banks to continue these investments. When I thought this was the right thing to go out for comment, I had no interest to send any signals or curtail anything.

One comment I have heard is that some bankers felt that they might be at the top of their [capital] headroom for these investments under the proposed rules.

For some institutions, that might be true; for most institutions, I understand that probably would not be true. The goal here is not in anyway to cut back on what the law allows, it is to make sure that it is done, as is our obligation, in a safe and sound fashion. As I've said, as far as I can tell from the early round of interviews, it seemed to reflect what a large number of institutions do anyway.

But the underlying thought clearly is that these are the times when one has to be particularly careful about making good judgements?

Well, let's not marry those two things too closely. Even is these weren't good times, if what one would discover was that the normal market practice is about 50 per cent capital and then you hear, from S&P at least, that they think it's reasonable, be it good times or bad, wherever it is in the cycle, we ought to set capital that reflects the long-term potential risk of such activities.

You have to recognize that these are, by definition, long-term exposures – I think the regulation thinks of them as being potentially up to ten years in duration – and so you can't set capital standards for only one part of the cycle, you've got to set some that you think, on average, across the cycle, work well.

You've said in a recent speech that good economic times can often temporarily mask bad economic judgements. Any worrying signs in the banking industry in particular?

Not really. I think the latest news that I've seen suggests that banks recognize that they've got to be realistic in these times of opportunities and keep their credit exposures and their pricing on their loans and their underwriting standards reasonably high.

Now, that is not to say that every bank is doing it exactly the right way, but I don't sense that the banking industry overall has lost track of the basic good banking fundamentals that allow them to survive in good times and bad.

RICHARD GRASSO

Chairman, New York Stock Exchange (NYSE)

INTERVIEW BY CAL MANKOWSKI

A SIA-ICI [Securities Industry Association–Investment Company Institute] survey showed more than 48 per cent of households in the US owning stock either directly or through funds. Is there such a thing as there being too much dependence on a stock market that has been going up and up for five years?

I don't think the change in demographics of stock ownership is driven purely by the cycle we've experienced since 1995 and actually a little bit longer. This cycle started in August of 1982 when the Dow was just a fraction under 800. I think what is more significant is the fact that America has converted over the last 20 years or so from a defined benefits to a defined contribution society. And as working Americans have grown more comfortable with the process of investing in their own companies they have increasingly broadened out to embrace the benefits of investing in the US economy and in broad-based economic activity. I think that to ask the question is to ask if there is a danger in a concentration. Clearly there is always the frailty that if one is overcommitted, either as to asset class or as to a specific sector within the class, there is what I call a multiplier effect on the downside. Certainly the history of the twentieth century has proven that long-term equity investing has been a terrific alternative to long-term fixed income investing. It certainly characterizes the period of the Nineties. We started the decade of the Nineties under 2500 on the Dow and closed at 11500. History has shown that prudent equity investing – not speculation, not day trading, but a prudent approach to capital management – with an asset allocation model that reflects the particular characteristics of the individual, is a rewarding strategy.

At this point in time, as a result of changes wrought in Washington last year, the financial services industry is going through a tremendous consolidation, where banks, brokers and insurance companies are merging with one another, forming larger organizations. As these organizations increase in size, what pressure for change occurs on the traditional venues for trading stocks?

I think it's clear that financial services modernization was a long-overdue reflection that the laws that went on the books in the Thirties had no relevance to the post-World War II economy, certainly no relevance to the global process of capital formation. Traditional platforms of trading probably were less impacted from the legislation and more as a result of the technology. The Internet has basically caused at least a rethinking of every business model in the commercial sector. What the Internet has fundamentally done is eliminate the separation of the consumer and the producer, whether you are a stock market, a bank, a broker–dealer or an insurance company. I think the whole model for doing business – the whole intermediate commerce model – is subject to a redefinition. I think that, more than anything, is driving the changes in the platforms for trading equities. For that matter, if you look at a bookseller, a suit seller or a book publisher, literally everyone is subject to displacement because the Net puts the consumer of your product or service literally in the manufacturing plan.

The traditional system for trading stocks in the US has been an auction market on the one hand and a dealer market on the other existing side by side, competing with each other for business. Do you see this 'two different competitive systems' model continuing indefinitely into the future and what role will the ECNs play as pressure for change goes on?

The permanent players – the ATSs, the ECNs, who fundamentally reference prices – I think they will always be here, but they may not be the ones that we know today. Of the nine ECNs that are there today, some may not be here but others will take their place. I would argue that the nine will probably become two or three. And the two or three will be absorbed by players we don't see in that space today. Whether it's AOL or Yahoo!, or Microsoft, it's hard to say. You have to know that the fundamental business model that we're in is moving financial data. Whether your name is NYSE or Yahoo! or eBay, or one of the international competitors out there, I think it's more important to recognize that markets today are an adaptation of technology.

You have said in the past that there will always be a trading floor. As the Exchange itself adapts to this technology, do you see any situation where you would be forced to reconsider that prediction?

I really do not, because if you look around the world, no equities trading system I have seen is completely without people. There is a human value-added component to virtually any trading system. It's a matter of dissecting and knowing where the technology does better in the execution process than does human interaction. As I have said, 92 per cent of our orders and half of our volume are electronically routed, price-discovered and confirmed back in nine seconds. That leaves another 8 per cent that produce half our volume where you have people exercising judgement. My observation is that no system is one without the other. It's a matter of blending technology and people and understanding where the people do best and where the technology does best and using the two together. In the Nasdaq world, the telephone has become a very major part of their communications and is getting larger every day.

Another part of the financial revolution is a rethinking of regulation. What sort of changes do you envision in regulation and from the NYSE's viewpoint what would work better than what we have now and what do we want to avoid in regulation?

I think it's important that the regulators and Congress have recognized the enormous changes that have occurred in the last 25 years. I think both Senator Gramm and Congressman Bliley have each said in their own words that the world admires the United States for having the best capital markets. I think that in the legislative process we don't want to throw what we have out the window and start anew. We're going to have to recognize the impact of technology, the impact of globalization, the impact of differentiated regulation around the world and fitting all of those environmental factors into what best grows the confidence of investors. We must look across the spectrum for a balancing, a mix of what I call legislative, regulatory, self-regulatory and marketplace-initiated change designed to enhance what is already in place – the best markets the world has ever known.

“It's a matter of blending technology and people and understanding where the people do best and where the technology does best and using the two together. In the Nasdaq world, the telephone has become a very major part of their communications and is getting larger every day.”

What would work best for the Exchange when and if the Exchange becomes a shareholder-owned public company?

The question is 'What do we want our marketplace structure to be in the first part of the twenty-first century?' From there comes the question 'How should we be governed once we create a structure? What form of competition serves investors best? How best should that institution be governed? And should it be a public company or a membership organization?' If our intuition is correct that we are going to be faced with a very different set of competitors – the AOLs – we better have access to public capital. We had better recognize that the Time Warner-AOL combination has signalled a very different landscape that calls for a very different NYSE. I can tell you that our Board is going to spend the better part of this year evaluating structure, evaluating governance and ownership. A public company has enormous advantages. And a private company has enormous advantages. If Alan Greenspan were to say something that surges the market in whichever direction, we have to be ready for a five billion share day. As head of a public company, sitting in front of analysts every quarter looking upon me as the chief executive of a 'manufacturing' company, their first question is, 'What is the utilization rate of your plant?' If I tell them it's 17 per cent or 20 per cent, that's usually a recipe for changing top management. As a private company you can do things, you can make investments you can't make as a public company. Today, if I want to build – as we will over the next 12 months – double our capacity from 1,000 messages per second to 2,000 messages per second, take our single-day capacity to probably somewhere in the 10 to 12 billion share level, I simply tell the membership, 'We're going to do that, it's an insurance policy, it's the right thing to do.' As a public company we don't have that flexibility.

Are you leaning one way or the other on this issue?

I'm leaning both ways.

What are you looking at if you decide to do an IPO [Initial Public Offering]?

There are three intertwined policy questions: structure, governance and ownership. It's not about selling stock. It's not about 'What are we worth?'

You have compared decimalization to May Day when fixed commissions were ended in 1975. Why?

Going from 16ths to 100ths, that closes spreads. Commissions are a function of spreads. That means you are going to have two engines of revenue that come to the equities trading product that are going to be influenced simultaneously.

As you forge global links, will you still trade ADRs [American Depository Receipts] as you do presently?

The real future is in DaimlerChrysler, the global share. Some companies do not need global shares. There is always going to be a space for investors who want the ordinary share and the depositary share. Some retail investors do not want to deal with currency transfers out of the US. For those, we will continue to have the ordinary share and the ADR.

Can the small investor really ever be on the same level field with the Merrill Lynch's, the big investment houses?

In many respects the well-informed small investor has a strategic advantage. It's kind of the equivalent of me coming up the Hudson River in an aircraft carrier and you're in a PT boat. If we were in the middle of the ocean, I'd rather be in the aircraft carrier. But, coming up the Hudson River, the PT [Patrol Torpedo] boat can run circles around the aircraft carrier. We have a $17 trillion market, but we only trade $40 billion a day. If a large institution wants to move 10 million shares of Microsoft or 10 million shares of IBM, that's going to be a much tougher job than you or I selling 100 shares. I really do think the information age we live in, the explosion of information, has democratized the process.

We saw some financial shocks in 1997 and 1998. Are you confident that the regulators, the Wall Street firms and the exchanges are sufficiently prepared should some unexpected event rock the financial markets?

I am as confident as one can be that we have the strength and leadership in the system that would allow us to deal with virtually anything. If that means that you're going to avoid a wave hitting the beach when there is a correction, the answer is absolutely not. In 1987 you had a single-day 22 per cent decline, which translates to almost 2,800 points on the Dow today. We also saw a 15 per cent rise. We haven't experienced moves like that since. What happened in 1997 and 1998, those were minor aberrations.

WILLIAM B. HARRISON, Jr

Chairman and Chief Executive Officer,
Chase Manhattan Corporation

INTERVIEW BY MARY KELLEHER

How will technology reshape the financial services industry? What are banks and brokers going to look like, and what role is the Internet going to play?

Technology has been one of the key drivers of the global economy. The whole Internet phenomenon is furthering a trend that had already begun, and will continue to have a huge impact on our industry. The Internet has caused a technology revolution that, when history is written, will have had a greater impact on change than the Industrial Revolution. If you believe that, then you want to make sure you're part of that process, doing whatever you can to get your company to understand the importance that the Internet carries. That's what we're doing at Chase.

How do you think the Internet will change Chase's business model and the business model throughout the financial services industry?

" The Internet will have had a greater impact on change than the Industrial Revolution. If you believe that, then you want to make sure you're part of that process. "

The Internet's impact on the business-to-business – B2B – model will be huge because the Internet is all about doing things differently and enabling you to think and leverage yourself differently. All of this creates huge opportunities.

We are seeing those opportunities. There are lots of examples with companies, such as Intelisys,

“Any smart management team has to encourage cannibalization of their business. We are great believers in cannibalization because the view is, if *you* don't do it, somebody else will, so you might as well do it yourself and get out in front of the curve.”

an Internet procurement company that we own a piece of and helped sponsor. The company allows corporations to go on-line to pay their suppliers, to shop for supplies. That's also a very good example of the convergence between the 'dot.com' virtual world and the traditional physical world. We, as a traditional company, bring a payments capability to the table. A big company would go on-line and buy something, they would have to pay for it, and we have the payments mechanism. And we would have access to the pool of corporate clients that would buy this service, access that a small Internet start-up wouldn't have. Our alliance with Intelisys is a good example of convergence between the physical and the virtual, the dot.coms and the legacy players, which is a key theme in the impact of the Internet on traditional companies.

It is more difficult in the business-to-consumer – B2C – space to come up with business models where you can easily convince others that you can make money on a sustainable basis, than in the B2B space. A lot of people are in the consumer space and it is hard to see how you can create a huge competitive advantage. Although people will do it at some point, nobody in the banking business has really created a B2C model that is taking big market share yet, like Schwab did in the securities market.

People have created business models that are enabling them to gain some market share and provide better fulfilment to their clients while creating a cheaper delivery system. But nobody has come up with a leapfrogging B2C model in consumer banking yet, so far as I can tell.

Do you see any cannibalization of the physical by the virtual?

Sure. Any smart management team has to encourage cannibalization of their business. If you look at past history, quite often the inability to let new processes and new thoughts cannibalize existing business has created major problems for a lot of companies. We are great believers in cannibalization because the view is, if *you* don't do it, somebody else will, so you might as well do it yourself and get out in front of the curve.

How do you get a massive company like Chase to adopt an Internet-driven strategy?

The question is, 'What is the future of traditional companies in this Internet-driven world?' The first questions you have to ask yourself as a leader of a company are; 'Do you really believe that there's an Internet revolution going on, is it real and is it going to change your competitive position?' My answers are; 'I do believe in the Internet revolution, I do believe it is sustainable and real and I do believe it will have major, major impact on our business and our future.'

Then you say, 'OK, so what do you do about it?' When I became CEO in June 1999, I launched a full-court press on the Internet, to develop a greater understanding and a sense of urgency around it because I believe it will have a major impact on our future. The question then becomes, 'You announced that, but what are you going to do about it to make it come alive?' In a big company, unless you get the whole company engaged – and not just pockets of the company or a few senior people – you won't be successful. This is all about major change, as a strategic matter and as a cultural matter.

After we announced this company-wide focus on the Internet, we announced steps to reinforce the process of becoming a more Internet-driven company. It started with the creation of Chase.com, which is our focal point for Internet-based expansion at Chase. It is staffed with talented people who have entrepreneurial types of backgrounds and experience. Their job is to Internet-enable the business take Internet ideas coming out of those businesses and make them come alive fast. So Chase.com is a place in the company where Chase has the special talent it needs to go out and really Web-enable things.

Parallel with that, we went to 15 key businesses and said we would like each one to take one of their top businesspeople – not a staff member or an IT person but a businessperson who really understands the business at a senior level – and pull them off their jobs to devote 100 per cent of their time to developing an Internet strategy and Internet-enable that particular business.

The third piece of our new economic strategy involves making sure we have a window to the external world, in terms of financial returns, expertise and knowledge. Chase Capital Partners, our private equity arm, created a special Internet group about four years ago to invest in the dot.com space. We own 100 dot.com companies. Not only are we getting substantial financial value there, but we also hope to incorporate and integrate some of the products, thinking and talent at these companies into processes going on at Chase.

And finally, the fourth leg involves our acquisition of Hambrecht & Quist. This not only gets our investment banking business into the Internet space in a serious way, but also provides a wonderful external window of expertise and knowledge into the Internet phenomenon, which is absolutely critical.

What is the next step?

We have tied the four pieces together with the Internet Council that I chair. On that council, we have the 15 businesspeople, the Chase.com people and a few other senior people. The council is meant to be the repository, the gatherer of inventory, for what's going on at the company with the Internet. The council members share information with each other as they develop business ideas and thoughts, to create common platforms so we do not have to reinvent the wheel every time we come up with a new idea. Over time, I will look to the group to help prioritize strategic investment decisions that Chase will have to make as we develop Internet ideas.

Imagine a big company like us. If the process works, you will have a huge amount of ideas arising from the different businesses about Internet strategies for particular products and services. And at some point, if that's happening, you can't do it all. You have to prioritize, based on your view of how you can win in the marketplace.

For example, you may have to decide of 25 projects how many you want to put serious money into. Somebody has got to take a view on that. In a traditional company, its management is not worried about those kinds of day-to-day operations; they are out running their businesses. And as CEO of a big company like this, I can't become an expert on it, but somebody has to and I want the council to help me do it.

You can't throw those kinds of decisions into your traditional management model, like our excecutive committee, because they are not spending all their time understanding the subtletier and the details of all this. It's a specialization that must be pulled together as a corporate-wide effort.

What has been the result?

The results so far have been very encouraging. First of all, the businesspeople have bought into this. They're excited about it, they are engaged and they own it. That is absolutely critical in a big company.

Ten or 15 years ago, the CEO at most companies stood up and said to the businesspeople, 'Technology is critical. I want you engaged, I want you involved, I want you to own it.' And guess what happened? The businesspeople didn't really understand it. Intellectually, they might have understood it was important, but they delegated it to the IT people. So, here we are today, and what's the outcome? Most businesspeople at most companies aren't very happy with the outcome. They still don't really understand technology – they think they are paying too much for a product that does not give them what they really need.

Contrast that to Chase's approach beginning with my announcement in June 1999 that the Internet was critical. Businesspeople have bought into it and gotten involved, perhaps because the Internet is a lot easier to understand. You use it at home, can understand how a portal works, and by thinking it through, you can see how the Internet could change a business. Understanding the Internet is different from trying to understand the details of technology. And the threat is much clearer today. If you don't adapt, youu could really lose out.

We have begun to see a lot of ideas percolate out of these 15 business groups that we need to take to Chase.com and say, 'Here's an idea – let's go out and do a joint venture or share the equity with another smaller dot.com and get their expertise.'

We can integrate these smaller ideas with dot.coms and, two or three years from now, we will have created a huge amount of value and a very different culture characterized by the things dot.coms ascribe to themselves – entrepreneurialism, speed, better decision making.

That's not to say we'll be a dot.com, but we'll have more entreprenieurial culture because of all this, which will be a good result.

What do you really want the Internet to do for you? Does it allow Chase to be more efficient or cut costs?

The Internet is another version of advanced technology that has a business model application attached to it, which is intended to create value in how you operate and in how you do business. At Chase, we're creating value both as an equity (investment) matter and as an ongoing business matter. For example, it's easy to see how value is being created in the B2B space, more so than in the B2C space.

Is the Internet push global or just centred in the United States right now?

Today, the centre of the Internet movement is in the United States, but Chase is organized around global business groups. If you take global investment banking as an example, we took one of our most senior bankers off the line, and this individual now has responsibility to develop Internet strategy and Internet-enable global investment banking, but not just in the United States. His charge is to get the whole global piece engaged. We'll cascade this around the world that way, and tie it back at the Internet Council level. The Internet revolution is spreading to different countries. The increase in Internet activity in Europe is quite high, as it is in the United States, where I'm told Internet activity doubles every three months. Europe is starting from a lower base, but the important thing is that Europe is now in the game. The same thing is happening in Latin America and will happen in Asia, too. Chase has a process set up to take advantage of all of this globally.

What does this mean in terms of consolidation? Are banks and brokers focused internally now, rather than trying to get customers through acquisitions?

I don't think most companies today are comfortable with the idea that the Internet by itself will leapfrog a company the way the right merger would. That view may change. But I still see consolidation between the physical firms happening. It's a trend that has been here for some time, and I think it will continue.

Do you expect the pace of cross-border consolidation to pick up in the financial services industry?

Cross-border consolidation in the financial services sector has not happened very quickly because there are huge cultural differences and, more importantly, different return-on-equity requirements, so it's just not as attractive to do.

What about acquisitions in the insurance industry, with the repeal of Glass-Steagall?

Insurance has not been a top priority for us. It is something we will think about at some point in time, but there are other, bigger, priorities for us, including the Internet and figuring that out with all of our businesses, developing a leading public equity platform over time, seizing global investment banking opportunities outside the United States, and further building out of our consumer business. Those are the top priorities of the firm and at some point we'll look at insurance, but right now it's not on the cards.

Is it worrisome to see mergers creating giant financial services companies? Is too much power concentrated in the hands of too few?

I don't see that happening yet. There is still fierce competition. There is a long way to go before one could become concerned about concentration of power. Nor has manageability been an issue after our mergers. In fact, I would say that the bigger we have become so far – and I would underline 'so far' – the easier the bank is to manage. Competing in today's world from a revenue and a risk perspective depends very much on how good you are, which is very dependent on whether or not you're a leader.

And if you're not a leader, which we weren't before our mergers, we found that trying to compete in categories where you did not possess leadership positions hurt your chances of winning business. And even when you did win it, the risks were much greater because you didn't have experts in all of these areas who knew as much as they should about what they were doing.

So, the big change with consolidation is that firms are created with a lot of leadership positions. Chase's leadership positions allow me to feel very comfortable delegating to the people running those businesses. What I work on is making sure we have a common culture of teamwork and partnership, so all the units can come together and share information and solve the clients' problems. If you build leadership and create the right culture, as Chase has succeeded in doing, you create a very powerful model. Few US firms have done a great job at that, especially in the wholesale investment banking business.

ALEX RINNOOY KAN

ING Board Member and Head of
ING Asset Management

INTERVIEW BY KAREN ILEY

What will the future business model of the traditional financial service provider look like in five years?

There is probably no such thing as a single model that will apply to a financial service provider, but it is equally true that ING has a very clear notion of what it wants to be – a truly integrated financial service provider, with integration in terms of both products and distribution channels.

In terms of products, we're talking about a very broad and complete range of wholesale and retail products stretching all the way from banking and insurance to asset management.

In terms of distribution channels, we include both the traditional distribution channels, such as the financial intermediaries, branch banking and the like, but also include more and more the Internet and related opportunities.

In terms of geographic coverage, we are not restricting ourselves to our home market, but also identifying and pursuing selected markets outside the Benelux with a view to ultimately becoming a leading provider in a number of these.

That is the model we have adopted for ourselves, but I'm certainly not pretending that this will be universally adopted. Indeed variety is probably a good thing.

ING has identified a few key business opportunities that are attractive and based on unique competences of the group. First of all, we have already been developing, with considerable success, the direct banking business under the name ING DIRECT.

In Canada, where we started out with the call centre technology backed up with some limited possibility for face-to-face contact, just adding the Internet has added considerably to the net inflow of funds. We believe this limited multidistribution model is going to be equally successful in other countries where we intend to pursue ING DIRECT. Right now, we have started operations in Australia and Spain and we are looking at other European countries as well. We really hope to turn this into a global retail label where the Internet will provide a very valuable addition to what the call centre offers us already.

Second, in the Netherlands, we have launched Freeler, a free access Internet portal. In a short period, it has gathered 400,000 subscribers. There will also be an effort throughout the group to adopt the Internet as a channel for communication and transactions, but, at the same time, a channel that will be specific to the business unit. We have no intention of telling a group exactly what they should and should not do. Web enablement is something we will carry out across the group, but, at the same time, we hope to identify a few special projects, such as ING DIRECT and Freeler, where the group can excel in certain areas and where individual business units might not be sufficiently motivated on their own.

“European financial service providers will increasingly feel the pressure and will need to position themselves in this oncoming distribution battle. It is not at all clear how successful they will ultimately be.”

I'm not sure how unique our total proposition will be, but this is certainly a formula I expect will stand up well against the competition that we will encounter.

What are the sources of competitive advantages for banks and brokerage firms in an environment of rapid technological change? how does such change impact the traditional intermediary role played by the banks?

You can't answer the question easily across the world. It is certainly true that the United States is leading the way in this technological development. Our US business units right now are feeling the pressure much more acutely than most of the Asian or European units.

In a sense, I think that gives us an advantage because we can learn from the American experience and apply it quickly elsewhere in the world. European financial service providers will increasingly feel the pressure and will need to position themselves in this oncoming distribution battle. It is not at all clear how successful they will ultimately be.

It is, however, very clear the Americans are trying to move into European territory, with mixed success. That pressure can only increase as we make further progress. It is not up to me to pronounce judgement, but one suspects that, at the European end certainly, the average financial group still has a lot of preparatory work to do to fully meet that challenge.

In the case of ING group, one source of competitive advantage must be the breadth of the organization, both in product range and geographical spread. We found that to be the case with our corporate relations where ING's traditional commitment to the emerging markets has served us very well. At the same time, we are also trying to establish ourselves as a European player. We've probably made more progress than most financial groups at establishing ourselves in a few large European countries – most notably Benelux and Germany – and who knows what else might happen? In terms of our product range, we hope the fact that we can offer this complete range of financial products, both at the retail and corporate end, will serve to attract customers.

Who are the new intermediaries? Can one envisage a future where intermediaries are no longer necessary because of technological change?

We suspect that the broad availability of very complex financial products creates opportunities for every type of customer, but to find your way among these opportunities is not an easy process. As much as the process can be accommodated through electronic means there will always be a clear role for a confidential personal adviser. Of course, we are as impressed as anybody by what can be done on the Internet. The more sophisticated Internet sites offer tremendous opportunities for tailor-made advice, but, at the end of the day, certain features of personal interaction are irreplaceable. It's a combination of all of these that will continue to work best.

We continue to believe in a lasting role for the more traditional intermediaries, provided that they can add value to whatever contacts they establish. Our experience so far has been that even in a successful operation, such as ING DIRECT, there are certain questions that people feel uncomfortable about putting over the phone or through e-mail, and a face-to-face conversation is the preferred way to proceed. I think we are as committed as ever to that form of financial intermediation.

I hope that we can adopt new distribution technologies and fit them in with the prevailing ones to create a harmonious whole.

What is the future role of information in global banks with large distribution networks and electronic transaction systems? Could proprietary information on transaction flows be used to generate information products?

On the one hand, financial groups with strong home markets are in a privileged position to acquire broad and detailed information on the financial situation of their retail and wholesale customers. At the same time, there are laws and regulations that prevent us from making full and complete use of that information. We obviously have to respect this as well. Nevertheless, one of our challenges will be to benefit from the opportunities of offering the right kind of advice, the right kind of suggestions, at the right time in a person's life or career.

Information technology is very helpful, if not crucial, in bundling that information and making it available to the right player at the right time. That is one of the reasons that we have been investing so significantly in IT and will continue to do so during the next years. [ING has invested around six billion guilders in IT in the last three years.]

The laws in the Netherlands are fairly strict about what you can or, more specifically, what you cannot do. We have to create Chinese walls between various sources of information and we are certainly not totally free to use it and apply it across the group. To the extent possible, we already use it. Postbank, as the first direct banking business in the country, has built up considerable expertise in datamining and datawarehousing for that very purpose. But to share that information with the insurance business and vice versa, for instance, is something the law will not allow us to do right now, so we have to be careful.

The rules vary enormously from country to country, but most 'sophisticated' countries have realized the potential but also the threat. There is continuing political pressure to make sure that the average citizen does not become a helpless victim of these international or national players that hold a terrific range of information. They can also manipulate it much more easily than in the past.

What is the future of traditional exchanges like NYSE and LIFFE?

They realize their position is not sacrosanct. They also have to accommodate the technological change that is taking place across the industry. Of course, electronic trading or variations on the theme are very visible on most of these exchanges. In Europe in particular there is the ongoing battle between Frankfurt and London on one hand and the relatively smaller players on the other, to gain and keep a place under the sun. Ultimately, there is going to be a role for the large exchanges in every conceivable economic order. New York, Tokyo and one big European player will not have to worry about their future, but it is an interesting question, who that European player will be and to what extent it will be a seamless combination of some of the existing larger players. Certainly the deals we have seen between London and Frankfurt suggest that they are seriously considering that scenario. But the European market as a whole is clearly more than large enough to support a strong stock exchange and, indeed, to support a few smaller regional ones at the same time, provided that they are properly linked into each other and can accommodate the needs of their local clientele.

If Amsterdam, to give a very specific example, were to make sure it offers the right price/quality level in terms of the services it provides, then there is no need to worry. But it will have to be a successful part of a larger whole to play a significant European role.

In isolation, it will be difficult for smaller bourses to survive. But if they hook in to a larger network, there is no reason why they could not provide tailor-made services in the region where they are active and as such enjoy continuing prosperity.

Will ECNs have sufficient liquidity to displace traditional exchanges? Are we likely to see consolidation among ECNs to achieve sufficient liquidity?

“New York, Tokyo and one big European player will not have to worry about their future, but it is an interesting question, who that European player will be and to what extent it will be a seamless combination of some of the existing larger players.”

If it concerns liquidity of the market, an electronic counterpart to the traditional exchange, then liquidity will be good most of the time. Compare this with the creation of Nasdaq, but also the development of private transactions with various electronic brokers. The flexibility and the volume function on the electronic networks is to the advantage of these electronic brokers. Consolidation will likely be very limited, just as with traditional exchanges, but there is a lot of competition.

If the question means to what extent large network providers – communication as well as information providers – have sufficient liquidity, traffic growth shows they have enough for expansion. Within this expansion you will also, of course, find consolidation taking place.

If the question considers purely portal activities, such as information and transaction portals, it will require a lot of marketing capital. At the moment, this is paid for by IPOs. If that falls away, a large consolidation wave will follow.

On-line consumer banking – what is its future in the US, Europe and Asia? Are there cultural, regulatory and legal obstacles to the proliferation of such services?

I don't see any major obstacles, other than the willingness of consumers to adopt these products and that willingness will vary from country to country. In sophisticated markets like most western European and the American markets, for many customers this is a tremendous, convenient opportunity they greatly enjoy using. It is totally within the domain and confidence of our group to provide these services whenever required. What we hope to do clearly is benefit internationally from what each of our national business units learns and picks up in the process. That is what we've done so far and ING DIRECT is perhaps the clearest example of an initiative that was benefiting from very modern call centre technology and a very modern back office and that has turned out to provide very satisfactory answers to consumer needs in these markets. We are very upbeat about on-line banking and hope to be among the first and foremost suppliers of that particular product range across the countries we are active in as a group. This is really one of our major ambitions for the coming years. ING has spent around six billion guilders [$2.8 billion] in the last six years on IT as a whole. We are investing a significant amount of money in developing ING DIRECT and establishing it in a large range of countries.

HENRY KAUFMAN

President, Henry Kaufman & Company Inc.

INTERVIEW BY ELLEN FREILICH

What lessons can be learned from the 1998 financial crisis?

“To some extent, risk management analytical techniques use historical benchmarks, historical time series, which cannot adequately capture risks when they go beyond these parameters.”

There really are a number of lessons to be learned from this problem of 1998. Among them are that you really, as an investor, cannot rely on the rating agencies to give you advance warnings of pending problems. They tend to be late. They don't have the capacity to get the data in time.

Second, you can't rely on the IMF or the World Bank to give you advance warnings, either. For a variety of reasons, these bureaucratic institutions did not put into place adequate advance warning systems, even though the IMF indicated it would do so when Mexico got into problems several years earlier.

Also, one of the lessons to be learned from this period is that the risk management approach by the various investing institutions and lending institutions were inadequate – and failed. To some extent, risk management analytical techniques use historical benchmarks, historical time series, which cannot adequately capture risks when they go beyond these parameters.

There's a dilemma associated with this: if you use a conservative risk management analytical technique, then you don't get the business.

Beyond this, there are a number of other problems that have cropped up. Where were the supervisors and the regulators when it came, for example, to the problems of LTCM? Here was a hedge fund that had huge positions in the derivatives market, estimated to be in the neighbourhood of $1.4 trillion on a capital base of several billion dollars.

Now there were two failings here: one, the various official supervisors, including the Fed and the various bank examiners, never called this extraordinary position to the attention of the senior management or the directors of the lending institutions involved. And then there was the failure of the senior management of these private institutions to recognize the risks that were being taken by the middle management of these organizations.

Let me make a note here because I have a chapter in my book [*On Money and Markets – A Wall Street Memoir,* McGraw-Hill (2000)] on lessons that we should have learned and they're spelled out in great detail in there so you might refer to that rather than my going on. Risk management analytical techniques are based on historical, quantitative statistics. The parameters that tend to be used is post-World War II information for which we have statistics. And, in many instances, the time series that are utilized maybe go back a decade at best. But the structure of financial markets over the last two decades has been changing rapidly and continues to evolve. Therefore, the full magnitude of these changes in the structure of the financial markets, and the impact of those changes on the behaviour of the financial markets in the future, is still to be fully ascertained and, therefore, is inadequately captured in the historical data that's utilized. And, as a result, the quantitative techniques have failures. Plus, as I said before, if you come out with risk management tools that are quite conservative and someone else will have risk-management tools that are somewhat more liberal, then you don't get the business.

So, there are two aspects to it. One is not only do you have to have the right risk management approach, but senior management: the COO [Chief Operating Officer], the CEO, have to fully comprehend what the data are all about and what their limitations are. And then there's a tendency to be romanticized by analytical tools that try to give you answers, actually, that are answers stretched out into several decimal points which tend to reflect really mathematical accuracy, rather than accuracy in analytical judgement. There's nothing like getting a number that says 35.22, which is very reassuring. But it's reassuring only in the quantification of the numbers that are there. It's not reassuring necessarily in the accuracy of the judgement that it's supposed to lead you to. I think that's one of the great problems.

How can risk be adequately measured in institutions engaged in a great diversity of financial activity?

I don't think it fully can. I think we are creating encompassing financial institutions or financial conglomerates where you have banks, insurance companies, security firms, finance companies, leasing companies – all under one umbrella. There is a dependence of the senior management on these various arms of activity – the dependence of the senior management of the holding entity on the senior management of the operating entities, which, in turn, is heavily dependent on the middle management of those subgroups. This dependence is probably greater than in any time in the post-war period. And the dilemma is that the middle management of these financial institutions has become all powerful because that's where the risk sits, that's where the reward sits. I do not believe you can really have a senior management that can be fully conversant in the magnitude of these risk takings of the financial conglomerate. And, therefore, that ultimately leads, as trouble brews, to more intensive official supervision.

“When we talk of process, you have to put in place all kinds of supervision and certain codes of behaviour in large institutions that makes them too good to fail.”

Do you think that this official supervision is in a better position to figure out what's going on?

No, I think it complicates official supervision, but it intensifies what has been called the moral risk. Because, as you create more and more of these big financial conglomerates, you create more institutions that are too big to fail. And that puts a much greater pressure, when you get into periods of financial strain, on smaller institutions that will be allowed to fail, which then furthers financial concentration.

When we talk of process, you have to put in place all kinds of supervision and certain codes of behaviour in large institutions that make them too good to fail, instead of too big to fail.

Do you think that risk management should, or can, become more centralized within an organization?

Certainly risk-management techniques are evolving. In order for risk-management techniques to improve, and to be more productive, it requires a much deeper understanding of a management of a financial institution. It also requires a significant improvement in accounting procedures and in accounting standards. The accounting profession is really running behind financial innovation. Official supervision is running behind financial innovation.

How do you begin to close that gap between financial innovation and the ability of regulatory bodies to supervise?

What this ultimately requires, among other things, is more conservative accounting standards, rather than more liberal accounting standards. By definition, you want to have financial institutions that have hidden reserves so that when there are problems, they're not exposed as much, they can write them off. The tendency is to go the other way. We ought to allow financial institutions to create somewhat more reserves. Unfortunately, both the governmental process and the desire of the management of financial institititions is against this. Because if you put more in reserves and tend to hide things, it lowers stated earnings. And I think there has to be a new mentality about this. Particularly, we tend to have greater risk taking in financial markets and financial institutions. Therefore, the accounting should be more conservative. And the supervision should be more conservative.

That's only one aspect. The other aspect is that, on the supervisory side, we have to increase the competence of the official supervisors. That means better-trained supervisors and better-paid supervisors. You can't fully narrow the gap between what a trader gets in a Wall Street house or what an investment banker gets at a Wall Street house and a bank examiner. That gap is enormous. But we can certainly pay up a lot more than we are at the present time.

Beyond this, it requires supervisors that really virtually reside in some of these financial conglomerates, to have greater intimacy with what's going on.

But also supervisors should be able to capture information – larger amounts of information – and they should be able to capture it more quickly. The transmission can be better. What difference does it make whether that information goes from a large conglomerate to its headquarters office and at the same time can go to the Federal Reserve and/or the Comptroller of the Currency and/or some other supervisory authority?

That should be quite possible.

In time it should be, so that supervisors get information that's very up to date and much more detailed than anything they have at the present time.

> “The structure of financial markets has changed. The structure of financial supervision and regulation is way behind, on a global basis. There's no reason why we shouldn't have it.”

I mean, such things as the call report that the banks provide to the Fed every three months or so. That's an archaic kind of reporting. The Fed gets other information on a more timely basis, but there should be much more. There used to be a tendency to worry about the amount of information that the examiners require from a financial institution because of the overload of paperwork. You can use computer facilities much more to transmit information and put it in analytical form. This should strengthen the supervisory capacity.

Do you think there is a need for a global body that monitors risk?

I have long advocated a centralized overview, a centralized body. I call it a board of overseers of major financial markets and financial institutions globally. We need uniform accounting standards, uniform reporting standards, uniform rating standards, uniform capital reporting standards for major financial markets and major financial institutions.

We now try to accomplish this on an *ad hoc* basis. It's a very slow, very imperfect process, waiting for the next crisis to happen. We don't have anyone that does this on a centralized basis, but, nevertheless, we have global markets. And money moves from one country to another country and financing is done in a global sense. The structure of financial markets has changed. The structure of financial supervision and regulation is way behind, on a global basis. There's no reason why we shouldn't have it. There are vested interests on a national basis that block this. Differences in liberality of reporting tends to encourage the financing and the borrowing to be done somewhere else than where the standards are somewhat more conservative. And, eventually, it produces risks that are very dangerous. And then you get back to that moral hazard and someone has to step in to bail it out. Also, as I have long argued – and I see the Meltzer Commission has now favoured many of these ideas that I proposed – is that the IMF should be overhauled, should be restructured.

How will insurance firms cope with higher levels of risk?

Insurance companies have a very fascinating challenge. On the one hand, they have to determine what the premium should be on the insurance they provide, and here, depending on whether it's life insurance, or whether it's fire and casualty insurance. If it's life insurance, actuarial

“The participation of the individual directly in the financial markets has extraordinary risks associated with it. It means that the economy itself will become more cyclical because greater risk taking means, on the one hand, greater rewards and, potentially, greater losses.”

tables. Actuarial tables – insurance companies have benefited for quite a few decades from the fact that life extension has been greater than the actuarial tables, but that's catching up, very quickly. And the pricing for that risk is under increasing competitive pressure – at least in the United States. So, it's the most efficient participant that's going to eventually get the business. Certainly, the Internet is pushing that very hard.

At the same time, it depends very much on the success of the insurance company, on how it manages its assets – stocks, bonds, real estate investments, and so on. So, there is a kind of a three-prong thing that these insurance companies have to be involved in all the time. It's two parts the liability side which they have – the premiums they generate versus the liabilities they have – and, on the other side, how they manage their assets. And this will induce more amalgamations and consolidations.

What's happening in the insurance industry happened to some extent at deposit institutions some years back. Some years back there were differences in the interest rate paid on the deposits between an S&L [savings and loans] and a commercial bank, between what was paid on the West Coast and on the East Coast on deposits. Much of that difference has disappeared because of the national sweep of the money market and the securitization of mortgages. And much of that will happen in the insurance industry.

A uniformity is going to emerge, more standardization?

That's right. And with standardization, more of this becomes a commodity business. And you can see some of these kinds of concerns when you look at the price of the stock of insurance companies today.

It's under pressure.

The participation of the individual directly in the financial markets has extraordinary risks associated with it. It means that the economy itself will become more cyclical because greater risk taking means, on the one hand, greater rewards and, potentially, greater losses.

That means, in the upsweep in a business cycle, there will be greater momentum. Just as we have seen, the wealth effect really is the result of the greater participation of the household sector in the equity market.

That's a good part of it, besides the impact on corporate investments and so on. But the wealth effect means there are powerful positive influences on the upside on consumption. We haven't seen the downside. Consumption for a long time has been a stable component of GDP when you look through the business cycle. This will make it a much more volatile component because, on the downside, when there is a major sell-off on the stock market, it will have a quick influence on consumption. That will pose, of course, in turn, a much greater responsibility and much greater judgemental problems on the official supervisors like the Federal Reserve, on the central banks. It has added a volatility dimension, the full impact of which we haven't seen because we have seen the pleasant side of that volatility – the upward momentum. But we haven't seen the unpleasant side – yet.

DAVID KOMANSKY

Chief Executive and Chairman,
Merrill Lynch & Co. Inc.

INTERVIEW BY JACK REERINK

How will the Internet and new technologies influence the business model of the traditional financial services firm?

You have to try to put the Internet into context. To me it's very much akin to the Industrial Revolution being accomplished in a very short period of time. It's probably the most significant enabler of the consumer in what I have seen in my lifetime. In our industry, it has made all information available to anyone at any time; it has made pricing totally transparent.

At the same time, it's the most destructive technology we have ever seen for those who cannot find a way to take advantage of it. It will force people to make very clear, concise strategic choices. It will force firms to move up-market, avoid the commoditized ends of the business, and focus on the value-added businesses.

What areas would these commodity-type businesses include?

Probably a good example would be the fixed income business. A non-structured product today can, and often is, offered to investors electronically. You really don't see traders intervening in those transactions. On the other hand, you have more esoteric products – whether it be emerging market bonds or structured investments, like swaps – where you have a value-added element. That puts an even greater premium on those who can flourish in those areas.

Are stock trades becoming a commodity, too?

Again, it depends what element of equity trading you want to look at. Pure execution has become very commoditized. There's no value-added in executing a trade for 1,000 shares. The value-added element would be advising the client what to invest in and using your own capital to get the trade done at a certain price. Straight execution is basically valueless today.

So how can Merrill's trading desk add value these days?

"There's no value-added in executing a trade for 1,000 shares. The value-added element would be advising the client what to invest in and using your own capital to get the trade done at a certain price."

On the retail side of the business, the greatest value-added service we can offer is the advice of what to invest in at what particular point in time. On the institutional side, the research product we generate is clearly value-added. So is our ability to sell a large order when the market doesn't provide the liquidity. We use our balance sheet to provide the liquidity and then trade out of that position. The more complex the trade, the more opportunity we have as a firm to add value.

Merrill Lynch last year introduced on-line stock trading, a marked departure from your traditional full-service brokerage model. What brought this about?

"For Generation X, or the next generation, strategically, it's critical for us to be able to build a relationship with these people early in their financial lifetime."

The reasons for being on-line from our point of view are simple. A certain percentage of our customers wanted to trade on-line. For several years, we chose to let them deal elsewhere as opposed to offering it ourselves because of the conflicts we had. It got to a point where it was foolish for us to continue that. No matter how many clients you have, a certain percentage are going to want to trade on-line.

Second, we're absolutely convinced that the next generation is much more likely to be found in the virtual world, and it will prove easy for us to move them into the advice model later in life. So, for Generation X, or the next generation, strategically, it's critical for us to be able to build a relationship with these people early in their financial lifetime.

What we attempted to do is offer the widest and deepest range of choice to our clients. You tell me how you want to approach the market, and we can offer a business model that not only suits your needs but also is arguably the best in its class.

For people who prefer the traditional model of approaching the marketplace, clearly we offer that. We have the Unlimited Advantage account, which is strictly fee-based – a certain percentage over the assets we hold for clients. We provide every service – which includes unlimited trading – for those clients. Third, we have the direct channel, which is purely online, without any intervention.

Most full-service brokerages now offer on-line trading and Internet brokers are starting to offer research and advice. How do you differentiate yourself?

I personally believe that technology necessary to compete in the on-line market will be totally ubiquitous in a year or two, if it isn't already today. Every firm that wants to offer it will be able to buy it off the shelf, so I don't think technology will be the differentiator. And we don't choose to wage the battle purely on price – anybody can price anywhere. There is a certain price where you can have a profitable operation and there's a price where you can't be profitable. That's purely an organization's choice.

What will differentiate us is the content we provide. First, we're the Number one research firm in the world. What on-line firm can compete with us? We have real-time research. I'm not talking about something that's three or four days' old, I'm talking about something that if our analysts publish at 8 o'clock in the morning and the biggest institution can see it at 8am, so will our on-line clients.

Second, our global reach. We can offer participation and execution in almost any market in the world. Not one of our on-line competitors can do that.

Third, the breadth of our product range. Be it mortgages, insurance, all the way to the traditional investment products, we offer highly competitive products in all of those areas, if not the best.

When an organization goes through changes that hit the very core of its business, how do you persuade your brokers or financial consultants to embrace the new model?

Clearly it's a major challenge. How do you introduce what could be a destructive technology in an organization and create the change that makes this technology additive? We certainly have had those challenges. It's an ongoing communications issue.

Those financial consultants who refuse to recognize the fact that a certain number of their clients want to be on-line, that a certain number of their clients want a different pricing mechanism; those people I think are fairly short-sighted. What we're trying to do is convince them over time that the future lies in a new paradigm, as opposed to the rigid, recalcitrant thinking of the old paradigm.

We told them [brokers] that the full menu of choice at the very least gives the clients you are going to lose to an on-line firm the opportunity to do business with Merrill Lynch on-line. Second, you should think about the fee-based accounts. There you have the opportunity to negotiate rates and provide a plethora of opportunities on the Internet. That has proved to be probably the most successful product introduction we've ever had.

Can the Internet help you sell financial products in areas where you now lack distribution?

Absolutely. We will be able to reach significant segments of the market with technology that we wouldn't have been able to reach before. In the US, for example, the small business market was very expensive and impracticable for us to try to cover. We now have financial consultants reach out to that marketplace via the Web.

Selling what types of products?

Cash management, many e-commerce offerings, 401Ks if it's a big enough organization, mortgages, certain credit products, all kinds of things.

How about using the Internet to expand in Europe?

Europe is probably one of the great potentials for us because it's very difficult to build a pan-European salesforce. There are fixed costs involved, language and cultural barriers. We cross those barriers much more efficiently on the Web. We think it will be an enormous opportunity for us.

On the institutional side, there are thousands of small- to mid-size banks, mutual funds that we don't cover with our institutional salesforce. We will be able to cover them with technology.

How important is brand in the Internet age?

We have probably one of the most recognizable brands in the world of financial services and certainly the most recognizable logo. That I think is going to be very important in our industry. The meaning of brand, the concept of branding and who you can reach, particularly as opposed to competitors who don't enjoy the brand recognition.

What does the future hold for traditional exchanges, such as the New York Stock Exchange, amid competition from alternative trading systems or ECNs?

I think back to when the push-button phone was first introduced. It was fairly unreliable and I remember vividly not particularly enjoying using it. I really liked the rotary dial phone. But once the push-button technology got into the marketplace, there was no going back from it. And in short order, the rotary dial disappeared.

I think the market structure environment is in the same situation today. Technology offers suddenly better ways to do it than it has been done in the past. Common sense just tells you that it's got to become different than it is. The ECNs are the embodiment of what technology can do to bring the barriers of entry down. They offer a sensible alternative, bring some real competitive advantages to the marketplace.

The New York Stock Exchange and the maintenance of the New York Stock Exchange is critical for a lot of reasons. Its brand and what that brand means for the peace of mind of investors, issuers, regulators and the trading environment. Now, unless the New York Stock Exchange changes its business dramatically, the ECNs will bleed off a large part of its volume. And it will be a problem to the New York Stock Exchange.

Are you foreseeing one central electronic US marketplace?

I'm not arguing for a central marketplace – that's the last thing I want to see – but what I *do* want to see is a mechanism put in place to avoid the fragmentation of liquidity. Let the markets compete, and those that are the best and most efficient will prevail. But if we don't protect pools of liquidity, if we don't prevent fragmentation, people are going to lose.

“Common sense just tells you that it's got to become different than it is. The ECNs are the embodiment of what technology can do to bring the barriers of entry down. They offer a sensible alternative, bring some real competitive advantages to the marketplace.”

Strangely enough, the trading firms would be better off if the markets became fragmented. Believe me, Merrill Lynch, economically, could earn far more money in a fragmented market because what you would be doing is making the markets yourself and you'd have more profit opportunity. So I think it's strictly an issue of what is best for the investor. I would say it's also best for the issuer. As CEO of Merrill Lynch, I don't want to see my stock trading at five different prices around the world at the same time. I want to see an orderly, transparent, disciplined marketplace.

What we are advocating and what we hope will happen is that the New York Stock Exchange will remain the fulcrum of the equity trading model. But in order for that to happen, it has to incorporate an element of an electronic exchange where small orders should be automatically executed in an electronic environment. And those orders that need help, or liquidity, should be executed in the specialist environment or another one. But, at the same time, ECNs are not going to go away. There have to be linkages between the stock exchange and the ECNs so that the investor will (a) know where the best bid/offer is and (b) so that the pools of liquidity are not fragmented.

Do you envision linkages that are now in place in the Nasdaq dealer market?

Nasdaq doesn't really have linkages. What's happening there is that that ECNs have disintermediated the dealers and now have a 25 per cent market share. I would like to see a really sophisticated system of linkages between the markets.

If Fidelity comes to us with a million shares for sale, we couldn't care less if we hit an ECN, a specialist or if we cross it in our own system, as long as we get the best price for our client. If we don't have those linkages, we are going to have to hit it ourselves, internalize the order. One way or another, the customer is going to be disadvantaged.

Banks in recent years have snapped up securities firms. Have these acquisitions worked and do you foresee more of them in the future?

It's fairly mixed. The merger of Citicorp with Travelers has worked out well. On the other hand, there's a raft of others that have not worked out well. It's clear that the banks prefer to be in the securities business. There will be further consolidation. There are still several European players who aspire to be global players. It's impossible to be a real global participant without having significant presence in the US market. So, you'll continue to see mergers and acquisitions, but probably not at the frenetic pace everybody had thought.

Why is it some bank acquisitions have worked whereas others have failed?

They are very different businesses, from the point of view of the acceptance of risk. We in the securities industry, trading and investment banking business accept a significant degree of risk as an integral part of our business – it's what we do for a living. On the other hand, banks don't. Some banks have successfully been able to acquire that talent, others haven't.

By and large, commercial banks employ a different type of people than securities firms and investment banks do. You have to find a way to be able to manage different people. If you spoke to an average commercial banker, he would tell you his most precious assets are in the vault. If you ask me, I'd say our assets ride up and down in the elevator every day. That's a stark contrast in value and style.

You are expanding your offering of banking products. Are you aiming to become a mini-Citigroup?

This has been an opportunity that has been obvious to us for many years. We had been precluded from it because of Glass-Steagall. Once we got the financial modernization bill, these opportunities became available to us and we're now taking advantage of them. One of the things we like to do is offer more banking products to our clients to broaden our product line. We see tremendous opportunity there.

We are already in the checking business, we are in the debit and credit card business, and we have a mortgage company. We also happen to have $150 billion in client assets in various types of money market accounts. There now is a way for us to take a portion of those assets, put them into bank deposits and pay the same rate as people get in their money market accounts. There is not a bank in the country that can do that because they have a cost structure to collect those assets whereas we can do it without any incremental costs.

What are some of the lessons you learned during the turbulence in financial markets in late 1998?

Clearly, our risk-management processes turned out to be inadequate – and I am not just talking about Merrill Lynch because it was an industry-wide phenomenon. Certainly the reliance on computer-driven modelling, to the extent that it was used, was a mistake. Clearly, good risk management is a heightened use of cutting-edge technology and people with experience and common sense. I don't think one or the other can do it by itself any more. It's too complex, too fast-moving.

The whole issue of liquidity in the marketplace was something that people had forgotten. That was a rude awakening. It seems to be one of the most fundamental things you would think about, but it was something people had lost sight of.

The third thing that I think happened was that banks and securities firms forgot how to price risk. In other words, if you are going to underwrite an AA corporate [bond] at LIBOR [London Inter-bank Offered Rate] plus 200 [basis points – additional risk premium], I don't think you should be underwriting the same kind of bond offering for an emerging market country at LIBOR plus 250 [basis points]. The differentiation between risk and what you charge; that skill became clouded. You saw the firms take on much too much risk because of mispricing.

What brought about the mispricing?

Competition. I can vividly remember pricing bonds from clearly not investment-grade countries at maybe a spread of 40 [basis points] against US paper. There's something awry here. But there was so much competition, liquidity in the market. It was a combination of those things. I wish I could tell you it will never happen again, but, human nature being what it is, some of that will happen again. We work very hard to make sure it won't happen again.

How can you guard against a future lack of liquidity in financial markets?

We've done a lot of things. You cut down on the amount of leverage you use and you cut down on the amount of assets you're carrying that are dedicated to trading inventories.

DICK KOVACEVICH

Chief Executive Officer,
Wells Fargo & Co.

INTERVIEW BY SUE ZEIDLER

Are US households too exposed to the stock market these days? What happens down the road when the boomers start to take their money out of the market?

History has shown that investment in the stock market over a long period of time has been the right thing to do. As long as people have a long time frame, it is the right thing to do. The danger or risk is if people are taking money they need in the short run and are investing in the stock market. I think some of that is occurring and is a concern.

I think the baby boomer situation is a concern, but I think most people are living so much longer today. People are going to keep a lot of their money in the stock market even after they retired because they don't know if they're going to have another 20 years of their life span or so. And you can't put that in fixed income. So I don't see this huge switch that is going to occur just because someone turns 65.

And, finally, because of the extraordinary change in the equity valuations, a lot of that money is going to get transferred to their children. So I do not see a huge bubble simply because the baby boomers are maturing.

Demographics are not something we can control. It's simply one of many factors we, as financial institutions, have to react to, but I don't see it as a materially negative issue. It will happen slowly. Money's going to be transferred to the next generation and we simply have to be there, allowing that to happen. The money isn't going to disappear. We just have to keep the customers' money for them.

How will creation of giant financial services companies affect the customers? What are the benefits and drawbacks for the customers?

The major benefit is that we can understand the total customers' needs and then help them and give them advice for the best way of solving those needs. If you are only dealing with a narrow portion of those needs, I don't think you can do that optimally. So, the more we know about the customers, the better job we can do to help them in terms of financial advice.

As we do more and more with fewer customers, we can do it more economically and give better value to the customer. I think there are tremendous benefits from both the value of the business proposition that we give to the customers and giving it to them less expensively. It's just more efficient to do more with fewer customers than less with more customers, that's just the cost dynamic.

The potential negative is that if you become so big and so removed from the customers, you don't serve them well, but, in a way, I don't see that as a negative. If that's what happens, the customers are going to go somewhere else. I think there's nothing but positive from the customers' standpoint of consolidation and being able to offer this. It might be negative from a particular company's standpoint because they fail to deliver good service or fail to be customer-focused, but there'll die and there'll always be someone to take their place. So, I don't see any negative from customers' point of view.

“Money's going to be transferred to the next generation and we simply have to be there, allowing that to happen. The money isn't going to disappear.”

How about the whole privacy issue?

Protecting our customers' privacy is a very important goal. It's all about trust. I think we need to distinguish between the use of information of a single entity and ensuring that we keep that information private and only use it for the purpose of helping our customers. If we don't, we'll lose the trust and it will be bad for us and the customers. Some people are saying that, within the whole corporate family, we shouldn't share information. I don't think that would serve the customers well. It's all about knowing more about the customers. Let's assume we have a customer that we believe has too much money in low interest rate CDs and believe that some of that money should be in stocks or bonds to something to get higher returns. Some would argue that to go to that customer and suggest it is an invasion of privacy. But not 1 per cent of the *customers* in the country believe that. Most people want us to do this. Giving CD balances and so on to ten investment banks would be an invasion of privacy, in my opinion. There's the difference. I think we should publish our privacy principles and adhere to them and the customers can decide whether they want to do business with this firm or not.

But to make it hard to use data would be a big step backward. We have to distinguish between true privacy and better information and advice and customer service. I think they're getting mixed up. I think it would be a disaster for the customers if an entity is not allowed to share information among its affiliates, its companies that it controls, in order to better serve the customers and give them advice and optimize their financial balance sheets.

If some corporation is not protecting someone's privacy, then the customer should go somewhere else, but to pretend that we can somehow write laws that would work in every situation is absurd. The world is moving too fast. In fact, customers often call us and get very upset if someone on the other side of the phone doesn't realize what a good customer they are or are treating them in a very narrow fashion.

You're saying the customers want their information spread within the corporation?

The customers want help with managing financial affairs and solving problems with one phone call or one statement. They want everything on one statement. They want to make one phone call and they don't want to go to their mortgage company, versus their credit card company versus their bank when they have an issue. People want to be sure their information is protected and not distributed to third parties or to parties within the corporate family who shouldn't have access. We have very strict security and access rules. In my opinion, if someone is not protecting that, customers should go visit with someone else and not write that off.

With all the news about hackers breaking into corporations, are you using consultants or specialists to build up guards against hackers?

We have all of the above, yet we're always at risk from this. New technologies and new procedures are always being developed to protect this, but it's a concern we take very seriously and spend a lot of money and effort testing to make sure our systems are as secure as possible. Thus far, we have not had any problems, but I can't guarantee that it would not happen. It's a very difficult situation.

Have you had any experience with people trying to break into Wells Fargo?

Sure. But I wouldn't want to talk about that.

Is the need for a supra-global regulator more urgent now or what is your argument against one?

I think there are aspects of regulation that need to be global. Certainly, from a competitive standpoint, you can't have different laws and regulations that would give one entity a competitive advantage over others because people are dealing in a global environment. From an information transfer standpoint, again, multinational companies and multinational individuals need the information and data readily available without restrictions. So, there is a need for some things to be globally regulated. I see an overview of global regulations and the primary part of regulations will be country-specific. I think we're moving that way. We have these standards that apply to all financial institutions – standards of information and communication – but about 95 per cent of our regulations are country-specific.

What things specifically ought to be globally regulated?

I think risk standards, capital standards, information and communication standards – those kinds of things level the playing field. But the actual details of supervision and regulation need to be country-specific.

You just mentioned risk management. When you look back at some of the economic shocks of 1997 and 1998, are there concerns that the next financial crisis could snare one of the giant players and have a systemic effect? What do you think needs to be done on the regulatory front to minimize the possibility of such problems?

“There is a need for some things to be globally regulated. I see an overview of global regulations and the primary part of regulations will be country-specific.”

I think the greatest danger to a systemic issue is the belief that some institutions are too big to fail and therefore should be supported in the case of failure. This belief gives a false security to those in the marketplace. The market is a much better monitor than a regulator. We've seen evidence in the US where very small banks – with $500 million or a billion dollars – have lost 35 to 40 per cent of their assets. It should be made clear by our insurance fund, the FDIC [Federal Deposit Insurance Corporation], that it will only protect $100,000 and below depositors and everyone else is at risk and should be forewarned – particularly at this time when times are good.

As long as there is an attitude of too big to fail, we are at risk for a systemic run.

Is there an over-reliance on quantitative models at the expense of human judgement?

I think there is an over-reliance that regulators or supervisors can do it and they tend to do it quantitatively. I think the only judge that can operate quickly and effectively is the marketplace. I think the market has this impression that we're going to be bailed out if there's a problem and they don't have to use appropriate due diligence and they can rely on regulators and supervisors and I think that's very dangerous.

Do you think we're on the verge of that happening?

I think it continues to happen. It happened in Asia and so on. It certainly is a possibility. I don't think it's any more serious than it was, but, because times are good, I think it's the time to correct the problem once and for all.

How rapidly do you feel is the consolidation occurring in Europe?

There still really isn't a European union. I think we're close to that happening. Once the laws and regulations do finally get harmonized, I think there's going to be vastly more consolidation. It's just beginning and that's because there really isn't harmonization of laws and regulation.

How important a role will national and central banks play in that?

I think the role they will play is not to impede it. I think the political environment is more of an impediment. I don't think the central banks will resist change.

Do you see similar explosion in the asset management industry developing in Europe?

Not to the same extent as we have here. They have a very different demographic picture. They have a huge ageing population with all sorts of social security issues and so on. The whole idea of who is going to support this rapidly ageing population in Europe with already a huge welfare state is a serious issue and much more serious than in the US.

What is the relationship between brand name and the size of the organization?

As our interactions become less physical and more cyberspace, and as people use a variety of channels to access information, brand becomes ever more important. As institutions expand their offerings from a product standpoint as well as from a geographic standpoint, brands grow more important . You don't want to brand each and every product. You do not need different brands for each geography, given the mobility of people.

So, whatever the importance of branding was 10 or 15 years ago, it has increased significantly 3, 4, 5 times – given the changes that are occurring from a technology, geographic and product standpoint.

Are you spending more resources on building brand awareness?

I think everybody is. You're asking a lot of questions on financial services and some people may think it's difficult to predict or forecast the future. But all we are is a distributor of commodity products. There are plenty of other examples of other distributors of commodity products and I would simply say, why won't we look more like what's happening in these other industries, where consolidation is also occurring?

“If you look at other countries where geography was allowed to expand faster or products were allowed to expand faster, the institutions do indeed have a larger market share and there are fewer institutions in those geographies. So, it's pretty obvious what's going to happen.”

People will buy more from a single supplier like Wal-Mart or Home Depot if they get a better deal. The brand becomes very important to that success. That's what convinces me that people will buy more under one roof. Brand will become more significant and important because it has happened in other industries with characteristics similar to ours.

You can ask, ‘Why hasn't it happened in ours?’ It's because we had laws and regulations that didn't allow us to. It was only just ten years ago that we in the US were able to expand geographically. It wasn't until last year that we were able to go to a broad product line. It was laws and regulations that kept it from going, not because the consumer wanted it that way. If you look at other countries where geography was allowed to expand faster or products were allowed to expand faster, the institutions do indeed have a larger market share and there are fewer institutions in those geographies. So, it's pretty obvious what's going to happen. I think we know directionally where things are going.

So how would you characterize what Wells Fargo will look like in five years from now?

I think it will hopefully have a much higher market share of our customers' business. Today, we have about 25 per cent of the financial services of our customers. We'd like to see that closer to 50 per cent, and that would still mean 50 per cent of them going somewhere else. Today, we may have 15 to 20 per cent market share of banking in our markets, but we only have a 3 per cent market share of financial services. I don't know if we will have that much more market share in banking, but I'd like to see that 3 per cent be more like 6 per cent. This is an important point. Citicorp only has a 3 per cent market share of financial services. It's really not huge, compared to Wal-Mart, which has a 40 per cent market share and Home Depot with an 18 per cent market share and General Motors with 30 per cent. Financial services just happens to be a huge business, but the big players have really quite small market share from the perspective of other products and services. That's why it has to get bigger. Why should financial services be different? The only difference was laws and regulations, not what the customers want.

And you plan to expand through acquisitions?

I think it will happen both ways – through acquisition and internal growth. That's the way it happened in the past and the way it will continue to happen. It will be roughly equal and not dominated by one or the other, although I actually believe that internal growth will be greater than by acquisition. But the point is, both will be significant.

Do you expect another major merger for Wells Fargo?

I think it's unlikely. It could happen, but geographically, we are about where we want to be. Maybe another three or four states, but we have no desire to be a national bank as such. We're a national finance company and a national mortgage company and we're in most of the products. Again, I don't see it likely that there would be a major acquisition, but you never know. It's much more likely that there will be a continuation of smaller deals.

Some people argue that all the info available on the Internet has put individual investors on a level playing field with institutional investors.

I think there is certainly no lack of information. And, certainly, it is both easier, cheaper and faster to obtain information today than ever before, and that's one of the great things about the Internet, but you can be so overwhelmed by information, it still doesn't help you to make an intelligent decision. I do not believe that providing advice to people on financial matters is going to disappear, by any stretch of the imagination. If anything, it will become more valuable because the world is becoming more complex and is moving faster. We're in a worldwide economy, not just domestic, but people will have a choice. People had less of a choice before because less information was available. There will be a bifurcated market, but advice will continue to be extremely important.

Do you think the traditional stock markets will be replaced by ECNs?

I think some of that will occur but the more traditional market will last for at least some period of time.

What are the competitive advantages of banks during this rapid period of change?

I think there are four core relationships. By a 'core relationship' I mean that if you have that relationship with the customer, the propensity of that customer to buy more from you is greater than a non-core relationship. A savings account, a credit card account, a personal loan are not core relationships. People are very happy to have just that account and may or may not buy another product from that company. The four core relationships are chequeing, mortgages, investments and insurance. Any one of these four categories has a somewhat competitive advantage because the customers are more loyal to that institution and have a greater propensity to buy from them. It doesn't mean that they just go in and give them all their business willingly, the bank will have to go after it, but it ties the customer in such a way that they're more likely to do more business with you. Banks have some of that, but so do some non-banks.

What percentage of insurance is your business?

We're very small. We only have less than 5 per cent of our customers' insurance business, even though we're the largest bank-owned insurance agency in the country and the eleventh largest of any kind. But we're still a peanut. We believe that our most important growth area for the future is insurance, and I would add the investment arena. Again, we are quite small in both of these areas because they haven't been our focus for the last 148 years. It's only been the last five years we've focused on the investment and insurance areas. We've doubled the size of those businesses in the last five years, but we need to step it up even more. So, those are two areas of increased focus for us in years ahead.

Are customers resistant to buying insurance from a bank?

No. We just didn't try it in the past, because we were so focused on the banking arena due to regulation. It wasn't resistance from the customers, although, now, once customers are used to buying something from somewhere else, it's hard to get them to switch. I'd argue, if banks 50 years ago had been allowed to be in insurance or investment banking, they would have the highest market share today, since it is easier to deal with one company. Most people, once they have a relationship with someone, will tend to give that company more business. We just weren't in that business.

Is there a specific type of customer or demographic that is buying insurance from you?

No. I think it's more a function of our people. The best people tend to be better at selling insurance and investments, but not all of our people are as well trained or can give as good advice or do as good a job at listening to customers and understanding their needs. So the challenge is more internal than external.

What is the future for on-line consumer banking in the United States, Europe and Asia. Are there cultural, regulatory and legal obstacles to the proliferation of such services?

I think there are obstacles, but the world is recognizing that it's important to use this technology. I think we have a good chance of getting it right around the world. Right now there are too many restrictions, but I think people are addressing that. It's important that we do not put handcuffs on this wonderful new technology that allows us to do so much. Although there are legitimate restrictions – like pornography for kids – that we want to address, there's got to be balance. With any laws, you have to be careful not to stifle the creativity and advantages.

“I'd argue, if banks 50 years ago had been allowed to be in insurance or investment banking, they would have the highest market share today.”

How much of a disadvantage are consumers who don't have computers?

I don't think it's a disadvantage. The greatest advantage is the convenience. I'm not into getting more information than my trusted advisers. I'm not going to out-doctor the doctor.

“Probably our biggest challenge, and one which always is, is to get more customer business and grow revenue. That's harder to do when you're doing lots of integration and conversions, but we expect to both walk and chew gum.”

A lot of Internet users do it because they enjoy it, but what I want to make sure of is that my provider of information gets access to this data. These are tools, not substitutes for human judgement. The greatest advantage of the internet is the convenience. It transfers repetitive transactions to electronic areas so that people can be freed up to really concentrate on what's important. I'm not sure that continuously cashing a cheque for a person or continuously looking up balances is adding a lot of value to society, but I do believe that all that human talent could be dedicated to helping you achieve your financial goals and that is powerful.

Are there conflicts of interest in bundling all these services under one roof?

I think just the opposite. If you're just offering CDs, that's a conflict. But now you can offer a wide range of products and that's the best thing for the customers.

Do you feel comfortable with analysts' estimates for fiscal 2000?

I think they're challenging but doable. They're challenging because we're talking about increases in the 14 to 16 per cent in earnings in a year where there's lots of competition and we're still doing about 90 per cent of all of our conversion. To have those levels of profit increases, which would be among the highest in the industry, while we're still integrating our companies and doing the conversions is very challenging.

The current quarter looks very good and we'll certainly be in the ballpark of everybody's estimates.

So your big challenge at this point is integration?

It's one of our challenges. Probably our biggest challenge, and one which always is, is to get more customer business and grow revenue. That's harder to do when you're doing lots of integration and conversions, but we expect to both walk and chew gum.

Do you feel that the intense competitive nature of financial services render many institutions less fit to cope with a downturn?

I think people are not pricing for risk. They are assuming the economy is going to go up forever. They are loosening covenants, particularly on commercial lending, beyond prudent means and not pricing for risk. Eventually, when the economy doesn't bail us out from these bad decisions, there will be significantly higher credit losses. We've been in an unprecedented [span] of low losses and this cannot continue.

Your institution is being more cautious.

We think we do a better job than most. Mainly, again, because we have such a broad product line, we can decide to do less in an area that doesn't make sense. Also, we have one of the highest loan loss reserves. But I'm sure we're guilty to some extent, too, because it's a competitive environment. I believe that because of the pricing we're using on the commercial loans, that product itself is not making the profit it should. To make up for that, we cross-sell so the overall profitability of the client is still good, but the commercial loan is almost becoming a loss leader. If you don't cross-sell, for sure, you're underpricing and you're going to get hurt. We make up by selling him other things so overall customer profitability is still OK, but the loan is being subsidized, if you will, by other products and services.

Do you see this trend reversing any time soon?

It will only reverse when problems occur and then we'll go the opposite direction and people won't make any loans to anybody. That's why the old traditional banking has been a cyclical business. We go too far in both directions. In good times, we lend too easily and in bad times, we shut our doors. That's why, generally, you have recessions in this country. The banks have done too much or too little and this has exacerbated the situation. If you do better than that, then you're in great shape. If everyone else is pulling in and your bank is getting out to the customers, you can really gain market share, so there's a real advantage. The only way to get out of this trap is by having a diverse earnings stream. So if one part of the business is being irrational, rather than having fewer earnings by pulling back, which takes a lot of guts, what we simply do is shift our resources over to all the other businesses that we have where the competitive environment is not as irrational and produce steady earnings.

An example is our consumer finance company. When all these sub-prime lenders two or three years ago were doing crazy things, our volume in consumer finance declined. We just didn't play that game. Yet, the corporation's earnings still increased because our mortgage company was booming and our banking business was booming. The opposite can occur when banks get irrational. Right now, our consumer finance company is growing . That's the kind of balance when you have diversity of earnings stream, which allows you to be a much more rational player and shift resources when irrationality is occurring in other segments.

What is your loan loss provision?

It's about 2.7 of loans and 500 per cent of non-performing. Its very high compared to everybody else.

What is your most vulnerable area?

Commercial lending. Many competitors are using price or covenants to gain market share that aren't prudent and they will pay the price one of these days as soon as the economy declines.

Any idea when the bubble will burst?

I have no idea. I've been predicting a slowdown for three years and it hasn't happened, so it shows you how smart I am.

Usually, there is something that occurs that sets one off. The greatest vulnerability we have to a significant slowdown is the stock market. I really think the stock market is cushioning the economy to such a degree – much more than ever – and, should that decline in some way for a period of time, that could trigger a significant slowdown.

If the GNP was growing between 1 and 2 per cent, that's half of what's growing now, and that would be a significant slowdown, but wouldn't be described as a recession. Second, if anything happened internationally, but international is looking pretty good so now it's even less likely that a recession would occur. It appears that Asia is coming back and Europe is getting stronger and so on.

There's already been a correction in the technology sector. I personally don't believe in these businesses where there is no business model that makes any economic sense. I don't believe there's a new economy. I do believe you have to make money and I look at these business models and can't say how they're going to make money. Some will, but people who have the best opportunity to take advantage of this technology are the clicks and bricks. Why do we need more warehouses, fulfilment centres, telephone customer service centres? What we want to do is marry those infrastructures with this new channel so everyone wins. I think its going to be the traditional companies that have the greatest opportunity to use the Internet for their advantage than the pure plays. Yet, it is the traditional companies that invest in the Internet and report lower earnings and get killed. These other companies can lose lots of money consistently. It doesn't make any sense to me.

DAVID LI

Chairman, Bank of East Asia Limited

INTERVIEW BY DAVID LAWDOR

How do you view the development of the asset management industry in Asia?

We're in the infancy of asset management in Asia because unit trusts or mutual funds are still not as popular as they are in US or in Europe, but it's growing quite fast. The mentality of the Asians is very different from that of the Europeans or the Americans, or even the Latin Americans. They don't want to give money to other people to manage. They prefer to manage money themselves rather than trusting someone else, and feel that having to pay a fee for someone to lose your money is quite a daft idea. Therefore, the industry has not picked up.

Also, in this part of the world, the gambling instinct is a bit higher than elsewhere, and people like to say, 'I make so much money investing in stock.' If they lose money, they won't blame anyone else, but if they pass it to a professional manager and he does it badly, they would feel doubly ashamed and wish they had managed it themselves. So the mentality is a little different and you have to overcome that. If people feel they can't manage their portfolios, say, in the US because they only know the Hong Kong stocks or the Asian stocks or they want to diversify their portfolios, they may want to give it to professional managers. If you look at unit trust sales in emerging countries, they rely

“The mentality of the Asians is very different from that of the Europeans or the Americans, or even the Latin Americans. … They feel that having to pay a fee for someone to lose your money is quite a daft idea.”

on professional managers, but in those mature markets, like Singapore or Hong Kong, people always like to be in the driving seat.

Was the success of the Hong Kong Government's blue-chip Tracker Fund[1] *a sign that investors are willing to look more closely at unit trusts?*

The Tracker Fund is basically an index fund, and quite a lot of people in America and Europe like to buy index funds because it's easy to track – if the index goes up, I go up. But with the Tracker Fund, the big attraction was the big 5 per cent discount and the loyalty bonus that the Government offered. It also was quite heavily marketed and, according to one survey, something like a quarter of the people who bought it believed it was *guaranteed* by the Government. I think it will not be as popular the next time around because if you look at the stocks that have been moving in recent months, they have been the high-tech stocks and the high-risk stocks, rather than the ones in the Tracker Fund. Unless people are conservative, they will go for any stocks with a dot com in it. So we are thinking of having Bank of East Asia.com.

The Mandatory Provident Fund pension scheme should provide a boost to asset management in Hong Kong and Asia.

That will definitely boost the asset management industry, and that will basically be also good for Hong Kong. Not less than 30 per cent of the exposure has to be in Hong Kong equities and bonds, so I think that will develop the bond market in Hong Kong. There are 21 MPF providers and, within two years, there will be only 15, so there is fierce competition. If you look at the fees that are being charged, it's mainly on a break-even basis, but competition is good.

Are we getting to the point where we have banks that are too big to fail?

I don't think so. I think with the Internet and cyberbanking, it is going to level the playing field a lot more. To say that no bank can fail is like saying that no country can default on their debt. It's not true. Banks *do* fail and governments *do* default on their debts. A lot will depend on government policies and on the stability of their markets. I don't see that a Citicorp or anything like that will fail. Some years ago, Citicorp was having a lot of problems and, despite the fact that they had the problems, they came out of it.

Does the Internet make it necessary to have a global regulating body?

> "I think the regulations are not tight enough and people's mentalities are very different. I basically think there will be a lot more rules and regulations and China will go through a painful learning process to recognize normal practices."

I think the Bank for International Settlement is already trying to do that, trying to basically have a global standard on some issues such as capital adequacy ratios and making certain that accounting standards are harmonized so there will be much more fairness in reporting, but I think it will take some years before it can be done. Even today, the European and American standards of accounting are very different and the two giants are not getting together. The American standards are getting ahead of Europe, but Europe doesn't want to adopt the American standards.

I basically think Asia will more and more adopt American standards. If you look at China, the Chinese banking system is very much modelled on the Federal Reserve system and the Chinese regulatory system is modelled on the American regulatory system. My branches in China are basically supervised the same way as my branches in America. The regulatory environment in China is developing very fast. I sit on the Board of the International Advisory Committee for Capital Markets for the Federal Reserve Bank of New York and I know they have lot of Chinese executives from the People's Bank of China in training there, also at the IMF and the World Bank. They are looking at the American system, learning from it and taking it home.

What lessons has China learned from the turmoil of 1997–98, including the collapse of GITIC [Guangdong International Trust and Investment Corporation] and the costly debt restructuring at Guangdong Enterprises?

I think they learned that their currency is not quite convertible yet. There was a timetable that, by the year 2000, it would be convertible, but because of the crisis, they decided to delay that. If they do make their current accounts convertible they will have a lot more problems. Second, they realized that their accounting standards and their legal system need to be improved greatly. As far as problems with GITIC and the other ITICs are concerned, it's malpractice, fraud and corruption. People's greed, no more than that. I'm a director of GDI, Guangdong Investment. If you look at them, they made bad investments without too much research, a lot of 'You help me, I help you', and the Board was not informed. I think the regulations are not tight enough and people's mentalities are very different. I basically think there will be a lot more rules and regulations and China will go through a painful learning process to recognize normal practices. They are learning it from Hong Kong. For Hong Kong banks like us, it was a very hard experience. We had trusted some of the officials we had trusted some of the companies and, yet, they didn't pay the bank back.

Did most foreign banks assume that loans to GITIC, GDE and other State-run investment groups were guaranteed by provincial governments?

Sure. There was a lot of implication that these loans would not fail because these groups were backed by the provincial government and that is the reason they enjoyed low interest rates. Some of the signing ceremonies [for the loans] were in the provincial government headquarters, hosted by the mayor, the deputy mayor and the governor of the province. And Guangdong province is the richest of all the provinces and the closest to Hong Kong, so people thought that they had confidence in these groups. And knowing how Guangdong has progressed in the last 20 years, banking people were very surprised that they got themselves into this terrible mess.

Your bank has taken some of the biggest provisions for GITIC and GDE [US$ billion in 1998 and US$ billion in 1999]. Is the worst over, and what kind of due diligence is now being employed for Chinese loans?

I believe the worst *is* over. I think we believe that we are still on a learning process of what not to do, on the part of both Hong Kong people and Hong Kong companies, as well as for the mainland officials. But I can tell you that, from now on, in lending to mainland, the type of interest rate that they used to enjoy is really history. As far as due diligence, it's a matter of looking at the track record of the people you're dealing with and whether they can be trusted or not to run the company well. When we used to lend, we lent to organizations we thought were making money, but we didn't know some of the officials were so corrupt. There will be more asset backing, but people will also be looking at the cash flow of the companies and their earning capacity. But the main problem with China is that the rules and regulations keep on changing and the goalposts seem to be always moving, so you have to watch it very, very closely or there are certain rules and regulations that will work against you after you sign the loan.

One of the things I think we learned from this is that implicit agreements and implicit understanding from officials are not good enough. Even things in writing are not good enough because you may never get exclusion of judgement in China because of the legal system. So you are looking basically at lending to them, and, to make certain that they will be able to repay you, you have to watch the management and you have to watch their business even more closely than ever before.

What role will foreign banks play in the development of China's domestic banking industry? Will it be more of a teaching role or will they take their fair share of the market?

When China enters the World Trade Organization, after a period of time, the Chinese will need a lot more capital in order to jumpstart their economy and really expand it. There is great potential in China for banks, but also great risk. I think foreign banks will bring not only capital, but expertise, connecting China with the country in which they operate. At Bank of East Asia, we already have done a lot of liaison and we've become a bridge for the overseas Chinese through Hong Kong into China. We'll continue to be a bridge for overseas Chinese, wherever they are around the world, to China. We have an 81-year history of doing business with overseas Chinese.

Chinese banks may be looking at a serious threat if the WTO conditions are applied as advertised. But Chinese banks have one advantage: they have the customer base already. Governor Dai Xianglong [People's Bank of China] , who is very smart, is asking them to consolidate and to specialize.

Given what's happened in a number of sectors where local products are still preferred in China – the beer market being a good example – do you think Chinese will prefer to do business with local banks even after foreign banks enter the market?

If you look at how Japan and Korea were opened up after the Second World War, initially, the Japanese didn't want to deal with any foreign banks. The same thing was true of Brazil. But now they all have to for the simple reason that foreign banks give them better product lines and better facilities. It's a matter of competing on services and on products.

As the industry consolidates, you have to have a great brand to stand out. What is your strategy for building your own brand name?

We are the largest independent Hong Kong bank and we have a long history of successes and achievements. We are the first Hong Kong Bank to launch credit cards in Hong Kong, we are the first to go on-line with 'cyberbanking' in Hong Kong, we are the first bank to do electronic broking. We will continue to innovate and deliver services.

“There is great potential in China for banks, but also great risk. I think foreign banks will bring not only capital, but expertise.”

We do believe in first mover advantage. We had all these on-line banking services – customer deposits, bill payment, fund transfer – all in place before we even had a platform to do the cyberbanking.

How do you see the development of Internet banking?

All simple products such as personal loan applications, mortgage applications, will be delivered through electronic means. But certain products will still always need active marketing, such as insurance products or unit trusts, where you will need more discussion with the customers.

You also will need to add content [on the Internet]. For example, in terms of mortgages, we have a link-up between surveyors, appraisers and property agents. You have to add value before people are going to be really interested in using your cyberbanking products.

In e-commerce, right now we are now doing mainly business-to-consumer [B2C], but later on we need to cover business to business. B2C transactions, the bank always plays a role. The buyer's worry is receiving the goods, and the seller's is whether they receive the money. We play the role in between. We've had a virtual credit card ready, but we haven't been able to launch it because of the [Hong Kong Government] Y2K moratorium.

How does the Internet change the competitive landscape? How do you stay ahead?

By investing more, by knowing the market and jumping in before everyone else, and adding content so that people come to your website and having bonus points that people can earn by buying things through you.

The Internet is basically a quick leveller. We have no branches in Latin America, but people in Latin America can still know about Bank of East Asia and still deal with us through their credit cards.

Having a cyberbank alone is not enough. You also have to have bricks and mortar, so the customers are aware of what you are doing. You have to advertise on television and in newspapers so that people know that you have bonus points or other incentives to come to your website. We are adopting a multichannel approach.

How much do you have to invest to stay competitive in this area?

I basically believe that the more you spend, the better it is. And that is the reason why some smaller banks may be prevented from going into it. If you don't have the customer base, what is the point?

Even if you have a group of banks going in together on a homogeneous [Internet] product, how are you going to make certain that they all agree to the same policies when one is prepared to go lower than the others in price? The costs of an Internet banking system are pretty much fixed, regardless of the size of the bank, so if you are a very small bank, it's probably going to be unbearable. It will encourage consolidation.

NOTES

1 The Tracker Fund – launched in November 1999 with Asia's largest ever initial public offering at HK$33.3 billion – was developed to help the Hong Kong Government to begin disposing of its blue-chip stock portfolio.

WILLIAM McDONOUGH

President, New York Federal Reserve

INTERVIEW BY STELLA DAWSON AND MARJORIE OLSTER

The financial services industry has undergone rapid changes, particularly in the past few years. We are seeing mega-mergers – this week alone Deutsche Bank and Dresdner. There has been an acceleration in the quantity and speed of international capital flows, triggered in part by the rate of technological innovation. Against that backdrop, would it be fair to say that the level of risk that regulators must oversee in their supervisory role in the global financial system is far greater today than it was a decade ago?

I don't think it is necessarily greater, but it certainly is different. The regulators have to be able to keep up with the pace of technological change in the financial services industry, which is very demanding for us.

Why don't we start with the banking firm, because the firm faces the same challenges internally that we do externally as supervisors.

In every firm, you want to have the most creative possible people on the trading desks, providing advice and counsel to their clients. At the same time, the firm wishes to protect itself and its stability against excessive creativity involving a greater amount of risk than the management of the company is willing to take. So there is a dynamic tension internally in the firm – between creativity and control of risk. And every firm both does, and, in my view, should, take a certain amount of calculated risk in allowing new creativity to take place and requiring the internal control apparatus to be a little breathless running behind it. But you have to keep that margin between creativity and control of creativity at a reasonable level.

It has to do with the definition of reasonableness – with the strength of the firm in terms of capital, with the strength of the firm in terms of quality of management and with the strength of the firm in terms of the quality of its people throughout the organization. A very highly capitalized, very experienced, very well-managed firm, which tends to attract very good people to work for it will be able to take more of this creativity risk, than a smaller, less well-capitalized firm.

In the same way, the supervisors have to, first of all, be sufficiently well staffed that they are capable of understanding the developments in the financial services industry. And that's not just understanding it three months later by reading learned pieces on it, but by actually understanding how the market works, being very closely in touch with market participants, especially those they supervise. We have to be able to make sure that creativity in the financial services industry is allowed to thrive, and at the same time to protect the public interest – which is our job – by not allowing such a great degree of risk in the financial services industry to be present that there would be the possibility of creating systemic risk, which would be injurious to the people of an individual country or more, broadly if one is in international markets, to the people of the world.

“ Every firm both does, and, in my view, should, take a certain amount of calculated risk in allowing new creativity to take place and requiring the internal control apparatus to be a little breathless running behind it. But you have to keep that margin between creativity and control of creativity at a reasonable level. ”

Is that risk management task much harder for you today, to keep track of the creative ideas that are being generated within the financial services industry when the rate of change is so rapid, than it was a decade ago?

It would be easy to say it is more difficult. I think it's more challenging, and it means we have to be smarter, quicker and have better people. I think that's the challenge. I do think we have smarter, better, more capable people and, therefore, I rather obviously am objecting to agreeing to use of the word 'harder'. It's more demanding, more difficult, more challenging. When you say it's harder you're sort of building in an excuse for not quite doing it, and that's why I dislike the use of that word or the acceptance thereof.

Let's turn to the Basel capital standards that you've worked very hard on. You are reviewing the 1988 standards and are looking at switching from a capital requirement based on the quality of assets held to a multilayered system. Why?

Let me take the generic: why did we think the 1988 capital accord was no longer useful, recognizing, of course, that we are going to be using it for a number of years until we finish the new capital accord and then there is a lengthy period of implementation?

The 1988 capital accord is a one-pillar approach. It's a minimum capital approach, and a rather simplistic minimum capital approach because its purpose was to create a more level playing field by demanding a higher and a more appropriate level of capital in internationally active banks.

What we have decided is that capital accord, because of its simplicity, lent itself to capital arbitrage. For example, all commercial loans are considered equal. So, if the bank is making a loan to the single best credit in the country and the single worst credit in the country, the amount of capital required for each loan is identical. Obviously, that doesn't make sense since the highest risk will pay you a minuscule margin, and therefore a rounding error to zero return on capital, then obviously you are pushed towards taking the higher risk to get an adequate return on capital with no adequate compensation for the amount of risk involved.

We think that a three-pillared capital accord approach is necessary because, even though we can get the minimum capital pillar – the first pillar – to be much better than it is now, we will never get it to be perfect. We will never get it to absolutely perfectly measure relative risk. Consequently, we need the second pillar, which is a much more actively involved supervisor. And, third, we need the market discipline that comes from greater transparency. So you are looking at minimum capital, which is very much concentrating on the management of the firm; you are looking at a more active role of the supervisor; and you are looking at the marketplace to provide discipline. And we think 1 + 1 + 1 = 4 – and that is what we are doing.

Now, in the first pillar, we are heading towards a rather more complicated conclusion than the proposal of last June would have indicated. At that time it looked very much as if the main body of the new accord would be what we call a standardized approach, and there would be probably a relatively small number of relatively sophisticated banks who would be able to use an internal rating system. We are now evolving in a direction in which there will be a much larger number of banks that will be able to use the internal rating system, and a relatively smaller number of banks that will be using the standardized approach among the banks in the G10 [group ten] countries.

We believe that the standardized approach has to be very strong. It has to be considerably more given to robustness and actually relating capital to risk than the present accord. But it won't be as good as the internal rating system, but it has to be a lot better than the present one. We are still working on all these things, but we are particularly working on the standardized approach, and we'll be able to talk about that more intelligently probably in about July.

On the internal ratings approach, the banks will divide themselves into two groups: those who are in favour of such an approach and those who aren't.

In the internal ratings approach, the bank will, as the word implies, use its own internal rating system. You divide your risk portfolio into various groups, which we call buckets of risk – and we will have to have some guidance so that Bank A and Bank B have a rather similar notion of what buckets ought to be. (We won't make that absolutely identical because we don't want Bank A and Bank B to have invested a lot of time and money in developing their own system, then we come along and say, 'No, no, no that's not all right, you've got to have it our way.' Well, Bank A has to have it Bank B's way or visa versa.) So, we will allow a certain amount of flexibility, but with a fair degree of guidance.

The key judgement that has to be involved is the probability of default in each bucket. Then there is the next step, which is – if you have a probability of default in Bucket 2, if the default actually takes place, what is the level of loss? – the so-called loss-given default analysis. The loss-given default is very, very much more difficult to calculate for even an individual bank and there probably will be a relatively small number of banks whose internal rating system will be so advanced that they will be able to use this whole approach. We are very happy to have as many as can qualify. We have no sort of magic number. But, in the case of a probably considerably large number of banks, we the supervisors will give them the loss-given default assumption that they should use in each bucket.

In this way, we will have two levels of internal ratings – a reasonably sophisticated and a very sophisticated version. So we'll have three approaches within Pillar One – the standardized approach and then these two levels of internal ratings. We think that, or are convinced that, that will give us a very, very, very much more powerful Pillar One.

There's been a good deal of controversy on the use of external ratings in two areas. One, external ratings of sovereigns, and then external ratings of banks and firms – private-sector and public-sector firms.

The reason that we wanted something different from the present accord for external ratings is that, in the present accord, there is an 'on and off' switch. If you are a member of the OECD [Organization for Economic Cooperation and Development], you're a good sovereign credit; if you are not a member of the OECD, you're not quite as good a sovereign credit. There are certainly some non-members of the OECD who think, rather accurately, that they are at least as good a credit as members of the OECD. Therefore, this seemed like a rather simplistic approach.

Then the question was, 'What do you put in its place?' We've explored 'Would the IMF be willing to do it?' The answer is 'No'. 'Would the World Bank be willing to do it?' Also the answer is 'No'. 'Would the OECD export credit rating agencies be willing to do it?' 'No.' So, we were left with the only thing that seems to be there, which is the sovereign ratings of the rating agencies. We are very well aware that is less than perfect, but it seems to be better than what's available. We are working with the IMF [International Monetary Fund], World Bank and the private-sector banks – mainly through their association with the Institute of International Finance – to see if we can come up with a better approach to external ratings of sovereigns, and I don't know if we'll be able to get a better one than we have.

In terms of external ratings of individual firms, there there's an issue of fairness, because, in the United States and in the United Kingdom, a very large number of firms are rated. Elsewhere in the G10 countries a very small, much smaller, number of companies are rated. In any event, for a lot of the medium- and small-sized firms that are really the main credit counterparties of banks, there are no ratings. So, we have to come up with a methodology in the standardized approach which will make it possible for this to be deemed to be fair, objective and a real step forward. It's a very considerable challenge. I'm quite confident we'll make it, but don't ask me how, because I don't know yet.

Has one provision not been that the bank itself issues subordinated debt, which then gets rated, which will provide an external debt? What is your view on that?

That is a way of doing it. People are also looking at 'What does the equity value of the bank's stock tell you about the markets appreciation of relative risk?'

It is much more complicated than looking at subordinated debt, but every bank has loads of capital trading and actively in the market. Subordinated debt will trade much less hecticly and, therefore, I think that subordinated debt is a useful tool. I don't think it's a unique answer.

Let's look at the second pillar: supervisory review. With global banks, are we expecting too much from the national supervisors in overseeing complex and far-flung operations? Do we need a global regulator?

I don't think that it's at all possible to have a global regulator. We exist in a world in which the market is the world and in which the nation state is still the dominant, controlling vehicle. Nobody is going to create a world government, and you probably couldn't have a world regulator in the absence of a world government. Even in Euroland, the European Central Bank is not a supervisory body, the individual national central banks are. So, I think we will continue to have the active supervisor at the nation state level.

“Nobody is going to create a world government, and you probably couldn't have a world regulator in the absence of a world government. Even in Euroland the European Central Bank is not a supervisory body.”

But then one might ask, 'What about a Chase, a Citigroup, a Deutsche Bank, which are truly worldwide?' We supervisors have worked out that challenge quite well in the home country, host country, with a balance of supervision. The home country supervisor is the one where the institution is incorporated, so the United States does Chase and Citi. The Germans do Deutsche. The British do Barclays, etcetera. However, since the banks are also active in other countries, we as host supervisor – we at the New York Fed being one of the most active host supervisors anywhere because of the amount of foreign bank presence in New York – in the case of a British bank, we operate very closely with the FSA. In the case of a French bank, we operate very closely with the Commission Banquier. And it works amazingly well, and I think it does not leave the world's people sort of unprotected by the fact that you've got banks operating globally but no single supervisor acting globally. It demands a lot of goodwill and a lot patience and a lot of understanding, but it works.

With national bank regulators, however – even if you agree on something like minimum capital standards – how the national regulators apply those standards might be quite different country to country. How does that assure the safety of the global banking system?

Well, they can't really be terribly different when the new accord comes out because, remember, the third pillar of transparency. In order to be able to operate in the international marketplace where your counterparts have to be willing to work with you, you're going to have to have a degree of transparency so that your counterparties can say: 'We'll deal with them' or not. And, if we deal with them, up to what amounts, what maturities, etcetera?

Part of that transparency is going to have to be – especially since the more active banks will be using internal ratings system – almost certainly part of the transparency will be, 'How does my internal ratings system work and what does my supervisor have to say about how it works?'

Now, if you had a country where the banks didn't have much of an internal ratings system and the supervisor was sort of winking at that, then the third pillar – the transparency pillar – would bring in like a shot a risk premium for the country. And risk premiums for the country or, let's say, all countries that don't behave . . . in the interbank deposit market, the country will pay 50 basis points, 75 basis points, 100 basis points or nobody will deal with them. That's the importance of the third pillar.

I think it highly unlikely that you'd have any country that anybody would want to do business with in which the local banks and the banks supervisory would cooperate to ease supervision. But, if they did – which would be an inordinately dumb thing to do – the third pillar will catch it. And the third pillar will be brutal because the third pillar will throw on a risk premium and the spreads in the international market are such that if you have a country premium, you're dead. You simply can't make any money.

Why, though, will the third pillar work? The critics of transparency – which has been strongly espoused in the international finance community ever since the 1998 crisis – say it is anti-competitive for a bank or a firm to reveal its trade secrets – who they are lending to and how.

They don't have to. You don't have to tell me what your positions are or what your trading strategies are. But you do have to tell me what is the strategy of your firm, what is the risk appetite that you have in order to achieve the strategy that you've set out, what is the amount of capital that your internal rating system says that you need. As far as I'm concerned, if you're not willing to tell me that, I'm not willing to trade with you. And I will do anything in my power so that any bank I supervise won't trade with you. We are quite serious about this stuff.

On the other hand, there is no need for you to tell me exactly what your trading positions are. I don't care what your trading positions are. All I'm interested in is, 'What is your appetite for risk? Have you demonstrated an ability to manage your bank within that appetite for risk?' Presumably, your confidential trading positions are within that. There the critics are absolutely right, except they don't quite understand the issue. The issue is not that we want to know people's trading secrets; we want to know enough about them to know whether we ought to deal with them or not.

“The danger doesn't necessarily come because the managers of the fund would like to get highly leveraged; it comes from the fact that they become highly leveraged, which means that they've got counterparties who are willing to do that.”

How would this strategy have enabled you to head off the Long-Term Capital Management debacle?

Well, LTCM – or any fund which we in the Basel Committee have labelled highly leveraged institutions (HLI) rather than hedge funds – largely because there are some hedge funds that have practically no leverage at all or none, and there are some things that are not called hedge funds but which have an immense amount of leverage. But we define a highly leveraged institution as highly leveraged, incorporated in a place where there is little or no banking supervision, and therefore they are not supervised by anybody. Those were the three characteristics in the Brockmeyer Report, which came out in January 1999.

LTCM and any other HLI cannot become highly leveraged unless its counterparties are willing to make a very large amount of leverage available to them. So, the danger doesn't necessarily come because the managers of the fund would like to get highly leveraged; it comes from the fact that they become highly leveraged, which means that they've got counterparties who are willing to do that.

As we made very clear in the Brockmeyer Report, there was a failure of judgement on the part of LTCM counterparties in general because they agreed with LTCM's rules that LTCM only told you so much and not more, and if you wanted to know more, you didn't trade with them. I've always said that that means anybody with really good judgement should not have been trading with them, but there were some very fine institutions that were.

There was a lapse of judgement. We have made that as clear as we possibly can. You should not be dealing with a firm unless you know what I've described before. Namely, what is the risk appetite of the firm, what is the ability of the firm to manage its risk, and, if the firm is not willing to tell you that, there's only one answer – don't deal with them and if everybody had done that, LTCM would never have gotten as highly leveraged as it did.

Let me go back to what you said in the very beginning about allowing creativity to thrive in institutions, and that the strongest institutions are those who have room for creativity, that have excellent people in them and that have excellent management. Working at LTCM, you had the best minds in the industry and, in the beginning, excellent capital. What then was the regulatory failure?

I don't think there was regulatory failure, because the regulators that were supervising the American institutions involved in the recapitalization of LTCM – the supervisors were looking at concentration of risk. They did not have a concentration of risk with LTCM or other hedge funds that were such that they were in any danger. We made it very clear in our involvement in LTCM's recapitalization that we were not concerned about the failure of the individual firms. What we were concerned about was the macroeconomic effects.

But what we did chide the banks for when we did target examinations of them after the LTCM event is that they didn't know enough about the counterparty and they were going much to much on LTCM's claim to fame – Nobel Prize winners etcetera, a very successful track record. Therefore, I don't think we had a regulatory failure. I don't think we necessarily had the counterparties being anything other than, by hindsight, a little unwise.

What we had was, in a rather dramatic moment in world financial markets, an institution that had become so highly leveraged that its failure because of its size in various markets, the size of its positions could have endangered the world economy. And that's why we encouraged – we invited people for lunch of sandwiches and cold coffee – so that they could see if they didn't prefer to do something about it.

So it wasn't a regulatory failure, it was a banking failure?

No, I don't agree.

It was a failure of the bankers in properly assessing the risks.

Yes.

Has that risk assessment problem been adequately addressed so it won't happen again?

What the Brockmeyer Report recommended – and every report written since then, and there have been quite a number – they have all come to the same conclusions. Whether or not it would be a good idea directly to control highly leveraged institutions, nobody really knows exactly how to do it. Therefore, the moral issue of whether you should control them or not I find interesting, but not very relevant, because if you say, 'Yes, we should control them', then you better know how, and we don't. So what we do know is how to get at them indirectly – through this supervision of their counterparties, which is done by the securities regulators and the banking regulators in the major countries.

“We, as the supervisors, remember that part of our responsibility is to have better memories than those who are in the marketplace.”

We did a one year after Brockmeyer Report, which is 'How does it look a year after?' and it looks a lot better, but not as good as we would like it to be. There still are people who are not quite as demanding and insistent as we'd like them to be. So, there's been a very, very large amount of improvement and clearly the level of risk is considerably lower. That's not surprising since, so close to the fact, even people with poor memories don't have *that* poor a memory. But I think the challenge will be that we have to keep on top of this issue to make sure that the indirect approach is working, that their counterparties are not letting them get overleveraged and that, as time passes – and hopefully nothing like this happens again – that we, as the supervisors, remember that part of our responsi-bility is to have better memories than those who are in the marketplace.

Have you noticed that this sort of risk appetite has been decreased in the wake of LTCM?

Yes.

Mr Greenspan, Chairman, Federal Reserve, the other day gave a cautionary warning to bankers about the bad loans they are making good at times.

You have two different things going on. First issue that we have been talking about until now is dealing in the marketplace among counterparties. I think there the risk appetite has clearly been reduced, and you see that in the fact that clearly there is much less leverage by those who like a lot of leverage. The spreads in financial markets are still quite wide, and that indicates that the degree of liquidity that you had pre-LTCM – really pre-Russian debacle in August of 1998 – that lesson continues to be learned.

Then you shift to another area of risk and that is the more traditional loan portfolios of banks. After nine years of economic expansion in this country, you probably have a lot of people making loans who never made a loan before the economic expansion started, and therefore have no experience whatsoever in an economic cycle bringing about a credit cycle which brings about loan workouts – and that's what really tests a banker. Anybody can make a loan to a company that looks good. It's dealing with the damaged customer and deciding which you are better off doing – lending him more money because you will get more back at the end of the day, or say, 'It's gone' and bankrupt him. That needs experience.

And Mr Greenspan, being very famous, when he makes such a remark, everybody pays attention to him. But I think every bank supervisor who's worth a damn has been making those speeches for several years now.

Is there adequate stress testing going on? He's concerned, but how do you ensure that the banks are stress testing their portfolios?

When we supervise them – we now have an approach to banking supervision called 'Risk Approach to Supervision' and we look at exactly those things: 'How are the bank's internal controls? Is it stress testing its own portfolio? Is the stress test meaningful enough?' – I think we, even though the banks I think are doing a better job, I think the supervisors are even more on top of them. It is still a good idea to make public speeches reminding people that there is risk in this world.

I remain unconvinced that transparency will work – that, as a number of people have described it, get that blast of cold air in there and the market will discipline the institution. Why is that going to prevent a future LTCM?

It won't, it won't. It's part of the larger puzzle. There are true believers in transparency who say all you need is transparency, and who needs supervision and regulation? I think they're crazy. What you need is transparency, very good supervision and regulation, and better bankers. You need all three. None of the three alone will work. You say, let's have better bankers. Well, sure, that's wonderful. Let's have a better bank supervisor. Great. Well, you can have the best bank supervisors in the world, but if you have lousy bankers, it's not going to accomplish a whole lot. And if you have nothing but transparency, that won't do the trick either. So, when you say, 'I don't agree that transparency itself will do the trick', then, 'Amen' say I. On that I couldn't agree with you more.

That's why the three-pillar approach we think is absolutely essential. It's like the three-legged stool: all three legs better be strong and the same length.

Why can't highly leveraged institutions be regulated and why is that so difficult? And a related question is, with individuals investing so much now in pension plans, 401K schemes, is a lot of money management now being transferred to the non-bank realm of financial institutions? Are those being adequately regulated and those types of investments being supervised adequately?

I don't pretend to be an expert on the supervision of money managers. My impression – but it's not a whole lot more than that – is they are adequately part of the SEC's brief. And I think that the answer is that they are adequately supervised, but that's a bit of a leap of faith in my fellow regulator.

Why can't you control an HLI? Our definition of a highly leveraged institution is lots of leverage in an offshore centre and not supervised or not supervised much. It's an economic definition, which I think all of us can understand. But if we said that's what an HLI is, and an HLI is controlled, any lawyer who has gone to the worst law school in the world can figure a way out of that definition within about 30 seconds because it's not exact enough. So, by the time you get to a point where you would have brought down the specificity, I think the thing would have disappeared.

I actually would like to control these things. There are those who say, 'No, you shouldn't', the true believers would have the marketplace doing everything. That's why I've rejected very strongly, in anything I've been involved in, the pure pragmatist saying 'No, you can't control these things, you shouldn't control these things.' I don't agree with that. But, on the other hand, I don't want to hang around until we figure out how to do it and let them do their merry thing in the meantime. It's principled pragmatism, if there is such a thing.

So they basically found a way around the system?

Well they haven't had to because there's nothing for them to work their way around. There are proposals but none has been enacted to regulate highly leveraged institutions. Whether or not they will be able to be precise enough that they'll actually work, is a very large question.

Then they do still pose a risk and you haven't yet a way to handle that?

In theory, yes, but I think, in practice, the indirect approach is enough for safety and soundness, and is enough to protect the people. Are there people who could invest in these things, most of which demand that you be fairly seriously rich in order to invest in them? I've got sort of an Everyman's view of the world: the rich can take of themselves; I'm worried about the people.

The obvious question, with the Gramm-Leach US financial modernization Act taking effect in March that allows brokerages, insurance companies and banks to merge – are these bigger institutions more able to engage in riskier behaviour and doesn't that pose the 'too big to fail' problem for regulators?

I don't think that the existence of the new law will encourage people to engage in more risky behaviour. Remember, Gramm-Leach, to a very significant degree, codifies that which already existed in regulation. For example, the only thing that it did for the only model that exists, which is Citigroup, is it made sure that Citigroup didn't have a law saying that it had to divest any of its insurance interests, but the company was already operating with all of those activities.

I think that the number of companies that will do the full range of activities permitted by Gramm-Leach will probably be rather small. And that does not mean that there will not be quite a large number of financial holding companies, because there are certain advantages to being a financial holding company without necessarily having to do everything. I don't have any notion that people are going to be doing unwisely risky things just because there is an Act to that effect.

I am vehemently opposed to the notion that anything is too big to fail. I believe that any institution, however large, if it is sufficiently badly managed, that the people who run it bring it to its knees, it should fail. The only question is, is there a public interest in having a winding down of the institution be sufficiently orderly that it doesn't send shockwaves unnecessarily to the rest of the financial industry and, eventually, at the cost of the people that are served by the financial industry?

I think there's no question that any institution's failure is one in which you would wipe out the shareholders. You would probably have a significant portion of the debt holders not get a full return on the debt they hold, and there might very well be a method by which the winding down of the firm is done by selling off pieces and so on in the way that a failed bank is disposed of. The FDIC comes in and makes an evaluation on whether it's better to keep the bank alive and dismember it, or whether it's better to just sink it and allow it to sink and pay off the insured depositors.

But I think any time that we have a notion that anything is too big to fail, it's just terrible public policy. It would encourage people to take risk on the notion that they would be saved. I just don't think that we can do that. It would be a desperate extension of the possible use of taxpayers' money and very unwise.

How widely is that view shared amongst your fellow regulators in other countries?

I don't know of a regulator anywhere who thinks that anything is too big to fail. If something has a universal scope and it fails, a winding down of its activities would be very complicated because of competing legal jurisdictions and having the assets of one side of a trade in place X and the liabilities in place Y. Winding down an internationally active financial institution would be very complicated and demands great skill. It still should be done. The fact that something is difficult is like writing a great story.

You've had about a year now with Citi, Travelers and Salomon Smith Barney. What lessons have you learned in regulating Citigroup?

Well, first of all, we now know that it's quite possible to do so. We [at the Federal Reserve] have the umbrella regulator responsibility for Citigroup under the Gramm-Leach filing. We had it before when it was, as it still is, as of today, a bank holding company. It demands that we have people who understand the complexities of the business they are in; that we have very good, cooperative relationships with the functional bank supervisors, which, in Citi's case, since its bank is a nationally chartered bank, is the Comptroller of the Currency. Since it is very big in the insurance business and their insurance activities are in a number of states – but, as you know, in this country, insurance is regulated only at the state level – it requires us to have very good working relationships with the insurance superintendent in two states, especially in Connecticut and New York, which we have. And it just means that we have the capability to work with the institution and work with the functional regulators in a way that there is an adequate degree of supervision in the public interest. I am absolutely convinced that we have that.

Would you like to make a forecast on whether you think we will have an accelerated pace of mergers in the US now the legislation is in place modernizing the banking laws?

No, I think the answer is probably not. The act is not the main thing that is pushing the mergers. For example, it did not affect Deutsche-Dresdner, except that they operate in the United States.

I think there are things going on in the world economy, forces in the world economy, which will result in a relatively small number of very large, powerful financial institutions, but leave a very considerable place for medium-sized institutions that specialize and know very well how to do what they decide to do and don't want to do the other stuff.

> "I think if you're medium-sized you better be specialized."

I also think it will leave a very important place – certainly in the United States – for community financial institutions, community banks. If you know what you're doing as a community banker, it's a very good business to be in. There will be some medium-sized banks which can do quite all right, but that is probably the toughest place to be.

The big banks, if they get it right and put it together and execute the merger well, can be very successful. I think what the community banks – as well as the medium-sized banks – have to be careful of is that they are not trying to be in all the lines of business that large banks have without the capital underneath them and all the expensive systems. If they need to have the same systems and they can't in effect use the systems on as broad a base, then the transaction cost to the system is higher. I think if you're medium-sized you better be specialized.

RICHARD MEDLEY

Chief Executive Officer and Chairman,
Medley Global Advisors

INTERVIEW BY ANDREW PRIEST

What are the lessons learned from the global crisis of 1997 and 1998?

The lessons of that crisis were that very simple fundamentals in terms of risk management and conditions of the marketplace will always end up catching up with you, no matter how sophisticated and how thorough you are and how much you think you are hedged. You can't hedge the entire world.

Have there been measures taken to tighten the monitoring of firms such as LTCM and their relationship with banks?

A lot of the portfolios that were constructed around that time by Long-Term Capital Management, especially on the derivatives side, and a lot of the investments being made by very big investment houses around the world, ignored the basic fact that you only *think* you're hedged against a five sigma event, but there's no such thing as a hedge against that. If you're in an illiquid market with massive leverage, you're going to be caught eventually. One fundamental truth that we try to stick to around here is 'free money makes you stupid'.

What were investors like LTCM doing wrong?

Across the board, people were ignoring the fundamental things that financial systems and financial businesses are supposed to do, whether it

> “No matter how sophisticated and how thorough you are and how much you think you are hedged ... you can't hedge the entire world. One fundamental truth that we try to stick to around here is 'free money makes you stupid'.”

was investing in the fourth hotel on a particular intersection in Bangkok – which is one way of saying there was simply too much money available for these kinds of projects – or people buying GKOs [Russian government bonds] in Russia that were yielding 80 per cent without wondering why in the world someone was willing to pay that for a loan. Both these ignored the fact that there are basic risk management tools that need to be imposed. All these heavily involved the banking sector not doing what it is supposed to do in terms of examining the credit worthiness of the loans it is making and the credit risk on its books.

What are the problems with the current quantitative methods of risk evaluation? Should more qualitative methodology be used?

There was this notion that there was an artificial net exposure that could be calculated from different market positions. As long as the world was working in normal ways with normal, bell-shaped curves, you were hedged, but it didn't allow you to understand that if all your bets went wrong at the same time, that the net figure was nowhere near reflecting the total exposure.

When there is so much free money around, people start relaxing all kinds of risk standards. There has never been more credit available in the world than there is now. Leverage in total terms is more than ever, even if individuals are not as leveraged as much as they were. Raising money is easy now. We are in a situation where we could be moving toward a new kind of credit bubble.

Do regulators have adequate means to measure risk in financial institutions? Is there the need for a global body that monitors risk?

They have learnt the lessons on leverage limits. It is now much less likely that we will ever see another LTCM-type situation again, where one institution is able to get such great leverage. Regulators have learnt that there's an impossible gearing ratio and have done a lot to encourage banks to cut any exposure to any one fund. In the past, banks were willing to lend without first checking what other loans a fund had, how many times it had pledged its collateral to other institutions and how many other lenders there were out there.

Do regulators need more powers, more teeth, to cope with growing globalization?

Regulators have got enough teeth – it's a matter of catching up with the reality before it becomes a problem. They need to focus more on credit. For instance, German and Japanese insurance companies have programmes where they guarantee a certain yield to investors. To meet those yields they can't go buy JGBs [Japanese government bonds] or bunds to get the needed return, so they have to go out and find higher yields and that means that they have to move out further into the risk spectrum.

It is very hard for a regulator to say, 'No, you can't take any more risk.' One of the problems is that, in a world when everyone is making money, it's very hard to get people to agree to stop making money in order to take precautions. When Alan Greenspan said Internet stocks were like a lottery, in the papers the next day the reports were that Greenspan said Internet stocks could be a winner on the grounds that someone always wins the lottery. What are you supposed to do? You give about as explosive a warning as you can give as Fed Chairman that you're worried about the risks being packed into these markets and the response is to take it as a bullish phenomenon.

Is there any other legislative action that could be taken?

You can't legislate against exuberance and still have free markets. You can warn, you can force people to take a more conservative stance. If you raised margin requirements on stock buying, then people would just start buying stocks in a different way, using derivatives, for example. You don't fix the roof when it's sunny. You think about it a lot when it's raining, but then it's too wet to repair it. There's a certain element of that in any regulation.

Instead of thinking of new rules for the new era, we have just removed the old ones. Capital controls are falling around the world and, in terms of flow of capital and funds, I don't think there has ever been more freedom. The regulators are just standing by and seeing how this shakes out. They don't know which lever to pull right now.

What should regulators focus more on?

“One of the problems is that, in a world when everyone is making money, it's very hard to get people to agree to stop making money in order to take precautions.”

What regulators can do is try to get reporting up. If there's an emphasis they're coming down on hard, it is increasing transparency. Is that going to make players behave more rationally? No. Is that going to give regulators the possibility of spotting trouble earlier or at least once it starts to stop it getting serious? Well, you hope so, but I don't think anyone has got any illusions that you can keep up with the market enough to truly protect itself when there is so much money being made as now.

The market is still operating with interlocked positions that the regulators don't understand. There is a fragility in the market now. Even three years ago you would get nice long trends in all the markets. All the challenge was at the turning points. Now you're seeing much bigger movements. One of the reasons is that, because of the pain of 1997 and 1998, the tolerance of institutions of any kind of loss is much lower.

How are modern risk management techniques helping or hindering the greater control of risk in the global economy?

Risk management systems may actually be adding to the greater volatility. We talk to people who years ago wouldn't have taken losses at a 1–1½ per cent move. This means you have to take smaller positions and, also, you have to catch it just right. There's no ability to build into a losing position that you think will go right. One of the functions of hedge funds which the market needs is to take positions and absorb these movements and act at the very least as a circuit breaker, but you can't do that if at each 1–1½ per cent move players are being forced out.

LEO MELAMED

Chairman Emeritus and Senior Policy Adviser, Chicago Mercantile Exchange (CME), and Chairman and Chief Executive Officer, Sakura Dellsher Inc.

INTERVIEW BY BRAD SCHADE

As Chairman of the CME, in 1972, Leo Melamed launched the first futures market for financial instruments, the International Monetary Market (IMM), to trade futures on foreign currencies.

The first area is technology and e-commerce, which is a threat to the Chicago Mercantile Exchange?

Absolutely, but only . . . you know, it's like in all things, a threat can be a stepping stone to greatness if you view it correctly and accept it and understand it. Let me underline accepting the reality of it – that is exactly why I came back. I saw the Exchange in self-denial. I saw the Merc., which, arguably, when I left it in 1990, was on top of the game, with having launched Globex and Globex was the first mechanism of its kind for futures. When to the world a black box was the equivalent of Darth Vadar, I led the Merc. to launch Globex, in spite of that, and the membership approved it.

Which is something in itself.

Which is like selling ice to Eskimos. So, having done that, I thought, my God, now it's just a question of carrying forward the momentum and the direction and the road we were on and, instead, we almost reversed. We let Globex languish – we gave lip-service to technology, but I don't think anything happened for the next five years. Everyone around us who saw the truth, bypassed us. Eurex is the best example. I remember in fall of 1996, as late as that – probably October, November – there was a futures industry expo here in Chicago – and I was chairing a panel that was on electronic trading versus open outcry. It had on it all of the heads of the exchanges of the world. So, Jorge Franke was there from DTB [Deutsche Terminebörse], Jack Wigglesworth was there from LIFFE, Bill Brodsky was there for the Merc., Tom Donavan was there for the Chicago Board of Trade. Everybody was represented, but only my voice, as moderator, and Jorge Franke because of the DTB philosophy, were the only voices for electronic trading. David Hodson of LIFFE was in the audience, and David, in the question and answer part of it, raised his hand and said, 'But surely, Leo, you must admit' – I'm paraphrasing what he said – 'that in moments of upheaval, electronic trading can't work. Only open outcry can provide the liquidity when it's a real moment of crisis.' That viewpoint was verbalized by the head of LIFFE as late as fall of 1996 when, by June of 1997, they lost their own bund contract to the DTB. So, he verbalized what was, in fact, the viewpoint of all exchanges except one.

So, your question is, does technology, in fact, mean the death of the exchanges? And my answer that I'm trying to get to is 'Not necessarily', but you first must accept reality.

Let me go on. No, not everybody has accepted it. Not every faction within every exchange has accepted it. They've accepted it in Europe, they've accepted in Asia, but they did not have to deal with an establishment. Don't forget, futures exchanges in Europe and in Asia are of short duration. They didn't have a long history of open outcry and the establishment to deal with, except SIMEX (and, arguably, that isn't that long since it has only been around since 1984).

> 'Only open outcry can provide the liquidity when it's a real moment of crisis.' That viewpoint was verbalized by the head of LIFFE as late as fall of 1996.

So, SIMEX was the last to accept it in Asia. In the United States, we are still wrestling with that. I think, today, the Merc. has gone further, at least in the last three years, than any other exchange, to put itself in a position to accept the reality and there's more to it than just simply saying 'I understand'. You've got to be in a position to understand and do something about it.

For instance, we always had Globex, but we never had the capability to do anything with Globex in large volume form. What good is an instrument of electronics if the minute you give it order flow that it can't handle it crashes? It is of no consequence.

At least now we have the capability. What other exchange has that? In the United States? Nobody. Project A at the Board of Trade couldn't.

That's one of the reasons they made a deal with Eurex, to get technology. But even Eurex will admit to you that they aren't yet with the new technology that would allow all of the stream and the capacity that they need for a world-class market – they're working on it. They're going to release it some time in June or July of this year. So, in the United States I think, today, we have moved Globex to a position where, in fact, it is robust. It could do all the things that you need it to do and we proved it. What I said is it's not merely a philosophical understanding of the fact that you need technology in the new world, but it's a capability of using technology that I'm talking about, not just the philosophical understanding of it. To use it, you also have to prove to your community that it's usable and that it works and that, contrary to what people think, it will give you liquidity.

So, two years ago, we launched something called emini S&Ps [smaller version of S&P only traded electronically] and, guess what? It has become – it was, from day one – the most successful contract ever launched in the history of the Chicago Mercantile Exchange. We've recently, because of its success, launched the mini-Nasdaq, which is rivalling the success factor of the emini S&P as we speak, and there is now a clamour for e-mini contracts in currency and even agriculture.

So, the proof of the e-mini deserves a little bit of conversation, a little more definition than just simply to tell you that it was the most successful, because it did lots of things for us. By launching an all-electronic trade, the Merc. was forced to face the reality of a needed capability, so we had to build on to Globex to be able to handle 70,000 to 100,000 contracts a day in rapid fashion. That's wrestling with the reality of the capability and the robustness of the system.

We have to train our membership to not only accept it, but learn how to use the screen. Some of these guys never even pressed a button on a computer, believe it or not. Their kids did, but they didn't – they were computer-averse – but, suddenly, here was a contract that was very attractive, but the only way they could handle that was on a screen. So, all of a sudden, they have this big contract and they needed to learn how to use a screen. From a membership that was electronic-averse, we now have a waiting list of something like 200 members lined up for screens because we don't have enough of them on the floor or in their homes.

So, that was the other thing that we had to do, we had to mass produce screens and get them out there for the purpose of advancing this technological understanding. And, in doing this, there was another thing we were forced to learn, that no other exchanges learned yet – the rule book about electronic trading. There was no rule book about electronic trading. How do you handle out-trades? How do you handle errors? What are the rules? What are the agreements? What are the issues that we have to deal with? We had to create a new committee that had to create a new constitution about that. We're the only exchange that did that. We have now got the rule book and it's going to be copied, of course, and it's going to be used by others, but somebody had to do the leg work. So, there is a Globex oversight committee that was born in the process.

“We have now got the rule book and it's going to be copied, of course, and it's going to be used by others, but somebody had to do the leg work.”

Another side-benefit to it, again, wasn't simply an understanding. Our IT department had to hire personnel because we didn't have the kind of personnel who were needed to do the things to make this system work. We didn't even have the technological capability inside – people – so, we had to go out and get people. Today, we have that kind of crew – we have a very good crew. I would say we have the best in the business.

Now, I'd probably get an argument from Eurex, but they would be the only ones that would make that argument, that would even take us up on it. Certainly, nobody in the United States would argue with that. All of that was the result of the e-mini contract. You've got something out there, it's really working, you have to make use of it and prove it. To a very large extent, it belied the argument that electronic trading couldn't create liquidity in a crisis moment, because we have lots of crisis moments.

And one more thing it's produced – I'm giving you all these points of what that understanding meant. The other thing that it produced is this: there's a universe of users that we have never had before, those who want to apply their beliefs, their opinions, through technology. They have not only the ability to trade an Amex technology stock, but they also have the ability to use the screen to hedge that in a futures market. That was another by-product of this. Something like 40 per cent of the volume that is being produced by the e-mini is from users who never traded futures before. So, we're talking about a whole new universe – in fact, the very universe that is doing the day trading on the technology stocks.

Since the e-mini has started, there is a new – and I hesitate to use 'a trend', but it is a trend – from electronic communication networks. They seem to be catching on.

Whether there had been an e-mini or not, they would've caught on. We recognized that there was a problem when EBS took the currency contract from

> “The guy that wanted to produce a buggy whip when somebody invented the motorcar, either he's going to produce tyres or a steering wheel, but if he continues to produce buggy whips, he's going to go out of business – and we were producing the buggy whip.”

us. In my 1995 article *Wakeup Call*, I pointed out that the Merc. – which had invented the idea of currency futures; it was just an interbank deal before that – lost that business unconscionably to an ECN called EBS. I said it was going to take it all from us if we let them, because we ignored their threat and what they represent. Again, there is this belief that there is something magic about open outcry, that it'll be here forever and it will prevent an ECN from taking our liquidity, but they did it. Our currency market – I don't know if it can be resurrected. I don't know if it's still alive. Yes, we do some trade and we're trying to resurrect it, but the guts of it we lost to an ECN world – not just EBS, others who took it from us.

Well, it's interesting volume is picking up in currency futures at the Merc.

But compare what the world is doing in currency.

Part of it is legislative. Part of it is this internal stupidity, internal refusal to accept the change in technology. Listen, throughout history, anyone who ignores technological change is dead, in time. I mean, the guy that wanted to produce a buggy whip when somebody invented the motorcar, either he's going to produce tyres or a steering wheel, but if he continues to produce buggy whips, he's going to go out of business – and we were producing the buggy whip. Maybe it's a bad metaphor for what was happening, but it makes the point.

So, ECNs have eaten our lunch in currency. The currency market overall in the world continued to grow and is growing, and will continue to grow.

The Merc. market has been somewhat resurrected in the last couple or three years, again, because of a variety of things. Let me tell you one of those things that we did to solve it and, again, it's a technological solution.

While you saw an increase in volume, nothing magical about it, one of the first things that I pushed for was something called GFX. GFX[1] is an arbitrage unit that brings liquidity to our Globex plan.

GFX has been an enormous success in feeding liquidity to our structure through the Globex screen, so it's a technological fix that helps the overall market stand. You know what the obvious next step is? It's to bring GFX quotes to the pit. Why only during non-open outcry hours? Why not feed GFX into the pit during open outcry hours? How do you do that? Again, through technology. You build a hand-held instrument that allows a local in the pit to see the cash market quote and to deal against it as he is bidding and offering in the futures market so, he can do both from the pit.

And to trade?

And to trade. That is our next step. It may be that all of that is not going to preserve open outcry anyway, but at least it gives open outcry a better chance if, in fact, it has this technological tool that can deal against the cash market quote – and we do have an arbitrage unit that is giving those quotes – there's a better mix involved and he can compete better with EBS. EBS is doing that very same thing in a more sophisticated fashion, but this'll be very sophisticated and it's in the works.

We have that instrument done, it's our hand-held – it's the Merc.'s hand-held. No other exchange has that – we got it and it's coming. Not only is it just going to be for currency. Why stop there? Why can't we do the same thing in cash in the Eurodollars? We can and we will. And why can't we do something else with that same hand-held? Why can't the local link-up to any market he wants to trade? Usually a local is trapped in his hog pit or in his S&P pit or in his Eurodollar pit, but with this instrument he can, in fact, trade anything. Why not? There is no reason – and we will do that.

So, through technology we can make the argument – I'm not going to buy into this, but I'm going to make the argument – that we will preserve the open outcry environment much longer than it would've otherwise been preserved. The reason I don't buy into it is that I believe, ultimately, there's an end in sight for open outcry. It's so much more efficient, it's so much cheaper, it's so much better to do that technologically that some markets will not remain in an open outcry environment and those markets are, in its largest sense, the financial market.

There's some reason to say that agriculture does not have the competitive push to move to a technological environment – it may be so – it may be so forever, I don't know. Although, there's a Texas outfit that wants electronic trading in cattle and they may be successful. The minute they're successful, we're right there, we have to face the enemy.

There's an argument that our S&P contract can't be taken from the Merc. because it's on a contract with Standard & Poors. That's true, there is no competitive reason that we have to go electronic with the S&P contract, but there is an efficiency reason. If we're allowed, for instance, to expand into narrow-based indices – as I hope and am pushing to get – or even single stock futures, they're going to go electronic. They're not going to go in any pit. It'd be crazy to try and trade single stock futures from a pit, it's impossible, but it can be done electronically. So, I would make the argument that, within a time frame that's within our immediate life, like two to five years, it's all going to, on the financial side of things, move over to an electronic environment. In spite of the fact that we're doing what we're doing to preserve open outcry and we're doing that because it's good business to do that.

We want our local community – and I think I have to get to that point in a minute. What about our locals? What about our professionals? What's going to happen to them? But it is our obligation to try and preserve their business. It is our obligation to make it possible for them to have a fighting chance and so we're doing this, through a technological fix. If the world shows us that we can't succeed that way, then we must have the instrument of Globex so robust, so ready, so that there isn't even a blink of time lag in the transference that would have to occur. Should that occur tomorrow, I can tell you tomorrow we could transfer on to the electronic screen and not feel too much of the pain.

Well, let me ask some other questions and feel free to pass on them if you feel they don't apply to your area of expertise. I think what you're saying is pertinent. What will the future business model of traditional financial service providers look like in five years?

Well, this is the $64 million dollar question that everyone is wrestling with. You and I see that Eurex, for instance, probably has a mindset to go directly to the end user – what do they need Merrill Lynch for? The end user is a customer of Merrill Lynch though. It is a regional bank somewhere or a financial institution of some sort, and no longer an unsophisticated customer that needs Merrill Lynch to hold their hand. The institutional end of our business is so sophisticated, they don't need much help. So, if they had the screen they'd disintermediate the traditional brokerage firm. If that is the view that Eurex has – I'm not suggesting they have that view, but they might have that view and others might have that view – we don't, the Merc. doesn't. It isn't a subject that's taboo, we've talked about it, but I'm a practical kind of guy and I think the Merc. is a kind of practical institution. And there are several good reasons why we're better off, not in an attempt to disintermediate, but, rather, to become partners of.

How would that work?

Well, the brokerage firms are like the client – they have the order flow. So, if that were true, it's something you want if you're an exchange. Why fight with the guy who has the order flow. Bring him in. Say, 'Hey, let's make a deal, bring us the order flow.' It might not, in fact, be the truth, though, and we don't know. Do they really own the order flow or is it just a convenience that they have right now? Again, that same sophisticated end user might say, 'Hey, if I can get a better deal without you, direct to the floor somewhere, goodbye.' But, if we're the one that's going to give him a better deal and if we stay with our partner, that end user might be happy to continue to do business that same way. We've got to make damn sure that we're efficient, that we are technologically at the cutting edge of everything and that we give them the best price possible in the process.

“In our world of futures, we proved something beyond any doubt. We have a clearing mechanism that takes that risk factor off the books of the user and they like it.”

But there's another reason that we think we ought to stay together and that other reason is the one you touched on in your paper [pre-submitted list of questions]. And I'll give you this example. About a week before LTCM broke in the world, I was in conversation with a bunch of foreign banks – subjects that have to do with futures and this very subject – and they gave me, in no uncertain terms, the understanding that their concern was cost. Number one concern was cost. That's all they cared about. About two weeks after LTCM broke, those same people, in another form, told me unquestionably that the only thing we care about is the creditworthiness of who we deal with. Forget costs, screw costs, at whatever costs necessary, we must have protection for counterparty risk. What a brand new reality and, all of a sudden, clearing houses were a meaningful thing because, in our world of futures, we proved something beyond any doubt. We have a clearing mechanism that takes that risk factor off the books of the user and they like it.

There's an argument to be made by some that if LTCM had had an ability to lay off its risks on a futures clearing end, they wouldn't have had a problem. The market would've sorted out the risks involved, they would have had to pay as they went along and, if they didn't have the money, they wouldn't have been able to make any more deals and they wouldn't have gotten into the risk that they got into.

So, we, the exchanges, today, have an enormously valuable resource. Now, I'm not saying it can't be duplicated and I'm not saying others can't do it and I'm not even saying that the banks among themselves can't do it themselves, as they are trying. Take Broker Tech or Blackburn, maybe they will create a clearing-type facility on a bilateral basis. On a multilateral basis where anybody can play – not a limited, 'We agree to each other's creditworthiness' basis, which is easy enough to do – the minute you get beyond a certain small group of users, you run that risk. Yet an exchange can do that. We know how to do that.

There are, today, GSCC – the Government Security Clearing house, which is super, AAA – the Merc., Eurex, Board of Trade, I would say – that's it. Maybe NYMex, but, you know, it starts to get of lesser quality as you go – so, there aren't that many. I will argue that there is room for two or three of these kinds of clearing associations/organizations to exist in – and that's a reason that the exchanges must bear in mind, that's a reason that they have a role to play, even in a technological world.

Do you think regulators are aware of this and it's something they want?

Well, we hope so. We're trying to poll them about it – we don't want to surprise them, but that's an important function of an exchange. Some of us believe it is the most important resource we have at the moment. I want to tell you three resources traditional exchanges have in the broad sense. The clearing entity that I just talked about. Liquidity, which is sort of an indefinable, intangible, but we've got it. So, as long as these contracts provide this enormous liquidity, that's where anyone who wants to trade will trade. Very hard to move liquidity, very, very hard. Can't be done. Wait, I didn't mean it *can't* be done, it's *hard* to do, but Eurex proved that it could move it, didn't it? So, it can be done. The only thing is that it's hard to do it – it took them six, seven years to do it – so, maybe it'll get faster, but it's hard to do. And then we've got a pool of expertise within our locals and market makers and brokers, so that's our third element. These are the three elements that an exchange has in a broad sense that are important resources. And the clearing resource, I think, of the three, is inviolate – we must not lose that resource and it must not become a utility, we can't give that away. If we give that away, where do we get our income from? This is it – the liquidity which is so difficult to get a handle on. But while we've got these successful contracts, we've got to make sure that we provide the environment for them, whichever way the world wants to go. Does it want to go electronic? Give them the electronic environment, but keep the liquidity – move with it. Does it want to stay where it is? Let it stay where it is, but give them efficiency, give them hand-held instruments, give them whatever technological assistance they can to keep it liquid. So, liquidity is a very, very important thing. I think it's hard to take away from someone, but it can be taken away and you've got to be ever on guard to provide the mechanisms that best serve that liquidity.

For our locals and brokers, this is the most difficult part. There are many that make the case that, well, they're history. Not so fast. Technology doesn't really ever take away a job – usually it *creates* a job, but it's a different job. Maybe it's a more sophisticated job, but it creates – technology doesn't work without people. So, I will tell you that I am an example of the trader mentality. I've learned something of my 20-odd years on a floor – I learned how to trade. It took me a while to transfer that knowledge to trading on the screen, but I learned how to do that. The rules are the same, you get a different feel from an electronic quote than you do from seeing the eyeballs of the guy next to you, that's true, but you can learn that difference, the instincts will develop, and so a local community that is a trader mentality can learn to transfer its trader mechanism or its trader instinct or its trader expertise to the screen. Not all of them – it depends on what kind of trader you were. If you were a trader standing next to a broker and leaning on him and offering a one tic buy/sell kind of situation – you know, 'I'll buy at tic difference' and he's feeding you on this kind of trade – you're history. There is no room for you, there's no broker to lean on in an electronic screen. But if you are a trader anywhere in the real sense of the word, whether it's a position player or a momentum player or an arbitrageur, a spreader or whatever, those things are transferable to the screen.

“Technology doesn't really ever take away a job – usually it creates a job, but it's a different job. Maybe it's a more sophisticated job, but it creates – technology doesn't work without people.”

“If you are a trader anywhere in the real sense of the word, whether it's a position player or a momentum player or an arbitrageur, a spreader or whatever, those things are transferable to the screen.”

So, I would make a very strong case that not everybody, but the bulk of traders can transfer their ability to the screen. The e-mini proved that. God dammit, if these guys aren't *great* on the screen. That was one of the missions that I had and the e-mini is to prove to the locals that they're not dead just because they moved to a screen; they've got a whole new life. In fact, it's a better life. Why? Well, because, first of all, they can trade from a screen in an environment like in an office, they can trade lots of things they can't in the pit – you know, the whole world's their oyster, whereas in the pit, they've just got one instrument. So, there's a lot more available to them from a screen point of view and they can transfer their expertise.

The broker is a little bit of a harder mission. To transfer his or her expertise will require some doing, but it can be done in this fashion. If the broker was only a paper shuffler, standing in the pit because he was tall and strong and had sharp elbows and a strong voice and all he did was shout and so forth and so on, he isn't going to fit. What he has to become is more like an account executive. Maybe he has to go back to school, maybe he has to get a degree, maybe he has to become a market master, so that he can deal with the customer in a fashion in which he not only pushes the button on a screen to buy or sell, but also gives the customer ideas, information, general conversation. People like to schmooze.

Traders are traders and if the trader is a bank trader somewhere in Tennessee or North Carolina talking to an account executive who used to be a broker in the pit but now is a broker on a screen-based technology, he stills wants to talk to him about what he thinks – 'What's going on? Who's doing what? What kind of formation, technically, does this look like? You got any ideas? What have you heard on the street?' Conversation and expertise is never in disrepute, and if our brokers, the order fillers in our community, can learn to gain this knowledge, this ability and not just to stand in the pit with paper and shout their bid and offer, but, in fact, talk conversation to the end user, that customer will stay with them, and he'll pay him something for that. To just press the button, the customer can do that himself – he doesn't need that kind of help.

But if you're going to give him some value-added and you've got something to offer, you've got some training, you've got some expertise, you can transfer what you've learned on the floor. Through osmosis even you've learned a lot on that floor. Add to that as a base of knowledge information, whether it's school-learned or otherwise, and bring that as a sales tool, you will get the customer back or keep him and he'll pay you for it. And he may pay you more than the damn 80 cents a trade that you get. He may pay you a buck, a buck and a half, maybe two bucks, maybe five – who knows? Depends on how good you are, how much information, how many ideas you can plant in this guy. Hell, that's worth a lot. That's cheap to the customer, in fact.

So, that is arguably the potential role of the order filler in a non-open outcry environment. There is hope. None of that's easy. I've painted it to make it look easy, but it isn't easy, but it's doable.

Some people will do it; some will go off the boards. For some, this is a world they don't want or can't do or can't handle – I understand that. But, getting back to the three elements that the exchange has and why it doesn't necessarily want to disintermediate anybody, in my view, it doesn't, and it may be better for it not to.

What are the sources of competitive advantage for banks and brokerage firms in an environment of rapid technological change? How does such change impact the traditional intermediary role played by banks?

The answer is 'Yes, they have an advantage in that they have this pool of knowledge, experience and credibility.' That's an advantage. If they continue to provide the technological capability that the world is giving them, that will be enough to keep them alive. If they ignore technology, then the credibility and expertise won't go very far.

You know, I see what happens on the Internet. I'd rather deal with an established bookseller, but if he isn't on the screen and I want that book right now, I'm going to just deal on the screen. So, it requires Barnes & Noble, so to speak, to also be on the screen. It isn't just good enough that we know his name.

And there are elements of establishmentarianism, that are kind of important. If you are a bank that's a supermarket, your chances of succeeding in this new environment are better, because that's the other element that allows a bank to stay in business. Look, we give you full service. Look, you've got everything here. What do you want, do you want your mortgage, do you want your insurance, do you want your trade, do you want your account, do you want – dammit, we can do it all. That's a very important, attractive element.

And I think that that coupled, again, with technology is basic to me. If you're going to ignore technology, none of these things will be enough. But, if you combine it with a technological fix, then the fact that you are a supermarket offering all these things, you have this enormous advantage of your brand name credibility, expertise. Otherwise, you allow the EBSs of the world to step all over you – or the Eurexs to grab away the business from you. Again, the difference is the quickness by which the establishment recognizes that things are a-changing and you better go with the change. Those that don't go with the change don't go anywhere.

Can you ever envision the future of banking – or brokerage, for that matter – where there are no intermediaries? Where customers go right to the source.

I always thought the source *was* the bank. You know, I always thought that was the owner, eventually, of everything. Maybe it's the insurance company as the owner of everything. But in George Orwell's – was it George Orwell's – world there were only three or four left, the big supermarkets and that's all that counted? I don't think so. I think, although that's the case that's being made and I can see that, there is some sort of conflict here.

I think that if the banks continue to do innovative and aggressive things and are not blinded by their own largess of past reference, then they can succeed and I think some of them will. Will there be many? No. There aren't going to be the mom and pop banks of the past. Whoever said that we're over-banked in the United States, is certainly correct – and that's probably true of Europe, as well. I think that the new world will have a very, very limited number of banks. They will be supermarket banks.

One more thing, and that's the interesting thing, it's what the Internet really is best suited for, is to provide a new entrepreneur with an idea, the ability to advance that idea, to create a little niche for himself. That will eventually force the banks to either buy him or create a similar niche of its own. So, it does provide a competitiveness that I love. The consumer will make the difference because the consumer can say at some point, 'Hey, look, my superbank, it does all these things, but this guy has created something else and I really like what he's created something that the superbank doesn't give me.' So, in this area, I'm using this little guy.' Well, the Internet allows that because in no other way would a consumer have ever even known this guy existed, except for the Internet. So, there will always be the ability for an entrepreneur to create something new and to force the establishment to either accept him, beat him or buy him.

Do you think that's what happened with Eurex?

Of course.

Why – was it more efficient?

Hey, no fuss, no muss – you got bids, you got offers, you push a button, it's done. You don't have anybody screaming. You know the instant you made the trade or didn't make the trade, what the price is and who you made it with. You know the whole thing and there is no out-trade ever, there is no pit cost – it's there, it's on the screen.

There's a fairness factor to it. Look, we've always had these complaints – legitimate complaints. My God, in the pit, it's who you know that gets the better fill. A better broker is standing next to the guy with the better order flow. There's so much of that that's involved in the pit. I mean, it was the best way and it is, in many respects, still the only way, but it has these deficiencies and these deficiencies are all cured on the screen.

Now, the screen doesn't always have the liquidity, so that takes precedence. If you don't have the liquidity, these cures don't mean diddly. You've got to have liquidity along with it. But, if you have liquidity along with it, then you get all these other bells and whistles. No outtrade, no fuss, no muss – you know exactly and nobody takes advantage of you. Nobody. There is no broker that's standing in a better place with the keyboard. You press the button. If you're first, you got it and you beat everybody else. And all you have to do is be first to do what you have to do, on top of it, it costs less. So, you put all that together, why would anybody not want to use that?

What's the future role of information in global banks and brokerage firms with large distribution networks and electronic transactions systems? Could proprietary information on transactions flows be used to generate information products?

Well, of course, the answer is 'Yes', because the answer has always been 'Yes'. In fact, the large entities, like J.P. Morgan or Goldman Sachs and Morgan Stanley, they've always used proprietary information to their advantage – whether they admit it or not. There's a constant use that goes on within the firm to its customers' advantage. That will be as important, if not more important, in the world that's coming. I think it's really too obvious. What does Reuters do since it doesn't have proprietary informational advantage? It has two choices. Either it provides some substitute, something that's better – and I don't frankly know what that is – or joins them. Isn't the mission of Reuters to own an exchange, own a bank – doesn't it behove Reuters to think along those lines. If it doesn't, certainly someone else will. Bloomberg is thinking on those lines – clearly, you've got to protect yourself that way.

Instinet is somewhat of that and I've always felt that it should expand into clearing and other things and should move in the direction of exchange trading, of other instruments.

We've touched on this before, but will ECNs have sufficient liquidity to displace traditional exchanges? Are we likely to see consolidation among ECNs to achieve sufficient liquidity?

In time, it's not easy to do, but it can be done – that's all I'm saying. It's not easy to do, but it can be done, and it's been proved that it can be done.

Do you see a day when we'll see consolidation among ECNs?

I think so, I think there'll be a dominance. Here's the thing about ECNs that seems to be clear to me. A trader, a user, a participant, would like to have everything on one screen – it's the most convenient way to trade. Besides that, the real estate of a desk is very limited – how many screens can you get on a desk? So, that prescribes the formula that the ECN world is going to have to get together to provide that trader with that result. But, first, we're going to have to sort out which ECN is going to be the best to do that. The ECN that provides all the markets, all the capabilities, on one screen or as close to one screen as is conceivably possible – because maybe it isn't possible, but variations of that are possible – that's the ECN that's going to drive everybody else out of business. A trade doesn't want 10, 12 different ECNs on his desk that he has to deal with. He wants one. That's the theoretical best. And the ECN could be an exchange or it could be a Blackbird.

A what?

'Blackbird' is a name for a technology that is offering trading in swaps electronically for the bank market. Not futures people and not bank people – this is a trader technology that was developed, technology that was developed not by traders but works quite well and is a very serious competitor to the exchanges because swaps, by any other definition, are a future.

The reason it's called Blackbird is because it's the fastest – you know, what the Blackbird is, the missile, the Blackbird is the fastest missile and they took that name. They're a very serious competitor because they're doing swaps and they have very good technology – better than what we provide, but we have to provide it.

So, it could be an exchange or it could be something like Blackbird, but they're limited, they're only swaps. So, I'm saying the Reuters or the Merc. or the LIFFE or the Eurex or the Broker Tech that provides completeness of the ECN capability is the one that will succeed. And does that mean, by definition, that there will be few of them? Of course. Once you have that result, you're in. And maybe there'll be always more than one because competition sort of demands that there be two, three or four of those, but there won't be a dozen. If there are, they'll be niche players that have some specialty that they provide – only a few segments of the market want that, but large portions want it all. And I want, for instance, the Merc. to provide it all. I don't want the Merc. to be just in the markets that we are in today. If we only provide for the markets that we have today, we will not survive in the future. We've got to be all the markets to everybody. That's the only way.

Let me turn to another area. Are risk management techniques too heavily dependent on quantitative models and, therefore, lacking in qualitative human judgement?

Absolutely true. It leads me to the same conclusion that I've reached before, and *that's* the reason exchanges have this advantage in risk management. They're clearing organization is not simply formulaic, it is with people that make judgements – they know who the players are and they make judgements. Yes, they have formulas, yes, they have prescriptions, but they also have a judgement factor based on a great deal of experience. And I think that's very, very important. Also, of course, you speak in here [referring to list of questions] about the fact that the regulators are demanding more risk regulatory application, but they're not.

Should they have different methods of testing?

Well, I think they're leaving it to the market.

Is that good or bad?

I like it because it forces a discipline on the marketplace, but I also like it because we have something to offer the marketplace in that respect, and its called a clearing corp. If we gave this field over to the regulators, it would be the biggest mess possible because things change too fast and, again, it's the judgement factor that they wouldn't have – they're not players.

But the regulators, on the other hand, have also adopted, not formally, this 'too big to fail' mentality.

Well, that's an unfortunate adoption. It's a trap that we started years ago. In recent vintage it was Mexico. We bailed them out to save some American firms. It didn't result in not giving Mexico a depression, it gave Mexicans the same recession they would've gotten anyway. South-East Asia, now we've bailed them out. I'm doing it in broad strokes and this isn't with any degree of specificity, but it is true, I believe, that we had the same mentality – it's called the IMF, etcetera – to go in and save Thailand and Indonesia and whatnot.

There was Chrysler and Continental Bank.

It started with Chrysler – it was Continental Bank, you're right, but we've gotten bigger. Chrysler and Continental Bank were small potatoes compared to Mexico – in the billions we're talking about – and Mexico is kind of small compared to South-East Asia. And Russia then came along and now we really threw money down the drain. There it was – the most ridiculous thing yet in Russia. So, the answer to your question is, it clearly is the wrong way to go. In some points, discipline will be achieved if you let somebody big fail.

I think we missed the boat on the LTCM, although it's an argument that the government didn't provide money. That's true, it wasn't government money. Except a little bit of it was, when we lowered the discount rate and we didn't tighten. In fact, we increased the money supply and, at the same time, offered the offices for all these guys and said, 'Here, you bail them out.' Well, we did get involved.

NOTE

1. GFX stands for Globex Foreign Exchange and is a facility that allows trading in the cash foreign exchange market over Globex terminals.

HANK PAULSON

Chief Exective, Goldman Sachs Group Inc.

INTERVIEW BY JACK REERINK

How will new technologies change financial services firms in the next five years?

We are in the information business, the people business and the advisory business. The growth of our profitability was largely the result of big breakthroughs in technology.

A couple of years ago, I talked to our people about technology. I told the story about foreign exchange trading. This was an example where technology really helped Goldman Sachs.

In 1990, we had about 190 people in our foreign exchange area. We didn't rank anywhere in the top ten in terms of foreign exchange trading. As a matter of fact, we weren't even a price giver; we were a price taker. If a client wanted to a do big foreign exchange trade with us, we had to go to one of the big commercial banks.

We were forced to develop superior analytics. We created a very complicated option pricing model and technological link-ups with our clients.

What happened was the market changed; you can now get foreign exchange quotes right off your screen. The banks went through a tough period – their distribution force was disintermediated. We still have about the same number of people in foreign exchange, but for the last three or four years we have been well in the top ten and it's been one of our most profitable areas.

You mentioned technology cut out banks as middlemen in the foreign exchange area. How will technological changes, such as electronic stock trading, affect your other businesses?

I would expect, looking ahead, that technology is going to cause a very significant change in our industry. Financial services lend themselves to the Internet, so I would expect that there are going to continue to be very big efficiencies coming out of this.

The businesses that will change the most are the sales and trading businesses. There are certain businesses – what I call the commodity-type businesses (small stock orders and government bond trades) – where trading should be done largely electronically. The revenues we would reap would come down, but the costs would also come down.

I think we will see disintermediation in sales and trading. It really comes down to adding value. We can do things well, have historically done well as a firm, very high value-added, complicated transactions. We put very smart people on those transactions and get relatively high revenues per transaction.

How can a Goldman Sachs trader who must process an order to buy 1,000 shares of Cisco add value?

If someone goes to do a commodity-type transaction – whether it's to buy government bonds or 1,000 shares of Cisco, it a matter of giving the client the best price for the lowest cost. Even in a trade like that, there's room for an intermediary to take credit risk and operational risk.

But I've always thought Goldman Sachs' role is one of an adviser, being able to add value through advice on portfolio management and tax advantages. You're not going to add a lot of value by executing the transaction.

“ Financial services lend themselves to the Internet, so I would expect that there are going to continue to be very big efficiencies coming out of this. The businesses that will change the most are the sales and trading businesses. ”

The key to running an investment bank is to hire the best people. You have to train them, motivate them and make sure they are where the opportunities are. We are doing commodity transactions as much electronically as we can to get the costs down. There are huge opportunities to get costs down and put our people and resources on transactions that are more complicated. That to me is what it's all about.

How will technology affect investment banking? Human intervention in that area seems all-important.

It has sure helped us a lot to date. I don't think we could have been as profitable or as effective. It made a huge difference. I just got back from Asia. When you are travelling across the region, it's wearing. It used to be you had to be in the client's office to get things done. Technology has made communicating easier – sending e-mails and voice mails.

I was just talking to people in Tokyo about how we add value. On the one hand, we're a Japanese firm – we've been there for 26 years, we have the relationships, we understand the culture and we understand the laws – but we've got global reach, so we have an understanding of global markets; we have industry knowledge on a global basis.

It's an information business. Some of it is in numbers, but a lot of it is in explaining the numbers and judgement. There is no doubt that technology helps us gather that information and transfer it to the client in a way the client understands it.

When I talk to our people about technology I also often tell about my early days in investment banking. I went down and talked to the Treasurer of Caterpillar. I was 26 years old and he asked *me* whether to sell five or ten-year debt. I quoted him prices of corporate and government bonds; I was a fountain of information. Pretty soon I almost cried when he got a terminal with bond prices on his desk, but it helped me that I wasn't able to do that any more. So I moved up and did something that added value. At the end of my career there, I was sitting next to CEOs helping them restructure their companies.

Goldman Sachs has made many investments in new technologies, such as alternative trading systems. How will technology affect traditional stock exchanges in the next five years?

We are making minority investments in electronic communications systems and alternative trading systems because we want to be part of the order flow, learn about it. We are not saying, 'We have to make these terribly successful.' They are a hedge against different outcomes in the future of share trading, but we are hoping that the New York Stock Exchange and Nasdaq will keep doing what they need to do so they can remain successful. In terms of where the exchanges need to go, we need to have a lot of these trades done electronically. Why do you need to go to a specialist, to buy 100 shares of IBM? As a specialist, you need to add value, maybe in stocks that trade less frequently.

I believe there should be strong linkages between the different trading venues, because the interesting thing about the markets is that they need liquidity – being fast, cheap and transparent alone doesn't do it. Otherwise, it can be disfunctional, running around from one market to another.

Do you think that individual investors in the future will be able to have their stock orders filled directly by a counterparty, without the intermediation of a market maker or broker?

If you want to just execute a trade and it's a commodity trade, there should be some way for you to do it efficiently, quickly and electronically. The idea of wanting to buy 100 shares of IBM, going to a broker who then goes to a specialist on the floor of the New York Stock Exchange just doesn't make a lot of sense.

“ I believe there should be strong linkages between the different trading venues, because the interesting thing about the markets is that they need liquidity – being fast, cheap and transparent alone doesn't do it. ”

Until you get something where there is a central limit order book, where there is time and price priority, you're not really helping investors.

Can the alternative trading systems that have cropped up in the United States over the last three years survive or do you see a need to merge them?

It's inevitable. Why would you fragment the market? Why not put liquidity together, aggregate orders and get the efficiencies?

Do you foresee more consolidation in the US financial services industry?

Big organizations are hard to run. You have to remember that we can restructure very quickly. We as a firm are able to re-engineer businesses in months.

It's all relative. You've got to be big *or* little – it's hard to be in between. There are two ways to think about scale. The way we look at it, we have scale in the merger business and we have scale in our various businesses. Another way of thinking about it is just size, but I'm not impressed by the arguments. In other words, if Goldman Sachs had a credit card business, would we be able to do a better job, would we have more staying power, would we be able to use one of the businesses to subsidize others?

The basic challenge we have is to continue to grow as rapidly as we are growing. Our existing businesses are so attractive, there's plenty of room for growth.

Another strategy, which I think works, is to be a niche business. As long as you have very good people, niche businesses are going to do well. It really comes down to talent. That's where there is a shortage.

The commercial banks bought up the boutique securities firms in the technology area – Robertson Stephens, Alex Brown, Hambrecht & Quist – and you see new ones emerge because there is a need for that. The world is filled with very large financial institutions that do nothing particularly well. That why I don't think just being big does it.

Some of the large financial services firms, which are built on the promise of cross-selling financial products, have done well, though.

Cross-selling is easier said than done. I think we cross-sell better than anyone in the world. Whenever we hire somebody from outside the firm, they always say, 'One of the things you do well is that you have teamwork and you cross-sell.'

I realize how hard it is for us to cross-sell, and if we had insurance and credit cards, we could theoretically cross-sell more, but I don't want to compete with AIG or American Express.

Will new US banking laws that allow banks, brokers and insurers to enter one another's businesses spur more industry mergers?

You had a back door in our industry. The Federal Reserve let the banks buy securities firms, but where the new legislation makes a difference is in combining banking and insurance. It's going to be more significant in that area.

The 1997 merger between investment bank Morgan Stanley and retail brokerage and credit card company Dean Witter Discover seems to work. What does that tell you?

There have been very few mergers in investment banking because of the cultural issues. I think Morgan Stanley worked because the businesses didn't overlap. It is a strong firm, but I wouldn't want to have a retail brokerage right now, given what's happening in technology and on-line trading. The retail brokerage network is not something you need to have to have a successful strategy in our industry. In a bull market, it's a wonderful thing; in down markets it's one less thing to worry about.

Doesn't a network of brokers come in handy when you want to distribute financial products like stock offerings and funds?

Our number 1 issue is not distribution. We've got all sorts of people who want the distribution and we intend to aggressively sell stuff on-line.

What are the lessons of the turbulence in financial markets late 1998? Do Wall Street's computer models rely too much on historical data, for example?

Every time there is a crisis, everybody sort of learns and makes changes. A lot of us were surprised at how many of the firms in our industry had similar positions. So, when they lost money in one area, they all started selling the same things. Everything moved together.

The computer models did what they were supposed to do; they looked at historical data. But the things computer models said would have the same probability as a sudden impact happened. Everybody was trying to sell the same things and the only buyers were in the hospital.

So now what we are doing – and what I suspect a lot of other firms are doing – is to do a lot more scenario analysis, a lot more stress testing and a lot more work on credit risk.

Did the crisis spur any operational changes?

No. When we went through the crisis, there were no unpleasant surprises. We found the operational people work very well with traders.

Our issue was simply a miscalculation of how much risk we really had. We relied too much on value-at-risk analysis and we thought there would be more diversity in the way things moved, but they moved all together. When you stop and think about it, it makes sense: when there's a credit crisis, it does start to move together. It was a flight to liquidity and people in the industry had similar positions.

“Now what we are doing is to do a lot more scenario analysis, a lot more stress testing and a lot more work on credit risk.”

One of the things I learned is that there is a systemic risk. When you are a global financial institution, you are impacted not only by what happens at Goldman Sachs but what happens around you. If another firm blows up in the mortgage area because it takes all kinds of imprudent risks, you can run your mortgage desk very well and do a lot better than they will, but when they get into problems and have to sell everything they've got, it hurts the market and it hurts you.

What have you learned from the near-collapse of the Long-Term Capital Management hedge fund in that period?

One of the things we missed was what everybody else was doing. In the case of Long-Term Capital Management (LTCM), we had an equity arbitrage for years and years. We had several partners and departments running it. It turned out LTCM had bigger trades. They advertised themselves as a fixed-income outlet and yet they had huge arbitrage business run by relatively junior people.

So, what do you do? You do a better job at understanding what other people's positions are and what is happening in the market around you. We also have been much more careful about what we do with our counterparties. So, when we are doing business with hedge funds, we are much more insistent on not just seeing the positions they have at Goldman Sachs, but understanding what their overall picture looks like.

But hedge funds hate to give away their trading positions.

We don't ask for specific securities or who they do business with, but if they don't tell us their overall exposure, or credit exposure, we don't need to do business with them or extend a lot of credit to them.

Have you actually turned down business?

Sure. We're very careful. We're even more rigorous than in the past.

What else do you worry about?

We worry a lot about liquidity risk. When investment banks fail, they fail due to liquidity problems – not enough cash on hand. We always worry about our funding, staying liquid.

We think a lot about reputational risk, legal risk. Every time I speak to a group of partners and they ask me, 'What do you worry about?', I say, 'The sad truth is that because Goldman Sachs is such a great firm, every one of us has a lot more potential to hurt the firm than they can ever help it. We can hurt the firm through a careless mistake, doing something dishonest.'

“When investment banks fail, they fail due to liquidity problems – not enough cash on hand. We always worry about our funding, staying liquid.”

What we generally find is that people who get into trouble are lone rangers. When there is a problem, you need people to sit down and talk it through with a group and you'll do the right thing.

SIR BRIAN PITMAN

Chairman, Lloyds TSB

INTERVIEW BY CLELIA OZIEL

What are the demographic factors at work shaping the asset management sector? How are financial services groups responding to these challenges?

It is becoming a market sector for everybody, not just financial services, with different needs and expectations from other groups, and, therefore, you've got to shape your products and services to meet the needs of that particular group. They vary tremendously from very wealthy people in later life with most of their commitments out of the way with quite a lot of money to people who, on a pension, are really quite poor, but they are a different group of people. Take the other extreme of very young yuppies – they have totally different needs and expectations. The older age group are concerned about their future, how to make their life comfortable and secure, how to keep their income up when interest rates are falling, so you have to think in terms of that to begin with.

There are really two groups even within the wealthy group.

There is a group of people who can do, could do it all themselves, but can't be bothered and therefore want to give it to somebody else to manage their financial affairs, and there is another group who are not up to speed with all the things that are going on in the world and, therefore, they've got to get somebody else to do it for them.

The first thing to recognize is this is a very specific market segment who have totally different needs and expectations. If you treat them as one size fits all and everybody is going to get the same no matter who you are, I don't think you'll be very successful.

We're all moving into a world of market segmentation in a way that I don't think we had before. If you care to examine digital TV in any kind of depth, you will look at the programmes and at the one end just nothing but pop music from dawn til dusk and at the other end are movies attached to nostalgia, if you like, but which have a very big audience, so that some of the groups in the United States have gone to great lengths to make sure that they are going to make available these movies for that group of people. It's exactly the same in financial services – the needs and expectations are different.

We have certainly identified this as a key segment of the market and we are organizing ourselves. One of the reasons that we got ourselves more and more into financial services as opposed to being just a bank is that you can see that these people want financial services, not just paying in a deposit and taking the money out again, and I think we shall see a continuing process of this group of people wanting to get themselves into things like mutual funds and securities, which offer a better return than a bank deposit.

> “We're all moving into a world of market segmentation in a way that I don't think we had before. ... It's exactly the same in financial services – the needs and expectations are different.”

We have to go to great lengths, and we do go to great lengths, with all of these customers to understand what are their objectives in this. If they want to have capital appreciation, it will be a totally different investment portfolio from one where they want to maximize the income.

We also have to explain to them very carefully that there is no way we can get a higher return without taking some more risk, and it's very interesting how people's expectations vary. You can have some quite wealthy people who say, 'I'm not interested in income, but I don't want to lose the money.'

If you believe you're going to live to 90 and your income is quite limited, you're going to have a totally different attitude to life than if you have bags of money and you say, 'These are the golden years, I'm going to live it up now.'

I think governments have great dilemmas because they can see that if we look out over the next century, there will be more and more people who will not have provided enough for their own old age and the pension that they're going to get from the government will be modest, and therefore they have this question, 'Do we make some pension contribution compulsory?'

If you look at tables for what will life expectancy be in the next century, in the Western world, if you could cure cancer, then we would have phenomenal changes. There is plenty of evidence that we are well down the road of certainly arresting cancer, and of understanding what causes heart disease. I think most of us would bet the average expectation of life will increase, not diminish, beyond the expectations we've got at the moment. All of these people who are predicting that more and more people will reach 100 years are absolutely right. I see it in our customers. I write letters to everybody who becomes 100 years old – quite a lot of letters, it's quite remarkable.

“I think governments have great dilemmas because they can see there will be more and more people who will not have provided enough for their own old age and therefore they have this question, 'Do we make some pension contribution compulsory?'”

Do you think the growth in asset management will continue or do you see any factors that might restrict or reverse this trend?

If there was some terrible new disease discovered in the world. If we look at what causes death in the developing countries, malaria is still the killer. If you start to get more and more educated in the developing world, if we have better conditions – and I'm optimistic about it – we're certainly going to reduce the effect of malaria, and we're talking about some countries where average expectation of life is less than 40 at the moment. So, if you start to change things there – it's not difficult to see countries which are showing very rapid progress in all of this, the average expectation of life in these countries will change dramatically.

I think it will lead to changes of attitude by the governments in relation to how long people should work. The option, the time when people want to retire, will change significantly. I think it's highly likely that people will change from a world where they expect to retire at 60 to where they want to work until they are 70. If you are 60 and you look forward to a world where it's going to be very, very tough on you, and you're fit and you have the opportunity to go on working til you're 70, I think more and more people will choose that option. But I think it will be their own choice. Out of their own choice they will see that, 'If I retired at a particular age, I'll get X.' The government will have to make it much more attractive for them to carry on until the age of 70, but that would be difficult.

I think the growth [in asset management] will continue because, after all, it's an attractive market. It will become a terribly important sector in the financial services industry.

If I look at one of my favourite sports, golf, the explosion in senior men's professional golf where 50,000 people go and watch people play golf and they are 60 years old, this would be unthinkable. Why is it? It's because it's the same age group as them, and they see hope for the future that they are still going to play golf.

How important is it for asset management firms to secure large distribution networks?

Very important indeed. What will be the distribution networks is another, more important, question.

I have a different view here about things like stocks and shares and banking relationships, because stocks and shares are very much an instant thing. If I decide today that I want to make an investment in stocks and shares, I better do it now because it might be different in a week's time, so I need very very quick access.

It is really quite fascinating how many retired people are now, for the first time ever in their life lives, buying themselves a PC. I think that these kinds of transactions which require instant access, I think there will be much greater utilization of these things.

We have been computerizing all our activities behind the scenes for a long time, but we haven't had much technology at the point of customer interaction. We've now got at a point of customer interaction technology – it' a very, very different world.

We can give out of the cashpoint machine huge amounts of information if we want. With the latest mobile telephone, we can give even more information. I haven't even touched on television, which is a very, very new thing – to be able to have interactive use of the television, interactive use with a PC – so all those things where people want very quick response – and stocks and shares are a classic example in my view. We're bound to see a very big use of that as a method of distribution.

I think that human contact will remain very important. This is not for the quick transactions. If people want to discuss things face to face, I don't think that's going to disappear. I think we will continue to see plenty of distribution or discussion on asset management face to face because they will want that kind of discussion and, therefore, the ability of people to be able to do this, in my view, will continue to be extremely important.

How is this going to affect traditional insurance providers?

We have moved much more to a world where you have to be satisfied that the product you are selling to the customer meets the needs of that customer. I cannot see how that will diminish. Governments reinforcing regulations to protect the consumer – I find it hard to see how that will be reversed because consumers decide whether governments get elected and, therefore, making sure that the consumers are content with what goes on, whether it's labelling tomatoes or providing financial services, I think will be terribly important. This is bound to have a profound effect on the provision of insurance.

I think there is a continuing role for independent financial advisers – not just in insurance, but in all sorts of financial services. Again, you have to segment the market.

You decide how you're going to position yourself in the market – I'm sure some financial service companies will be only Internet companies. They know exactly which market they're serving and they're going to serve that group of customers very, very effectively. There will be other people like us who will become multispecialist, multibranded. We are organizing ourselves to provide a wide range of financial services, but as specialist products – whether it's general insurance, life and pensions policies, mutual funds, current accounts, travellers cheques or whatever it is. And the advantage we should have is that we will have the relationship with the customer, where the brand expectation will be that you'll get very good value for money.

Both can win – it depends how they can position themselves in relation to the customer.

How important is it for banks to expand into asset management?

It's very important for banks to expand into it if we're going to live in a world of low inflation, and I think we are.

“I am very much in favour of free markets, but we do have to find a way of avoiding these intensely abrupt movements that can destroy people's lives.”

Low inflation means very low interest rates on deposits so the customers say, 'I must be able to do better than get the return on this deposit.' If we do not offer very good mutual fund asset management products, they will go to somebody else, so not only will we lose the deposit, but we will lose the business to a totally different business and it will not come back as a retail deposit, it will come back as a wholesale deposit. In wholesale deposits, the profitability is very low indeed, so we don't want to lose the business. We want to give the customers what they want as a result of very low inflation.

The market in the US has expanded much more rapidly than the market in the UK, but I think there is a very good reason for that. Inflation in the US has been lower than the inflation in the UK. *The Economist*'s published figures showed that, over the past 60 years, we have had 4,000 per cent inflation in the UK and 1,000 per cent inflation in the US.

Now that people are becoming increasingly convinced – they're still not there yet because the inflationary expectations by the general public in the UK are well above the Bank of England's target – that we're in for a long period of low inflation, they are switching to equity investments and, indeed, bond investments, which will give higher returns than bank deposits.

The Japanese have had very low inflation – they've had deflation – therefore, mutual funds are going to be very important to them.

In the developing countries, it's very natural that, as you're beginning to get some money together, the first place you turn to is a bank, and it's only later on that you start switching to other things.

The propensity to inflation influences this enormously, but, if we're looking out over the next 50 years, I think in all those places there will be growth in mutual funds.

Has consolidation created global giants that are too big to fail?

It's perfectly rational to think that markets are just too powerful and point the finger at some companies that are too big. The basic point is that markets act very abruptly. The Asian crisis almost brought the world to its knees.

I am very much in favour of free markets, but we do have to find a way of avoiding these intensely abrupt movements that can destroy people's lives.

We will learn from this process, find a mechanism which will get the best of both worlds – free markets, but ones that have more information about things. In Asia, if we had a better information system at that time, people wouldn't have gone on lending.

Is there a need for a global financial regulator?

There is no magic solution for this. I can't see a global regulator – who is it going to be? Who's going to agree the rules?

Is competition making some institutions less fit to cope with a future economic downturn?

I don't think so. One of the changes in the last four or five years is that, before, only in a downturn did financial services firms get together. The next thing was the strong getting together with the weak. Now the strong are getting together with the strong.

The gap between the winners and losers is widening. You have to be willing to embrace very substantial changes to survive in today's markets. We shall see further substantial consolidation.

There will undoubtedly be some nimble, niche players that will give everybody a rough time. It will be very difficult for big companies to match that because they are very quick on their feet. They will be great competitors. At the other extreme, there will be big specialists.

The shop within the shop seems to be the way things are going. We are having shops within shops within our company. There is a Cheltenham & Gloucester shop and a Scottish Widows shop.

The middle is the place not to be.

But we have to be careful – the competitive equilibrium might change and we could find ourselves suddenly moving from being very strong to being weak.

Does the euro require a more centralized system of banking supervision?

It depends on how politically integrated these countries become, and it's difficult to predict how integrated these companies will become.

I don't think we are going to find ourselves in a world where people want more choice, that everything will be standardized.

Does achieving a strong brand name mean being all things to all people or are there niche markets where one can carve out profitable opportunities?

My own belief about this is that it's the strength of the products and services that make the brand. People buy the products and services because they like the products and services. They will not buy the products and services just because of the name on the door.

We start from that point. In effect, a brand is a promise of what a company will deliver and if you deliver that promise you will be successful; if you overpromise, you will quickly get yourself into trouble.

No matter how much we spend on advertising, at the end of the day, people go into shops of whatever because of the promise that they expect. It's exactly the same in the financial services business – that they believe that we behave in a particular way in relation to them and if we don't behave in that way, if we fail to meet their expectations, it won't be long before the brand is damaged, no matter how much we spend on advertising or anything else.

“A brand is a promise of what a company will deliver and if you deliver that promise you will be successful; if you overpromise, you will quickly get yourself into trouble.”

Undoubtedly one of the most successful brands in the world is Kellogg's. You go and buy your cornflakes, you have a certain expectation and as long as they meet that expectation you're happy with Kellogg's. If they started to make Kellogg's in a different way and you didn't like the taste, it wouldn't be long before you bought something else. It comes from your satisfaction with the products and services associated with it.

Coca-Cola sells other brands. They sell an orange drink called Fanta. They don't put Coca-Cola on it because it's got a different promise, it tastes different, it doesn't fizz in the mouth in the same way, so the expectation of this in relation to you is all terribly important for brands. So, the advertising should reinforce what you actually can do, not the other way around.

I think all the companies that I know are working at this in the financial services because some of the things we are doing are different from customers' expectations and the status quo is not an option. But when you make the changes, the changes have to be something that the customers feel comfortable with and they can understand why you're doing it and why you could't deliver it the way you did before.

I think the real challenge for financial services companies is to realize that when you're making these changes you must start with the customers – how to make your staff really customer-focused, that, in the end, is what makes the brand.

Branding is in its infancy in financial services. It is a huge opportunity for us.

How will traditional financial services providers compete with firms outside the industry with strong brand names?

If I take it that we are currently getting about 1,000 customers a day on the Internet without incurring any expenditure on advertising, that is a huge competitive advantage.

You can take years and years building up a brand, but the brand is very quickly destroyed if you don't pay attention to customers.

Is there scope for banks to form alliances with non-banks that have strong brands and broader distribution networks?

It's perfectly possible to do that. I think the dividing line between partnerships and outsourcing is a very narrow one.

“I think the real challenge for financial services companies is to . . . make your staff really customer-focused, that, in the end, is what makes the brand.”

Partnerships suggest that you would have shareholdings in it together, but if we use somebody as a supplier, that to me would be a kind of partner. You might not have any financial interest together, but you get so close and so dependent on one another, you're still in a kind of partnership. Will that grow? I think there is absolutely no doubt about it.

People banking with us in the UK or using the Internet in the US – it's a very, very short step from pushing this all over the world to try to attract customers to our brand here. Do we say that we're going to do this all on our own and not to think of using the Internet companies further down the road? I don't think so.

We should be the same in financial services. We should be very dependent upon people. It may be done through some sort of shareholding, but it doesn't have to be. A kind of networking arrangement to provide the best possible service to customers.

Already we do this, if we are going to develop some new computer system here, if somebody has already invented a part of this to be put into us, we don't say, 'Oh, we got to make it here otherwise it's no good.'

I think we're living in that kind of world more and more. The division between suppliers and partners gets very artificial after a point because you're so dependent on one another.

How about banks developing partnerships with, say, supermarkets? Do you see any risks in that strategy?

We have got a relationship with Asda, but we've got our own banks in Asda and that can be a variety of relationships. It could have been the Asda Bank, managed by us, but we're perceived as a bank and they are perceived as a supermarket. The promise made by Asda is that they are going to be open for very long hours, so if you have a bank in Asda you better have the branch open for very long hours because this is the promise being made by us, too.

Will there be more of these liasions? Yes, there will be.

There are risks in everything you do. The risk with such alliances is that you can damage one another.

How important is branding on the Internet where a wide range of products are available?

It's even more important. You become more remote if you are not careful. If I buy a book on amazon.com and the book doesn't turn up, I don't care what discount I got from them.

Distribution is key. People forget that even with the Internet there will still be physical movements of things. You've still got a lot to deliver in the form of customer support. Everybody underestimates this.

Is there going to be a different business model for traditional financial service providers in the future?

We are going to see a huge consolidation in wholesale banking influence by technology. I am nowhere near as convinced when it's business to individuals whether this will wipe out everything we've got at the moment.

The death of the branch network in my experience has been predicted for at least 25 years and it's still around and it's still likely to be around no matter what you do.

I have seen the cashless society going to be coming – I'm afraid there is more cash in circulation than ever. We were going to have a chequeless society – we haven't got the chequeless society. I know I sound like an old cynic in this, but I'm afraid that human beings want all sorts of things. Human beings still want stamps on credits. When you pay in cash, you are not willing to drop cash in a box and trust us, you're not even willing to drop cheques in a box and trust us – you want a stamp on the damn thing to show that we have actually received it.

It's very, very difficult to change the culture in these things. You're willing to take the money out of the machine, that's our money you think, but you're not willing to put it in.

It won't be so easy to change that. It is easy to change the staff behaviour but you cannot change customer behaviour very easily.

I think the death of some of these old systems that we have been predicting here is premature. I still think that we shall still have quite a lot of these things around well into the next century.

So, you don't think the business model for banks will change?

It will change. You can divide the customers broadly into four different groups. One, the people who use the branches all the time. Two, the people who insist upon having a stamp – what we call branch depositors. You've got the people who use every channel – Internet, cashpoint, mail, branches, telephone – and you've got at the moment quite a small number of people who are 100 per cent fully automated, never ever ring up a human being. That will change over time but it's not going to change overnight.

Do you see banks selling products other than financial services in the future?

It's unlikely that we shall start selling soap flakes or something like that. We have to be careful in defining what financial services are because some services which are very much advice services would not have been regarded as services in the past or even information services. I think I would still be able to define them broadly as financial services.

How fast will the growth of on-line banking be in the US, Europe and Asia?

It will be pretty rapid all over the place because, if you look at the percentage of population, you can see how it wouldn't be long before 20 per cent of the population will be on the Internet and then it will continue to grow. It doesn't mean to say that we'll use it exclusively.

Will financial-sector consolidation continue and are there limits to this trend in terms of efficiencies and economies of scale?

I think you could get to such a complicated Byzantine organization that diminishing returns would set in. If you wanted to be everything to every person, then I think you could get yourself to a point where you wouldn't be a very efficient organization, and there is plenty of evidence that the most effective mergers are those that have been really thought through to say where all these synergies are going to come from because bigger doesn't necessarily mean better.

“It's not size that people are after … We've seen, say, in merging two banks or getting an older and better product provider than ourselves as a way, ultimately, of improving what customers get and, therefore, producing better results.”

It's not size that people are after – certainly it's not size that we've been after – and, if you measure it by total assets, we're certainly nothing like as big as some banks. We've been after performance. We've seen, say, in merging two banks or getting an older and better product provider than ourselves as a way, ultimately, of improving what customers get and, therefore, producing better results.

But is there a size beyond which diminishing returns would set in? Yes, you can imagine you get to such an organization, it's so complicated and, as I say, so Byzantine that I don't even know what the effort of the people will be like, because people have got to feel they mean something for the company, that they have some ownership of the company.

I think in some areas of activity – in wholesale banking in particular – I foresee very substantial consolidation because you can run it in two or three places in the world, you don't need all these different places in dealing. You can organize a loan for somebody in New York whether you're in Frankfurt or London or New York.

I think we will see further substantial consolidation of banks that are similar in attitude, where you can get the economies of scale out and you can get the synergies out. I think we will see further acquisitions, as we've done here, of a specialist product provider in order to enhance the products you're selling to the customers.

How big will these banks and financial services become? Well, I think I'd like to say they'll become bigger than they are now. We haven't got to the end of this game at all, in my view, and what used to be big in the past is now not big. If we are going to go down this road, you can see that 50 billion pounds or 100 billion dollars, as we look down the road, will not be big.

How many of these financial services giants will there be?

You've got about 100 mortgage providers in the UK. It's hard to see more than 20 substantial mortgage providers if we go down this road. We've got over 100 insurance providers – it's hard to see more than 20. There is a smaller number of banks and, therefore, I think the question of choice with the competition authorities will continue to get in the way of very much further rationalization.

If we start to see things on a European basis, if we're looking forward to next 50 years, then you'll see another wave of consolidation across Europe. There are already plenty of signs of consolidation in different parts of Europe, and then you could start to see what is a very fragmented market in Europe still have further very substantial consolidation.

I wouldn't want to name how many, but I think what we can see – as we look at it over the next two decades and further – is substantial consolidation in practically every one of the financial services organizations.

From a customer's standpoint, what are the benefits and drawbacks of having all of one's financial needs serviced by the same company?

I don't think there are significant drawbacks as long as you are willing to shop around so you're getting very good value for money. That seems to be the key to me – can you get very good value for money from this one supplier? That's the test all the time.

We're having to provide more value for less money, not just value for money. We're currenly providing an Internet service free, a telephone banking service free, a cashpoint service to our own customers free, a current account service – if the account is in credit – free. There is absolutely no doubt that, from our customers' point of view, they have had more and more for less and less.

If we now add up individual products, they've got mortgages from us where the mortgage margins in the UK are lower than the mortgage margins in France or Germany. There's practically nowhere else in the world where they can have a current account which is free and they get some interest on the current account as well. The customers, although they don't believe it, have got more value for less money than they've ever had before and I think that will be a requirement; I don't think it's going to go away. I think the customers will continue to demand more value for less money. The challenge will be to provide that to them at a reasonable profit to ourselves.

What are the systemic risk implications of larger global organizations?

If one of these major organizations got themselves into difficulty, it would have repercussions all over the world. I don't see it because the regulators are tougher on everybody now than they've ever been and they know much more about our companies than ever before. It's not just the books that we've got, they want to know what the strategy is, people being appointed in the company, etc.

So, I think it's extremely unlikely to find a major player in the world going bust, and it will be in our self-interest for that not to happen anyway. It wouldn't be altruism for us to rescue a major corporation because the knock-on effect to us, even though we might not be directly involved, would be highly negative.

While there is pressure on banks to achieve higher and higher returns on equity, consumer groups see this as a rip-off. How can banks find the balance?

There is no magic number. There has always been a conflict between shareholders and customers, but most successful companies earn the highest returns and consumers will get the benefit.

ROBERT POZEN

President and Chief Executive, Fidelity Management & Research Company, investment adviser arm of Fidelity Investments

INTERVIEW BY CAL MANKOWSKI

The stock market has been doing wonders since 1982 and, particularly in the last five years, the returns have been out-sized. Do you think the American people have becoming a little too dependent on these big returns?

Well, we've seen from surveys, and I've talked about it, that it seems – if you put all of the surveys together – there is an expectation now of somewhere around 20 per cent returns per year and we know that, historically, over long periods of time – 30, 50 and 70 years – that returns have been more in the 11 to 13 per cent range, so there clearly is considerable tension between those two numbers and, hopefully, people will become educated as to the fact that this has been an unusual period. It's a big issue for all people in the financial services when expectations are so high one wonders whether or not they can really be met, and I think no one wants to be in a position, where the market goes up by 12 per cent, for everybody to say 'Oh, it's terrible,' when, in fact, if the market goes up by 12 per cent, that's a reasonable year.

One of the drivers, according to many experts, is the demographics, and the baby boomers in particular. There will come a point in time when they will be taking money out. Is this a big problem for the financial services industry when that happens?

Well, there two points. One is as to the baby boom generation – the ones born after World World II – we really don't know what their behaviour is going to be. It's possible that some of them will take the money out; it's possible that some of them will keep the money in and just live off the income through distributions; it's possible that some of them will transfer the money to their children. To the extent they do the second or third thing, then, obviously, there won't be that much impact. So I guess we have a lot of question marks there.

The second factor that's, I think, significant is – the generation in their teens. I read something the other day which suggested that the baby boom generation is no longer the biggest generation in the country and that the generation that's now somewhere in the teens is becoming a bigger generation. By the time those people who are around 20 – the time that generation gets to be 30 or 35, then the baby boom generation will be more in their sixties. So the other big question mark is whether that group, which is slightly bigger than the baby boomers, will serve as a replacement investor.

And, another big driver of the market that we have seen pushing stocks higher has been the shift to the defined contribution plans. I wanted to ask you how much of a global phenomenon that is going to be; the United States seems to be ahead.

I guess you would say the shift is prevalent in the Anglo-Saxon countries. Canada is already in a DC mode, the UK is already in a DC mode and Australia is already in a DC mode. Hong Kong is now starting its Provident Fund, which is in a DC mode. I think we already have a DC model in large parts of the British-related world. I think you also see that Continental Europe – in France, Germany, and other countries – have begun to move toward defined contribution systems, mainly because they have very difficult old-age problems. France, for example, is not reproducing its population and it has some pretty big pension obligations, so that the numbers just force you toward a DC system; you can't continue to have this indeterminate unfunded obligation. In Japan – the other big pension market – we've been told that legislation will go into effect at the end of this year, or perhaps next year. As you know, everything goes a little slower in Japan than one wants– one has learned to expect slower in Japan – but I think Japan, over the next two or three years, will start a defined contribution system. So, I think that there is a global trend already toward DC systems and this trend will become more accentuated. The one caveat is that sometimes people think, every country is going to do DC just like we did in 401k, but each country has a different approach to DC. If you look at Canada, the UK and Australia – each one has its own variant. These are quite complicated plans and there is no uniform worldwide type of DC system, and I don't expect there to be one. I think there is going to be a different DC system for each country and that has big implications in terms of costs and in terms of computer programs and all sorts of things like that.

Notwithstanding that there may be variations as various countries go to DC, these would be big opportunities for the American companies who have the expertise.

It's absolutely a big opportunity, but whether the opportunity will be realized depends a lot on how the legislation and regulation of these plans occur. For instance, if countries decide to have very small account sizes, that will make the DC plan very costly. Or, if countries decide that they are not going to give very much choice at all, then they'll look more like DC plans. Or, if a country decides that the DC plan can invest only in bonds from that country or stocks from that country, that DC plan will not be attractive to American companies. So what I'm saying is, depending on how those sorts of issues get resolved, this global movement towards DC plans will either be more or less attractive to US companies; more or less of our American expertise may be transferable depending on how some of these issues come out.

Would you say, as a general rule, the mutual fund practices, as they vary internationally, that you have more differences from country to country as opposed to other financial services?

Oh, absolutely. I think that a share in a mutual fund is the least transnational security in existence. With stocks or bonds, you can trade them pretty much across the world, especially now that interest on US bonds paid to foreign portfolio investors isn't subject to withholding. There's a pretty good international market for most securities. But mutual funds are basically very parochial. I think it's because each country insists that mutual funds be incorporated in that country and that they follow the tax and accounting and regulatory rules of that country. Therefore it has been very difficult to have a true globalization of mutual funds. You still can't sell Magellan in Europe and you can't sell Magellan in Japan; and to be fair, you can't sell a Japanese fund in the US or a German fund in the US. A few years ago I was a member of something called the 'Committee of Experts' which, of course, made us all feel very smart and we had this international group that tried to reconcile and harmonize, mutual fund regulation around the world. But after a few years we gave up – the differences were so enormous. So people have become used to using what are called 'clone' funds – for example, if we go into Canada we have to create a separate growth fund that's patterned after the same growth fund in the US bit it's never quite the same. There are always differences in accounting and tax and investment rules and, of course, there are differences in local taste. So we've pretty much learned to live with what I called a modified clone fund system. Now what we're trying to do is to insist that countries be open to having clones of foreign funds. That's true in Canada; that's also true in Mexico since NAFTA [North American Free Trade Agreement]. But Mexico says it will treat US clone funds the same as Mexican funds and, at the moment, Mexican managers are only allowed to buy Mexican stocks and bonds. So the modified clone fund does not really present an open system in Mexico. In the EU, you can register funds in Luxembourg and sell them throughout the rest of EU. But each country maintains the right to control the marketing of the fund, and under that rubric, many countries impose lots of requirements that usually are not thought of as marketing. In Asia the entry barriers are the worst though Japan is now pretty opened up, and so is Hong Kong and Australia. But in Taiwan, Korea and Thailand, you still have a lot of difficulties as a foreign manager actually gathering assets in those countries. I should say that everyone is very happy for the US mutual funds to invest in their country, but when we get to asset gathering many of the Asian countries are still quite protectionist.

Do you think it will take a long time to change things?

Oh, yes. These are essentially long-term problems involving trade relations and many other issues that will take years to resolve. I think, for better or worse, mutual funds have to live with a modified clone system and try to make that work. I doubt whether there will ever be a true universal fund or worldwide distributed fund; I don't plan on that happening in my lifetime.

To shift the topic a little bit to the United States and consolidation, the key event last year was, in effect, the repeal of the Glass-Steagall Act. Do you think we are going to see true one-stop shopping financial service firms come to dominate the industry?

I really don't think so. To begin with, the repeal of Glass-Steagall, like a lot of major pieces of legislation, only occurred after the loopholes were so large that most of the reform had been accomplished already. There were some important changes – a key change is that banks can now buy life assurance underwriters and I think some of them will probably do that and combine life insurance companies with money management companies. Another big change is that now you can have a merger between a large bank and a large investment bank; but I still am of the view that one-stop shopping is not very attractive to most of the high net worth customers. Sears tried it several years ago and fell on its face and I think other firms would face the same results. The high net worth investor – who everyone wants – is very sophisticated about his or her use of financial services; they want the best deal in every financial service. While they may be willing to buy some closely related product from the same firm, the idea that they're going to do all of their insurance and all of their brokerage and all of their money management at the same place seems unlikely.

I think we at Fidelity have tried to be more focused. For instance, in the insurance area we do not try to sell all types of insurance and underwrite all types of insurance, though we are allowed to. What we try to do is to concentrate on variable annuities since that insurance product is closely related to mutual funds. But I don't think we have a comparative advantage in whole life insurance or other aspects of the insurance business. Moreover, I think that the Internet will make it even more difficult to have a financial supermarket. A big attraction of a financial supermarket is that it's very convenient when one person can give you all these financial services, so you don't have to go to a lot of different places. But the Internet makes it very convenient to buy from several providers. Another important aspect of a financial supermarket is that the consumer will say, 'Oh, this is a reasonable price for the other product and, since you are a nice guy, I'll buy this other product from you,' but, once you have the Internet, consumers do not develop a personal relationship with the seller. Also, consumers can very quickly see the offerings of many financial service providers, and they can see pricing for everybody. So, I don't believe that customers are going to stick with one firm for all financial services – the transparency of products and pricing has been so enhanced by the Internet. I think that what will happen is that you'll have clusters of firms – firms will concentrate on a few related products. And hopefully Fidelity will be one of the firms that will be good at mutual funds, variable annuities, and other closely-related products.

Could new players enter the market through the Internet that we don't even know about?

Yes, sure. I think that is possible. There's no doubt about it – it's possible, but I'll answer your question a little more broadly. I view the structure of the industry as the large players getting larger, mainly because they offer 401k, they make the investment in technology for service, and they go global – I also think there is still a tremendous opportunity for small players in the mutual fund industry because everybody is willing to make deals with people to act as distributors through structures like mutual fund marketplaces. Also, if you're a small fund company and you get a good performance record, you can get plenty of marketing. But I think the middle gets squeezed. We have already seen companies like Scudder and Dreyfus acquired by larger institutions, and I think we'll see more of that. So, there is plenty of room for people to come into the fund industry through the Internet as a small player; whether people can really become big players with the Internet, I think that's a more difficult question. I would say the factors against it are, first, that, basically all mutual fund companies are already adapting to the on-line environment and Fidelity is particularly in the forefront, so we're already assimilating many of the aspects of the Internet into our service and sales model. Therefore, somebody cannot come up with an Internet model that would be the first one. Second, if I get the gist of your question, companies like Microsoft, Intel, or one of those technology companies have found it very difficult every time they've tried to get into content rather than process. By 'process', I mean, broadly speaking, technology – on the delivery of information. Some of these companies have gone as far as to become good portals – meaning that they'll provide sources of information and then people can quickly pick among the menu items. But that's very different from getting into the actual business of managing money, which can prove a lot more challenging than being a very good processor or aggregator of information. So, I guess it remains to be seen whether or not technology providers can become money managers.

One aspect of the Internet is they're telling consumers they can name their own price or directly search out the lowest price from the array of providers. Does this mean that profit opportunities are being squeezed out of all the businesses that are affected?

Well, there's no doubt about it, the Internet is putting downward pressure on prices, both because it's allowing more productivity and because it's providing a great degree of transparency. However, contrary to what some people think, the segment of the industry that Fidelity is in has been reducing prices over the years and probably is already pretty price-competitive. Moreover, in mutual funds, we are not really allowed to have each shareholder pick and choose a price. So, then you say, well how do you know the whole mutual fund industry won't get re-priced? What's interesting is that the portion of the mutual fund industry that's sold with loads and 12b-1-type fees [rules of the Securities and Exchange Commission governing use of fund assets to pay cost of distributing the fund] is actually growing; If you look at net sales and these sorts of statistics, the direct-marketed portion of the industry was growing strongly say from 1985 to, roughly, 1995 or 1996. In the last few years, however, the direct marketing channel has pretty much plateaued and maybe even has been going relatively lower. Meanwhile, the funds with loads and 12b-1 fees have done better in sales. And I think that these numbers seem to say that people are willing to pay a little more in order to get more advice; that's what it comes down to. That shows they are willing to pay for advice and that's why we have so many mutual funds now with so many classes. Now people are wanting more and more advice and they seem to be willing to pay for it. At Fidelity, through what we call our advisor line of funds, we've done very well in the last two or three years, distributing funds through banks and broker–dealers and they are all sold with 12b-1 fees and loads. People seem to think that that's quite reasonable because they're getting a broader package of services than just money management.

“Once we are in this environment of open architecture, the possibility of distributing through multiple channels is much more viable.”

When a company like Fidelity uses a variety of distribution channels – and now the Internet is a new channel that you are using – do people working within each channel, are they in conflict or . . .

I wouldn't say that the Internet is a new channel of distribution; it is a more efficient way of delivering information and doing transactions for an existing channel. So, for instance, if you focus on the 401k channel, now participants can look at their accounts on the Internet or they can do trades through Internet. Similarly, if you focus on the broker–dealer channel, the broker can get more information from the Internet to serve the ultimate customer. Obviously, the Internet is important but I don't think the Internet is really a separate channel. The Internet is being used by the three main distribution channels – direct, 401k and broker–dealer – all in very different ways. I think that Fidelity is the only company that's actually in all three channels. There are other firms in two but we're in all three. That does create the potential for conflict. But Ned Johnson has personally decided that he is willing to tolerate potential conflict. When these issues come to a head, in regard to a particular policy, we try to resolve them. It's basically been our business strategy to be in all three channels. Historically, I guess it's fair to day that direct and 401k were our strongest channels and that the broker–dealer intermediary channel wasn't as strong because of this channel conflict. But I think now that almost everyone has gone to open architecture, this is no longer a big issue and people like Merrill Lynch sell our funds and so do people like insurance companies and banks. We in turn through our funds supermarket, will sell everybody else's funds. Once we are in this environment of open architecture, the possibility of distributing through multiple channels is much more viable.

To shift the subject a bit, another area where electronics and modern methods are having an effect is the way stocks are traded. It used to be the Stock Exchange and Nasdaq, and now the ECN. What sorts of changes do you see coming in those platforms for trading stocks and how does it affect big players such as Fidelity?

From Fidelity's point of view, we're going to be trading wherever trading is good. We're generally in favour of having as many alternative trading opportunities available as possible because at any one point in time, you never know which is going to be the best way to trade the stock. So we'll trade stock on the Exchange, we'll trade on the OTC [over-the-counter], we'll trade through ECNs, we'll trade through Instinet and Posit. We'll trade wherever we can get the best price. I think that the ECNs have surely brought a lot of pressure to bear on the established markets because they have taken away a lot of business from Nasdaq and the New York Stock Exchange. This pressure will produce some significant structural changes. I think probably the New York Stock Exchange is going to have to make significant modifications and they're already talking about making some – while maintaining the specialist structure, using technology to deliver trades and get them executed automatically. And, we're involved with those discussions but we're really not going to be the main mover of those discussions – someone else will. I think those people who think what we need is perfect time and price priority are essentially advocating one big black box. Although that's surely possible, I would tend not to be particularly enthusiastic about it for two reasons. First is that if you really reduced everything to one big computer, then we'd have a public utility on our hands. But I think that the differences in markets have produced a lot of innovation and have generated a lot of price competition. Just think what the ECNs did to reduce prices. And, second, a lot of these equity markets are very different. For example, look at something like Instinet. It's a different sort of market than, say, an ECN. An ECN is good at executing lots of small trades very quickly and very efficiently. But an ECN is really not in a good position to handle block trades of 200,000 shares while Instinet is. So, trying to push all trades through the same mechanism will not work.

“We're going to be trading wherever trading is good. We're generally in favour of having as many alternative trading opportunities available as possible because at any one point in time, you never know which is going to be the best way to trade the stock.”

Both Nasdaq and New York, they have different systems, but rely on monolithic technology that they each have developed already, but they involve people to a great extent too. What happens when markets become difficult?

I think that's important for us – we definitely believe that liquidity, the depth and volume of a market, is very important to us. So if you have a system which is merely a matching system, like what we have on the Tokyo Stock Exchange, you'll see that orders do not find matches in a lot of stocks, especially for thinly traded stocks or in difficult market situations, you just don't get executed.

What kind of systems in Japan?

The Tokyo Stock Exchange is based on a system that matches buy and sell orders for the same price. But there is no specialist system there and no market-maker system there. There is a computer together with a clerk. If the clerk sees a buy and sell order in the same stock, he'll match them and execute on the Tokyo Stock Exchange; but if they don't match, they don't get executed. Of course, in high volume stocks like Toyota, most orders get executed; but in lots of other stocks, many orders don't get executed. Moreover, if you have a crisis in the market – a financial crisis or some big event – then many orders don't get executed even in high volume stocks. So, we think there still is quite a role for market-makers and specialists and all these sorts of people though. But they will probably have to change and become much more transparent in the future.

“I think people have become much more sophisticated since 1987 about volatility. . . . So while we have good tools, I can't guarantee that there's nothing that could happen that would really throw us.”

You mentioned the financial crisis and how it makes things difficult. In 1997 and 1998 we saw some financial shocks – but not as big as happened in 1987, but do you think risk management and how it's used generally in the industry is sufficient today to avoid another shock like we saw in 1987?

I think people have become much more sophisticated since 1987 about volatility. I think we are used to more day-to-day volatility, and intra-day volatility on all markets. To deal with this higher level of volatility, we have developed more tools and we all monitor market movements pretty closely. But in the end it's always the unanticipated that gets you; there is always the possibility of something that we're just not smart enough to forecast. Or there's a possibility so remote that it's hard to plan for. So while we have good tools, I can't guarantee that there's nothing that could happen that would really throw us.

Is there anything that's needed on a regulatory front that would give us extra insurance or protection?

For me, the most undisclosed and unregulated entity we have is the hedge fund. And the number of hedge funds is going up rapidly and the amount of assets they manage is going up. We have to file so many documents with the SEC, and so do banks and pension funds with their regulators. But hedge funds don't have to file almost anything, so there's poor disclosure about their holdings. We saw what happened in 1998 because of the near failure of one large hedge fund. The other thing is that all mutual funds are required to have what are called symmetrical performance fees. Fidelity is one of the few fund complexes that have adopted performance fees because of this symmetrical requirement. In our performance fees, if a fund goes up, our management fee increases by a specified amount; if the fund goes down, our management fee decreases by a certain amount. Hedge funds, by contrast, have asymmetrical performance fees – meaning that they get paid basically 20 per cent of the upside and nothing on the downside. I think that encourages a lot of risk taking. So I think that the treatment of hedge funds is probably the biggest regulatory lapse within our control. Of course, there are factors like earthquakes and political revolutions which are not within our control.

Do you think they've been making it maybe easier for the hedge funds as opposed to harder?

I think you have two choices: either you can let all pooled vehicles operate freely like hedge funds or you can impose a stricter regulatory structure on hedge funds. I would predict that hedge funds are never going to be regulated like mutual funds. But if we could require quarterly disclosure of all hedge fund holdings and we could require that they have symmetrical performance fees, those two reforms alone would go a long way towards reducing the amount of risk that hedge funds bring into the financial system. In addition, those two reforms would have the effect of making the regulatory structure fairer to all pooled investment vehicles.

“The most undisclosed and unregulated entity we have is the hedge fund. . . . Hedge funds, by contrast, have asymmetrical performance fees. . . . I think that encourages a lot of risk taking. . . . There are factors like earthquakes and political revolutions which are not within our control.”

Is this something the SEC could address?

Absolutely. The SEC can do something on performance fees under the current statutes. But I think that quarterly disclosure requirements for hedge funds would probably have to come from Congress. There have been reports and some hearings, but so far there doesn't seem to be a high probability of actual changes.

Just one more thing on the question of how the technology is changing. One aspect of that is the move to extend the trading hours – before the open, after the close, the once-a-day pricing that's most prevalent in the industry, I know sometimes some funds have hourly pricing. What changes might be coming?

The only funds that have hourly pricing, as far as I know, are the Fidelity Select Funds and that's extremely difficult to do on an hourly basis. I don't think it would be realistic for us to do hourly pricing for most of our funds and it would be almost impossible to price a fund more often than once an hour.

I think people talk about continuous pricing. That's a pipe dream?

Remember, in an actively managed fund, there is a continuously changing portfolio, so while you can announce a price for the fund's shares, is it going to be the accurate price? The answer is if you tried to price an actively managed fund continuously, it would rarely be the accurate price because the fund would continuously be changing its portfolio. On 24-hour trading in individual securities, I think there's very little demand. People keep arguing that we need 24-hour trading in US stocks. But I don't think either the firms or the investors are very interested in that type of trading. There is some interest in trading a few hours before the opening and in the few hours after the close. But even then if you look at what's actually happened, the markets are very thin. Occasionally, of course, you'll have a company that makes a big announcement after the close, so then that stock will trade heavily, but that's really a special case. So, I think people who are predicting we're going to move to 24-hour global trading are just plain wrong. I think we will see, gradually, more interest in a few hours before the open and a few hours after the close.

Just one final question – something I noticed in your book [The Mutual Fund Business, *(1998), MIT*] *on the mutual fund business. You discussed how service became a product. How do you see that evolving?*

I think service is critical to the mutual fund industry; it's become almost as important as the investment decision. And the decision to invest has broadened to include advice on your whole portfolio and on lots of related matters like tax planning. As a result, you see even pure direct shops, like Vanguard and our direct shop, providing advice along with the fund product. Then, once you are in a fund already, there is the quality of service that fund shareholders receive – in getting information about the fund's performance, in getting tax reports about the fund and in being able to add money or make redemptions easily. These are very important services and I think that the quality of service will be a differentiator among firms. Every firm should try to get the best investment performance – we surely try to get the best investment performance and I'm sure other people do, and we succeed most of the time. But you can't always have the best investment performance. By contrast, you can have great service every day and every week. Great service is within your control. If you have great service, your customers will be much more likely to stay with you even if you have an occasional dip in performance. Because there always are occasional dips of performance, continuous service at a high level is critical to how satisfied your customers are. Obviously, if you have great performance, your customers are happy. But you can't always have great performance. If you provide customers with great service all the time, that'll be very important for their long-term relationship with the mutual fund company

“I think service is critical to the mutual fund industry; it's become almost as important as the investment decision.”

ALESSANDRO PROFUMO

Chief Executive Officer, UniCredito Italiano

INTERVIEW BY JENNIFER CLARK

Did banking-sector consolidation after the euro take place more quickly than expected?

Faster than expected, no. It happened very quickly in Italy, which had a very fragmented banking system that started reacting ahead of time, since consolidation started to take place before the birth of the euro. And the reaction of the banking system has been fairly adequate, I would say.

It was very quick, but that was expected because the market here was so incredibly fragmented it had a long way to go. Compared to other countries we've travelled a long way, but there's still a lot to do, especially in terms of costs. Italian banks today have good cost–income ratios compared to European banks, but have a cost structure that's still rather high. There's still room for work. So, we need more intervention on costs to maintain the cost–income ratios we have now, because we will see more pressure on income.

Where? From trading on-line?

Commissions will tend to get squeezed, while interest margins should improve. Interest rates and lending spreads in Italy are very low compared to other European countries. Total assets will increase and the spread will widen, while commissions will be under pressure.

So, you're telling me that banks will raise their lending costs in order to recoup commission margins that are getting squeezed?

Yes, I think that the spread for loans will widen a bit, but rates in Italy are very low right now.

The next step is cross-border mergers, and your bank is involved with what could be one of Europe's first, with Banco Bilbao Viscaya Argentaria. What would you say are the main forces driving them?

There's a fairly simple answer. First of all, you have to define what 'cross-border' will mean in five years' time. European integration is already under way, so more than 'cross-border' you might want to talk about 'cross-languages'.

The answer is this: price structure will become more and more homogeneous across Europe. We'll have a European market. The services we are offering are intangible – they can be supplied across long distances quite easily. So, there are two factors at work: one is the single currency and the other is technology. Moreover, we're selling a service and not an industrial product, like a car. For example, I can live here and have a bank account in London, pay my bills in London, manage my savings and assets there as well. This combination will result in a flattening of prices, particularly for the more profitable client segments. So, we need a cost structure that is homogeneous with basic structure – a European cost structure, not a domestic one. Alliances enable banks to achieve cross-fertilization in terms of know-how as well to share costs in order to be competitive in the market.

“There are two things to keep in mind. The first is the element of size – you have to try to have a partner that's more or less the same size. The second is the 'cost of complexity'. The increase in size always increases the complexity of managing any organization.”

There are two things to keep in mind. The first is the element of size – you have to try to have a partner that's more or less the same size. The second is the 'cost of complexity'. The increase in size always increases the complexity of managing any organization.

Which areas of your business are more affected by this process?

Investment banking certainly presents opportunities for significant economies of scale, as does asset management. Technology, payment systems, international banking activity are all areas in which economies of scale are important.

But certainly, in describing this scenario, you don't face competition from foreign banks in your home territory because that's not what's happening, banks aren't setting up retail networks in other countries.

Right, but, if you take the single currency on one hand and technology on the other, the interface with electronic support systems becomes quite simple (with a huge impact on traditional branch networks). The Internet, videoconferencing, telephone ... one of the most important services for banking that access to fibre-optic networks will give us is high-quality videoconferencing. I can be seated at my desk and interacting on-line and decide I need to speak to my bank teller or bank official by videoconference. If the quality is good, after we get used to it, it will be like being face to face. This could have a huge impact on banking distribution channels. I think it's possible we'll see the creation of banking networks with greatly reduced physical presence and a wide use of electronic kiosks.

All of these developments require significant investment on one hand. There are defensive actions on one hand and, let's say, offensive ones on the other hand. We need creative thinking on one hand, and more investment on the other hand. As always, joining forces doesn't hurt.

How important is the role of central banks in the consolidation process? UniCredito had a takeover offer blocked by the Bank of Italy in 1999 because the central bank frowns on unsolicited offers. At what point will local monetary and regulatory authorities start getting replaced by the European Union?

National banking systems will continue to exist, of course, and the subject of supervision of domestic banks by central banks or by other authorities is very important, but, certainly, once cross-border mergers start happening, the problem of how banking supervision is exercised at a European level must be raised. It could be in the form of coordination of national central banks or in another form is something I really can't say.

Which do you think is preferable?

I don't know. It's a problem that needs to be examined.

I think, however, that, obviously, the problem of creating European institutions will inevitably need to be faced in the wake of the single currency. Now that we've made a single currency, we're faced with a series of new problems that are extremely relevant. Just think of corporate law and the differences between Germany and the Latin countries. The takeover laws are different in each country. The theme of the passage from national institutions to supra-national ones will have to be faced.

At the Helsinki summit in December 1999, the EU failed to pass a Europe-wide takeover law. Would you have been happy to see one?

It's not a question of being happy or not. Increasing economic integration simply generates colossal problems. The problem is how to coordinate international norms. The single currency is an incredible accelerator. The economy is continually more integrated. Just look at the Vodafone-Mannesmann bid.

Having all of one's financial needs served by one organization seems to be the strategic goal of many financial institutions. From a customer standpoint, what are the perceived benefits and drawbacks of such an arrangement? At what point does this move towards a 'supermarket' model create new spaces for niche players? Is there this risk?

Yes. We made a slightly different strategic choice. We reorganized the bank on national lines by client segments. Then we asked ourselves which client segment wants integrated services and would be happy to be served by a single bank.

So we started from the client, instead of the distribution model – supermarket or otherwise. Clearly a mass market client has different needs from a private banking client. Therefore, starting from the client, we then reaggregated a group of services that we believe that type of client would be satisfied in buying from a single provider, and then we tried to supply them in an integrated way.

Certainly there's a problem of economy of scope in the distribution channel. In other words, if I have a distribution channel, if I am able to sell a plurality of services, I can achieve additional income flows. But I would call this model a 'co-marketing' approach rather than a 'supermarket' approach. They are specific selling initiatives that, on the one hand, benefit the middleman because he works on our client base and, on the other hand, benefits us because we give additional services to our clients that we have seen are well received and, in the meantime, we receive fees for these services.

“The fundamental point is to ask ourselves what the client needs. ... Ask yourself how to avoid creating confusion in the clients' mind while providing services they really want to have from a single provider.”

The fundamental point is to ask ourselves what the client needs. For example, in the high end of the market, simple asset management is not enough. For example, private banking clients want services like insurance, tax advice, art investment advice, real estate advice and so on. So the key point here is integrated services, if you're talking about a supermarket approach. The most important thing is to ask yourself how to avoid creating confusion in the clients' mind while providing services they really want to have from a single provider.

Do you find this approach works?

The fundamental thing is to segment your client base, create diversified distribution channels for each client group, provide the right services in that distribution channel. Yes, it works very well. All the most successful banks in the world are organized along these lines.

Are you satisfied with results from cross-selling of insurance products?

Yes, it works very well. You have to sell the right product to the right client, and that's where marketing comes in – you have to segment your client base very well.

This client-centred approach has come very late to Italy.

There aren't a lot of banks organized by client segments anywhere in the world. It's one thing to talk about it, another thing to do it. We carried out a radical reorganization of the bank, starting in 1995, and concluded it in 1999. First, we reorganized the bank into different distribution channels, but not organized into divisions, but now we've reorganized Credito Italiano into divisions – corporate, retail, private banking – each completely separate.

Across different industries, we're seeing consolidation into one or two or three big players. If we imagine a future in which there are just a few mega-banks in Europe, at what point will consolidation start offering new openings for niche players that step in to provide services that maybe the giants haven't thought of or charge too much for?

I don't think the level of consolidation will reach that sort of extreme level. If, however, there were to be the creation of a duopoly, let's say, prices will reach the stars and that would leave space for new players to enter the market, but I don't think we're headed for this type of scenario. Banking is partly a productive activity, with the resulting economies of scale, and partly a distribution activity. Distribution activity, by its nature, can continue to be carried out in precise niches, be they geographic or by client segments. All banks that have the intelligence – not just in Italy but across Europe – to understand what products they can produce in-house and what products they can adopt from outside will still be around for many years to come.

Do you see a point when consumers will find themselves facing big players that in some ways resemble the oil trusts in the US at the start of the 1900s, to name one example?

Antitrust authorities function very well in the US and function well in Europe, even though they have to grow a bit. But, apart from that, I'm convinced that the technological development under way will enable even the smaller companies to be strangely profitable. Therefore, quite frankly, the main thing to understand is how your business works and what value you want to give your clients. I'm fairly convinced that the development of information and communications technology gives everyone the possibility to clearly identify the portion of value they want to give their clients, and to be profitable in that portion of value and create a business niche around it. So, yes, there will be consolidation, but there will be also space for a group of players that I wouldn't exactly call 'niche players' because they will be bigger than that.

How do you plan to deal with the erosion of margins implicit in the boom of on-line trading. On-line brokerages in Italy have already reduced their commissions, but nowhere near to the levels we've seen in the US.

It's like when the big discount chains started opening up in Italy – everyone said it would be the end of the traditional retail chains, and that didn't happen.

In the meantime, the fundamental aspect is to concentrate on services rather than prices. On-line trading involves a very specific client segment. Charles Schwab makes a profit because it sells a series of services to its clients. On-line trading is provided at a low cost or even for free and profits come from other services. The important thing is to understand what is a commodity and what is a value-added service. Where can I give value to clients? That's where you have to look.

Apart from that, I'm also convinced that on-line brokerages are seeing their bourse values soar because they're the flavour of the month with investors, but the day of reckoning will come for them, too, when they have to start showing profits. There's a lot of confusion about prices right now, as there is in all moments of discontinuity, but, in the end, we need to make a profit.

We certainly need to keep a close eye on this business, but it's not our most profitable area. We have good margins from trading activity, but they're not incredibly high. If trading commissions were to be subjected to strong price pressures, we will have to have the capability to furnish alternative services that will enable us to maintain interesting margins.

Tradinglab [an electronic communications network that enables investors to trade stocks after the market closes] is not aimed at retail clients, it's aimed at wholesale clients. The main thing here is to understand what types of services retail clients want when they trade on-line, which in any case is a relatively limited market in any country in the world.

The main thing is to have a big client base and do a lot of cross-selling – in other words, accurately analyze your marketing database to determine which services are most suited for this channel. You have to re-engineer your activity.

Tradinglab is a wholesale service that goes to distributors – it's not aimed at retail investors.

How does it fit into your banking strategy, seeing you are the first Italian bank to offer this type of service?

It's fundamental. This type of investment banking is not being provided by other banks, its very innovative, even at a European level. We want to have a strong national market presence, but we've also started to present the project to foreign banks.

CARLO SALVATORI

Chief Executive Officer, Banca Intesa

INTERVIEW BY JENNIFER CLARK

Banca Intesa, now Italy's largest bank, was created in 1998 from a union of several smaller banks. Intesa has opted for what you call a 'federal' model that retains each bank's brand name and identity, rather than following the usual merger process, whereby one bank swallows the other. Can you explain how the federal model works?

Our model grew out of certain considerations made during the period when we integrated Cariplo and Banco Ambrosiano Veneto – two of the largest banks in the Intesa Group.

“A merger results in diseconomy of income, whereas the federal model, leaving the banks' individual brands on the market, results in the creation of added-value in terms of revenues.”

There were two alternatives: one was a full merger and the other was a federal model, which I prosposed. A merger is recognized as the solution that provides the greatest economies of scale and cost, but I believe that the federal model enables us to meet all our cost cut targets, or come very near, if we are extremely rigorous.

In terms of income, a merger results in diseconomy of income, whereas the federal model, leaving the banks' individual brands on the market, results in the creation of added-value in terms of revenues.

Can you elaborate on what you mean by 'diseconomies of scale' in a merger?

In a merger, the banks become a single bank and you have to close branches and unify profit strategy. With the federal model, each bank keeps its brand and strengthens the brands in their historic market – Ambroveneto in the Veneto, Cariplo in Lombardy, Cassa di Parma in its areas, Carime in the south.

We strengthen the banks' brands by applying best practice standards in the group to all banks. For example, Cariplo was one of the first banks to introduce phone banking in Italy. We can transfer its know-how to other banks in the group, in other regions in Italy, therefore increasing their market share without incurring the additional investment that would be needed to start up these services from scratch.

In that way, we obtain cost rationalization while we improve income because each single bank's market share improves in its own territory. We know from experience that, when a bank's market share improves at branch level, it brings a more than proportional increase in revenues.

Once you've chosen that model, how do you make it work?

We've established four rules.

First: the federal model has to have solid and indisputed goverance. Banca Intesa has to be the one that calls the shots. It establishes the strategy for the group, and all the companies in the group.

The other principle is that we centralize all support activity and product activity. We have centralized all support activity in a company called Intesa Systems and Services. It oversees all technology and telecommuncations platforms for the group. For Banca Intesa, the product companies, Cariplo and so on. We have a single asset management company, and so on.

Centralization of finance: a single group will handle finance for all of our units. Caboto, our brokerage unit, acts as a finance arm within the group's treasuries, and towards the external world as the sole intermediary.

Product companies: there has to be one for every business – a single factoring company, a single leasing company, a single consumer company, a single asset management company. And that will enable us to reach results that are very close to a merger.

This the basis of the federal model. If you respect these principles, you can reach results very near to those of a merger in terms of costs and, in terms of revenue, added-value with respect to a merger.

What is the drawback?

The drawback is that it's very difficult to make it work! You need a lot of rigour or else you run the risk of wiping out your results in terms of income and costs.

Ours is working. When we started, we said it would take us three years to reach our goal. Nearly two years have passed and we've made good progress, we're ahead of schedule. And we will certainly be able to make it within our timetable. What's behind it? There's the experience of several integration projects. With Banco Ambrosiano Veneto, there were three or four. Then, three smaller banks. They are smaller projects, but you still learn something from them. Then we did Cariplo-Ambrosiano. Then Cariparma, Friuladria. We've had the experience to enable us to be rigorous in creating our model and to manage it with effectiveness and efficiency. Now the Banca Intesa group has 48 subsidiaries if you include all its member banks and companies. The drawback is the difficulty, but we're not afraid.

What do you think about cross-border mergers, which are seen as the next big step in European banking consolidation? Banca Intesa already has several foreign shareholders, including Crédit Agricole and Commerzbank.

In Crédit Agricole, we have a strong shareholder and an ally with whom we are pushing ahead with common projects. Then we have other allies – Crédit Lyonnais, Banco Commericale Portoghese, BankAustria – with whom we are looking at common accords for services and products.

Here's how I see things. There's a trend towards increasing European integration and it will continue, but I don't think we'll see the creation of a European retail bank. I think the retail banks that have been successful at a regional level in the past will see that success amplified into a national level. The big retail players will be national players basing themselves on strong local market shares.

That's our model. Banca Intesa has very strong regional or inter-regional market shares. Banco Ambrosiano Veneto is a very strong inter-regional bank. Then we have some banks with a very strong local market share – Cassa di Ascoli, Cassa di Spoleto. They are small banks, but with a strong market share, and that's what we like. Retail will become a national business, but with a strong local focus. I don't think we would ever have success at a retail level if we went to Germany, France or Spain. Because there are already big German, French and Spanish players.

So why is there all this talk about cross-border mergers?

It depends on what you mean. There's been one in Scandinavia and that's it. I can understand share swaps that strengthen existing relationships. To establish even closer links, an Italian bank would take a stake in a foreign bank and vice versa. I can imagine a company with a European governance that would oversee asset management, that would combine know-how in areas like research and products. It would specialize in the product and each partner would sell the products at home with its own brand.

“I ask myself, if car companies like Fiat and Toyota have the same pistons, why can't we use the same underlying technologies?”

This is something I can imagine and I hope it will happen because it will create economies of scale and an improvement in overall quality. But I imagine it would have to take the form of a consortium. I can't imagine a cross-border merger being controlled by an entity in one country. I can imagine, however, a consortium in which everyone is convinced that, by pooling their resources, they will have better products.

In a joint venture, you mean?

In Italy, there is such a thing – it's a consortium. I think you can set up a European consortium for asset management, technology, brokerage for stocks and bonds. Here I can see enormous possibilities for recouping costs as well as improving quality of services.

I ask myself, if car companies like Fiat and Toyota have the same pistons, why can't we use the same underlying technologies? Once the basic international standards are defined, after that . . .

To do this, would you need a cross-shareholding internationally?

An international cross-shareholding is useful because it means that, once you do a share swap, both partners are committed on a certain project, but it's not necessary. I don't think, as things stand today, that cross-border mergers are possible. Perhaps in the future.

Why not? Because national indentities are still too strong. We have created a united Europe, but the single countries in Europe are much stronger than the individual states are in the United States of America. European nations have hundreds, and thousands, of years of history. Plus, today in Europe, there is no unified body of law, so, on the legal level, there are still too many differences. But even the structures of legal systems are different – we Italians know we have too many laws, and other countries have a lot less, and that creates structural problems right there. That's without taking into account the fact that legal systems are based on different philosophies.

Another element is the tax system. I can understand how a single tax system can have several different tax rates – that's possible – but I still can't imagine doing a cross-border merger taking into account different tax systems.

So it seems to me premature to talk about cross-border mergers. A few will happen, but there will be big problems afterwards in managing that merger. I think it would be much more efficient to adopt an approach that creates consortiums for managing cost centres – products and services – to distribute in each country.

What role do national authorities have in regulation?

As long as Europe doesn't have a single, unified tax platform, the national authorities will have a lot to say. As long as a single country – I'm not just talking about Italy, but also France and Germany – is operating without a supra-national regulatory framework, I don't see why countries shouldn't maintain their basic prerogatives. So governments, out of necessity, must remain strong at the national level. And their monetary authorities must remain strong. It's a contradiction. The path towards a united Europe in terms of economy, law and taxes is unstoppable, but it will take time.

“The path towards a united Europe in terms of economy, law and taxes is unstoppable, but it will take time.”

Are there physiological limits to consolidation, in terms of antitrust rules?

Yes, the limit of consolidation is essentially an antitrust question. It's a European and a national problem. It's still not clear, in my view, the jump from the national to the European level. We can have a significant market share in our domestic country, but not on a European level, and this relationship hasn't been clarified yet. We have a factoring company that has an important market share in Italy, but 5 per cent in Europe. But, to answer your question, the limits are the ones imposed by antitrust authorities.

Having all of one's financial needs served by one organization seems to be the strategic goal of certain financial institutions, but, from the client's point of view, what are the perceived drawbacks and benefits of this arrangement? From the bank's point of view, does cross-selling work?

I think cross-selling works, and I think it could work even better. I think we still use cross-selling relatively little in the bank, which means that I believe there are a lot of opportunities from cross-selling.

From the client's point of view, I think today's client has a lot more options than they used to have at a lower price. That's the result of competition. And this forces banks to be more efficient, to offer better products that cost less or else you risk getting pushed out of the market.

What role does technology play?

I am absolutely convinced that technology must be incorporated into the organizational structure in order to cut costs and improve efficiency. It must be incorporated into distribution systems and in products. If you don't do it, you fall behind.

So, can the consolidation trend also be limited by technology, because a bank could be huge, but, if it's behind technologically speaking, it has a weakness . . .

Technology is a critical factor of success or failure. I believe that technology must be incorporated into banking practice, and technology use can be projected outwards on a European scale. I don't see why technological platforms, IT solutions and telecommunications systems can't be shared by banking groups from different countries.

It's complicated . . . your systems have to be able to talk to Crédit Agricole's . . .

Yes, and to BCP, Commerzbank, BankAustria and other banks. It's a complicated problem, also because of a certain reluctance to face these questions.

DR HENNING SCHULTE-NOELLE

Chief Executive, Allianz

INTERVIEW BY TOMASZ JANOWSKI

While substantial inflows into the asset management industry are expected to continue over the foreseeable future, the baby boom generation will, at some point, turn from savers into dissavers. How will this affect competition in the asset management industry?

Although, demographically, the baby boom generation's ageing will ultimately have important impacts on asset allocation shifts and dissavings, the impacts are some time away and imprecise. When they do arrive, in roughly 20 years, the impact could be muted by a rise in the retirement age or general wealth increases that could ameliorate outright asset sales to fund lifestyle maintenance. Over the next ten years, projections indicate that privately managed assets in Europe will witness growth of between 15 and 20 per cent per year. Four important trends will provide engines for growth: a steady increase in private wealth, the inheritance of substantial sums by the younger generations, a shift towards professional management of private assets and fully funded old-age provision. And Germany has to catch up when it comes to asset management: the average per capita amount in an investment fund is around 5,000 marks in Germany. By way of comparision, an average individual in Holland invests almost 10,000 marks and in France, the figure is almost 18,000 marks. The top benchmark is the US, with more than 36,000 marks. Especially Europe, but also Asia and Latin America, are growth markets for the asset management industry. In these markets, the competition for customers has just started, whereas the US asset management industry, and US mutual funds in particular, have to cope with the truly enormous current size of the industry and the large fund penetration in the US population. Most people with assets are already mutual fund shareholders. Intensified market share competition among fund families will fuel further brand awareness efforts and promotional activity. Marketing expenditure will be necessary to maintain current client bases.

Europe is widely expected to see an explosion in the asset management industry. What factors might constrain the pace of growth? Regulation? Traditional saving habits? High cost of labour?

Europe has witnessed enormous growth in the asset management industry during the 1990s and this trend will be amplified, particularly during the first decade of the new millennium. The European markets, due to their diversity, will face certain challenges that will shape their development and differentiate the landscape of European asset management. Europe is not a level playing field, but, rather, a multicultural and multiregulatory environment with varying levels of sophistication, already visible in the various domestic asset management industries.

> “Meeting the mobility challenge means that the solutions must permit both companies and employees to ignore national boundaries. As companies become European and global players, providers will need to offer solutions and services that can follow both the firm and the individual.”

In the future, complexity will remain a core issue for Europe. The growing pension gap will challenge the first pillar system and increase the demand for new solutions from the second and third pillars. A vision no longer based on domestic view, but on a greater European perspective is to develop. The solutions proposed will need to address not only the well-worn worries of funding the existing PAYG liabilities, providing alternatives for defined benefit company pension systems and supplemental individual retirement planning needs, but will also need to address the more urgent issue of labour mobility. Today, our workforce in Europe is far more mobile than ever before. In addition, cross-border mergers increase the likelihood that the country in which we are born will no longer be the country in which we retire. Meeting the mobility challenge means that the solutions must permit both companies and employees to ignore national boundaries. As companies become European and global players, providers will need to offer solutions and services that can follow both the firm and the individual abroad. And as individuals become ever more mobile, new demands will be made on the existing State PAYG systems, as the national barriers are crossed more and more frequently.

What challenges will we face as we carve out the new European landscape? The most obvious are the regulatory and tax differences among the various countries, which remain the primary market differentiators. Regulatory differences have resulted in differing plans for second and third pillar solutions between the various markets. In the case of the two largest Continental European markets – Germany and France – no plan for pension reform has yet been decided upon. Taxation on retirement planning and investments is yet another challenge, and is far from harmonization. Europe will remain a complex region; however, the greatest challenge is to develop a platform which will permit us to efficiently manage this diversity. Today, the differences between markets remain significant. Over the past decades, however, we have seen the differences in the European financial markets diminish. This is perhaps best exemplified by the single European currency. We expect the trend in the European retirement and investment market to move toward parallel products and solutions with fewer significant differences.

While one can easily say that regulatory, tax and cultural issues are challenges for our industry in Europe, they only really define the more significant challenge, which is to develop the experience and capacity to build a flexible and efficient business platform that can meet the diverse demands of a rapidly evolving and globalizing investment business.

Is consolidation in asset management the most likely scenario or is there considerable scope for the growth of smaller funds? How important will it be for asset management firms to secure large distribution networks?

Consolidation is being driven by three key factors: the need to provide competitive pricing, which is clearly a function of investment size; the growing sophistication of investors, both on the institutional as well as on the retail side; and, hence, the increasing demand for more international investments and the need to accompany clients into whatever markets they go.

As a result of globalization, investment firms must be able to provide clients with more international products in their domestic market and, now, increasingly, must also be able to provide these products on a cross-border basis. This does not mean that small boutique firms will disappear, however, the trend is moving towards smaller niche product firms – as demonstrated by the proliferation of small independent hedge funds in the 1990s.

The middle market or purely domestic players will increasingly face problems in remaining on the cutting edge in this rapidly changing industry. Mid-market firms will have difficulty maintaining the level of systems investments that are an important part of providing products and services to an increasingly demanding client base.

On the investment side, building a robust investment factory requires attracting and retaining top investment professionals. For a pure investment company, such as Allianz Asset Management, the development of a proprietary buy side research team is a substantial investment, as is retaining top investment professionals. Furthermore, as the need to provide global products increases, firms which cannot point to the capacity to manage across all markets will find it difficult to retain sophisticated clients. On the institutional side, global investment capacity for large multinational clients with various asset and liability requirements is essential. Developing added-value products and services is, more and more, capital-intensive business, which argues strongly for size and diversity of market reach in order to best leverage these investments.

Large banks in Europe currently control the distribution network that asset management companies are seen needing to prosper. What does this imply for new entrants, particularly US firms wanting to tap the market?

US firms will likely have to partner with European banks and insurance companies and vice versa. In the global asset management business, it will be necessary to have access to a minimum level of distribution in any geographic region. Efficient transfer of know-how, sharing of distribution networks as well as equity linkages are basic parameters for success in this financial sector. The business is highly dependent on economies of scale, integration and bundling effects. Take Allianz as an example. By combining the expertise and salesforces of PIMCO and Allianz, our two companies are now one of the top international providers in global asset management. PIMCO, with its strong position in the US market, gives Allianz an entrée into the largest capital market in the world. Through Allianz, PIMCO gains access to the increasingly important European market. Together, both companies will become actively engaged in the Asia-Pacific market. Our clients will mostly benefit from the transaction: PIMCO will be able to supplement its product range in the US with attractive euro-products of Allianz. Allianz is in a position to offer one of the world's most successful investment strategies and fund products to institutional and retail clients.

How will the demand for such assets affect traditional insurance providers?

The trend will be the same as in the investment banking sector. A handful of very large asset managers will dominate the business, among them insurance companies. There are still more than 4,000 insurance companies and the fierce competition will force many of them to merge or disappear. Potential competition may be lessened by careful building of strong investment performance franchises, coupled with excellent multiplatform distribution channels. A couple of years from now, the markets will be less determined by geographic differences and more by customer attitudes. If we look at Europe, however, there is a nascent trend for a more open approach within traditional sales channels via specific products. In the near future, some clients will prefer basic financial insurance coverage and others will ask for full problem-solving services. Some will want to buy their insurance from the Internet or through the telephone and others will want to talk about it with a financial expert either working for one company or acting as a broker. Some will prefer 'one-stop shopping', the others will build their own menu of financial services providers. There is, however, a critical sales volume that an asset manager must have before it can concentrate on exploring these new trends. Asset managers have to maximize their comparative advantages. Therefore, they have to define their core businesses and to answer the question, 'Which financial product range will be the best?'

What are the lessons learned from the global crisis of 1997 and 1998? Have there been measures taken to tighten the monitoring of activities of firms such as LTCM and their relationship with banks?

While LTCM caused losses to their investors, other hedge funds and alternative investment funds provided significant positive returns. A lesson of 1997 and 1998 is that, while volatility can be high in any single investment or during any short time period, investors with a longer time horizon and a diversified investment portfolio will reduce volatility in their results and attain attractive, risk-adjusted returns.

“Asset managers have to maximize their comparative advantages. Therefore, they have to define their core businesses and to answer the question, 'Which financial product range will be the best?'”

Allianz is continuously making improvements to strengthen the company's risk-management procedures. We believe that good risk management requires good controls at a local as well as a global level. Good risk-management requires qualitative as well as quantitative know-how. Allianz monitors its global exposures on both the asset and liability sides of the balance sheet.

Are risk-management techniques too heavily dependent on quantitative models and therefore lacking in qualitative human judgement?

Risk-management techniques should give an overview of the current risky exposure of a firm and estimate the expected performance of this exposure in the near future as well as in the long term. This represents an enormous task since a typical financial services company faces various kinds of risk, like interest rate, liquidity, market or credit risks. All of those must be monitored not only independently, but also on an aggregated level. For several years now, the most common risk management tools have been in use. Firms have acquired a great capacity of experience. However, one has to be aware that the models only create a rather simplified picture of a world which can drastically change in the course of extreme events like market crashes or political crises. These events demand specific consideration in, e.g. stress tests. Finally, the models have to be improved in pace with our ever-changing world, doing so ahead of time rather than repairing damage too late.

How can risk be adequately measured in institutions engaged in a multitude of diverse financial activities? Should risk management become more centralized within an organization? Should it become an integral part of strategy?

Risk management within a wide range of financial activities has to deal with two contradictory objectives. On one hand, there is the need for risk measurement of all different financial activities; on the other hand, there is the need for an integration of these different risk sources. One solution could be that risk controlling and risk management become an integral part of the organizational strategy. In order to define a risk strategy which is able to cope with all types of risk covered by the organization, different risk categories have to be incorporated into one decisive risk model. This model, in addition to human judgement, has to detect interactions and, by means of scenario analysis, accumulation of risk. This could be the task of a centralized unit which not only recieves information about predefined key risk factors from each decentralized operating unit, but also delivers a strategic risk framework to each unit. An appropriate interaction between a centralized strategy-oriented risk unit and their operating partners at local risk-management units is strongly dependent on a common culture of integral risk management.

Do regulators have adequate means to measure risk in financial insitutions? Is there the need for a global body that monitors risk?

Indeed, we have seen a tremendous development taking place in our industry. Institutions are not only expanding geographically across borders and continents, but also across formerly rather separated business segments. In the Allianz group we are well aware that the consistent scrutiny and transparency of our cumulative risk profile is hindered both by the fact that our expansion has reached a global scale, and that our clients and business partners take on activities in many different areas.

Nevertheless, there is a common understanding that a simplistic unified regulatory regime across all financial business activities makes little sense. Risks originating from different kinds of services, like insurance, asset management or banking, should be measured and controlled, each by its appropriate means and methods.

Any global corporation is confronted with a variety of local laws, limitations and regulations, which reflect local opinions of how institutions and customers should be protected. Contrary to any globalization of monitoring authorities, we rather welcome any acceleration of the trend to convergence in the multitude of methods and standards applied internationally in separate business segments of our industry. In this respect we see not only a competition between the global players in our industry, but also between developing global regulatory standards as, e.g. the rating agencies, the Basle Committee or the US Securities and Exchange Commission.

> **“A simplistic unified regulatory regime across all financial business activities makes little sense. Risks originating from different kinds of services should be measured and controlled, each by its appropriate means and methods.”**

How will insurance firms cope with rising levels of risk? Securitization, etcetera?

Financial and insurance risk changes with market cycles, changes in regulation and product innovation. As risk rises or falls from market to market and product area to product area, risk-management monitoring tools and guidelines must change. Securitization is a good example. On the one hand, it shifts risk from the issuer of the security to the buyer of the security. Investment in securitized issues allow financial institutions to attain higher returns than investing in risk-free securities. On the other hand, securitization also allows for the transfer of risk to other market participants. In 1998, Allianz issued a $150 million catastrophe bond option that provided coverage for wind, storm and hail risks, written by the company's German subsidiaries.

Is the assumption of greater risk by individuals in managing their futures a positive or negative development for the health of the global financial system?

Rapid changes are transforming the financial services industry. Historically, retail and institutional customers left equity investing to banks and insurance companies. Today, individuals rely less on social retirement systems and invest in equity through direct investments or mutual funds. Financial institutions, accepting the trend towards disintermediation, have discovered financial market instruments that provide access to capital to increase profitability and manage risk. This trend presents great opportunities for the global financial system as it leads to growth and reduced volatility. The financial industry also profits, especially in the sectors of life insurance and asset management.

KATSUYUKI SUGITA

President and Chief Executive Officer, Dai-Ichi Kangyo Bank Limited (from October 2000, President and co-CEO of Mizuho Holdings)

INTERVIEW BY KUNIO INOUE

Are there limits to the trend towards consolidation?

No, not for some time. The trend will continue for at least the next ten years, and the pace will likely accelerate for the next five years.

The investment in information technology will become increasingly larger and the need to offer a wider range of financial services will get stronger. Against this backdrop, mergers and acquisitions, initiated primarily by major banks, will continue for some time, but it is not desirable for companies to become too big because they would be more difficult to manage.

Could technology lead to more efficient ways of servicing the financial needs of customers and thereby reduce the scope for mammoth organizations?

No. Mammoth banks are moving to expand into new business areas where new technologies, such as the Internet, help reduce transaction costs and increase efficiency greatly. But, at the same time, mammoth banks will also continue to conduct traditional business in which economies of scale offer an advantage.

Having all of one's financial needs served by one organization seems to be the strategic goal of certain financial institutions. From a customer standpoint, what are the perceived benefits and drawbacks of such an arrangement?

“The more cross-border mergers occur, the more companies go multinational, and this would require regulators of different nations to cooperate and work out unified rules.”

This is not an issue of merits and demerits. The point is what kinds of services individual customers would want. Average customers would normally prefer the ‘one-stop shop’ concept, because it is convenient in most cases, but certain customers, such as those who are very wealthy, would prefer more specialized financial services to meet their specific needs.

Are there competition issues that might arise from further consolidation?

Not necessarily. While further consolidation would create mammoth banks, there also exist banks and financial institutions that do business in certain geographical areas and specialize in specific financial services. Also, financial markets as a whole will likely expand as a result of further deregulation. Against this backdrop, chances are slim that mammoth banks would be able to dominate over the whole market.

From a regulatory perspective, what are the systemic risk implications of larger international institutions?

Systemic risk is irrelevant to whether institutions are large or small. It concerns the financial system. But as more cross-border mergers emerge, closer cooperation among authorities of different countries will be needed.

How rapid is consolidation likely to be in Europe, given the euro’s introduction?

Since the euro’s introduction, the integration of money and capital markets has proceeded rather smoothly, but, given that there still exist differences in tax systems and regulations, it may take more time before financial institutions can operate freely within the euro zone.

What are the obstacles to European cross-border mergers?

To some extent, differences in culture and languages.

How important is the role of national authorities and central banks?

There are two roles that are expected of authorities and central banks. The first is the role as supervisor, i.e. to help prevent any move that could limit fair competition in the financial business. The second role is to help promote various activities in the financial industry. The more cross-border mergers occur, the more companies go multinational, and this would require regulators of different nations to cooperate and work out unified rules.

JACOB WALLENBERG

Chairman SEB

INTERVIEW BY BARBARA TALTAVULL

What will the future business model of the traditional financial service provider look like in five years?

New technology forces traditional banks to rethink the roles they currently play. As a universal bank, you are playing all roles in the financial services delivery chain. Technology helps to determine if you should be a product specialist (key success factors = scale, a low-cost and fast product development) or a world-class distributor (key success factor = full set of products). Furthermore, should you be an independent adviser or an intelligent customer base (key success factors = full understanding of customers needs, use of customer purchasing power, and individualized packaging of products/services).

Getting closer to the customer will create most of the value-added. Hence, the business model will not be based on interest margins, but, rather, on value-added services related to the roles of the distributor or customer database.

What are the sources of competitive advantage for banks and brokerage firms in an environment of rapid technological change? How does such change impact the traditional intermediary role played by banks?

Execution, execution and execution are the sources of competitive advantage. The firm that can drive and adjust to change the fastest has the leading edge. Change forces banks to rethink their current roles. However, banks do have significant advantages in the financial service arena compared to other players in terms of credibility, trust and the ability to understand and price risk. Yet, new intermediaries will emerge, focusing specifically on individual pieces of the existing value chain and create new value chains. An example of a new value chain in financial services could be the demand aggregation model in the mortgage industry where a new player goes out on the Internet and aggregates enough demand for mortgages to push prices down.

Who are the new intermediaries? Can one envisage a future where intermediaries are no longer necessary because of technological advances?

Intermediaries will come from all industries – retail, media, heavy industry – as well as brand-new Internet players trying to capture a share of the consumer surplus which exists in financial services. You could certainly envision a future where technology is the intermediary. We are already seeing examples of that today where we see Internet banking customers handle 100 per cent of their financial services needs over the Internet. And, as technology develops, more people will move on-line. However, one should not underestimate the value of the 'human touch', which is unlikely to be replicated technically in the foreseeable future. Hence, there is a role for the human intermediary and most likely within the area of 'qualifying/assuring' advice.

What is the future role of information in global banks with large distribution networks and electronic transaction systems? Could proprietary information on transaction flows be used to generate information products?

Information plays a very important role in the new business model. More specifically, customer information – individual as well as corporate – is extremely valuable. This information would probably be used to improve the services to each customer, but not necessarily become an information product. However, customer information could be bundled and turned into a sellable information product to other players interested in getting access to the specific customer base. The higher the quality of information, the higher the purchasing power of the customer base.

On-line consumer banking – what is its future in the US, Europe and Asia? Are there cultural, regulatory and legal obstacles to the proliferation of such services?

Internet penetration – or new technology penetration – primarily drives the future of Internet banking. As the Internet becomes more commonplace, so does transparency in terms of comparing different services. Culturally, the customer segments are quite homogeneous in terms of the 'innovators', 'early adopters' and 'early majority' in each country. Hence, the customer demand is out there, but it is in different phases depending on the country/continent.

Regulatory and legal obstacles to the proliferation of Internet banking still prevail. However, the pressure will increase to abolish these obstacles – above all because of the transparency that the Internet provides. However, a new legal/regulatory framework will need to be put in place once you have players that have one Internet banking solution, with one offering, serving customers in any country in the world. Technically and culturally, this is doable today.

While substantial inflows into the asset management industry are expected to continue over the foreseeable future, the baby boom generation will, at some point, turn from savers into dissavers. How will this affect competition in the asset management industry?

The level of general underfunding on a global basis means that the conversion to dissavers will be regional and the overall growth of funding in general will continue. The baby boomers will certainly start turning savings into consumer spending, but this only affects areas where funding is already at high levels. Therefore, it will probably have a limited impact on economies, such as the US and UK, at certain times, but funding levels will still need to be maintained for the younger workforce. It will also be a factor of the ongoing age of the workforce. For example, Italy's workforce age will be stable for the medium term as the volume of young workers coming into the workforce maintains the balance of workers to pensioners. Therefore, competition will continue along the same lines of superior products/returns, availability of distribution channels, etcetera.

“A new legal/regulatory framework will need to be put in place once you have players that have one Internet banking solution, with one offering, serving customers in any country in the world.”

Europe is widely expected to see an explosion in the asset management industry. What factors might constrain the pace of growth? Regulation? Traditional saving habits? High cost of labour?

High costs of labour should not be a factor – labour costs, in comparison to potential earned income levels and volumes of scale benefits for assets under management, are minor and it is more the factor of distribution networks that will incur high costs. These distribution costs are borne by the asset managers and, therefore, should not halt the explosion in funding levels in the asset management industry.

Regulations and legislation are being amended widely throughout the EU in order to widen the scope for investment opportunities – for example, hedge funds and their related trading techniques used to be much more restricted, with regard to what institutions could do and which investors could invest – and current legislation is freeing up the investment tools that can be used and will help, rather than hinder, growth. All governments are looking to pass the onus of pension provision from State to the private individual and are therefore passing regulations and laws to ensure that passage.

The only potential constraint for growth could be if, on a national basis, union power and influence causes certain countries to slow down their changes from a defined benefit system, funded by the government, to a defined contribution basis, in which individual employees become responsible for a growing proportion of their pension management. Italian unions, for example, have opposed cuts to government pension payments, as have French unions, but this has not halted the move towards personal responsibility.

Italy and Spain, together with Germany, are switching from the historical defined benefit systems to defined contribution and this move is progressing smoothly to date. In addition, governments need to reduce their spending on social security systems in order to manage their GDP ratios for continuing membership of the euro. Unions will therefore face stiff opposition from the government to any backtracking that they, the unions, may require.

Traditional savings habits have often centred on government bonds and short-term money market investments. However, there is a continuing growth in equity investments in the regions experiencing significant growth in asset management, which is changing the nature of overall investment patterns, whilst also helping to fund economic growth through investment in industry and the stock exchanges.

Is consolidation in asset management the most likely scenario or is there considerable scope for the growth of smaller funds? How important will it be for asset management firms to secure large distribution networks?

> “The principal drive for all funds will be the availability of distribution routes. The major asset management companies will be those that are able to construct successful distribution platforms and a number of different drives are presently taking place.”

Yes to all. On the large, industry-wide scale, consolidation will be essential for economies of scale, and this will lead to consolidation of groups of major asset management companies, but, on the other hand, the demand for variety of funds is so great and individual traders will operate niche products or funds on a smaller scale [US$ 25–500 million under management] which will ensure that smaller specialist funds can continue to thrive. Thirdly, pooling of resources, in the form of funds of funds, will allow tailoring of risk or product profiles and will allow small companies to band together in groups, cooperatives. Funds of funds allow investors and fund managers to diversify their investment in a single fund – the fund of funds – by the fund manager investing this capital in a wide variety of funds [the individual traders referred to above], with different trading strategies and risk profiles. The idea is that the diversification of risk and trading strategies irons out the highs and lows and provides the investor with an overall balanced portfolio risk. So, it will be horses for courses.

The principal drive for all funds will be the availability of distribution routes. The major asset management companies will be those that are able to construct successful distribution platforms and a number of different drives are presently taking place. Depending on the development of the various asset management services in different countries, different distribution routes are operating. In Spain and Italy, for example, the majority of distribution is arranged through the national major banking systems and these operate a near monopoly. Access to these distribution routes is jealously guarded from newcomers, but the major international players are pushing to get into the high growth investment markets prevalent in much of Europe. In the US and UK, by contrast, a wide range of distribution routes, which is also a factor of the maturity of the markets, is available. Japan is experiencing deregulation of the financial industry and therefore is both developing a very restricted personal investment market – over 60 per cent of investments are in bank deposits earning practically 0 per cent – as well as the securities house – previously the only entities that could distribute investment opportunities – opening up to outsiders through agreements or joint ventures.

Large banks in Europe currently control the distribution network that asset management companies are seen needing to prosper. What does this imply for new entrants, particularly US firms wanting to tap the market?

See above. Also, the major US asset management houses have been making marketing pushes into the European markets for several years, sometimes directly, at other times through acquisition of local companies or via joint ventures. It is, or can be, a slow process and overall success can be elusive.

How will the demand for such assets affect traditional insurance providers?

The insurance companies in the past have not really provided the same kinds of products. Endowment policies – products that look to provide an investment structure to an insurance product – probably bear the greatest resemblance to asset management products and will continue to be offered by insurance companies as one form of asset management product. Insurance companies will be in the forefront – as has been SEB/Trygg Hansa's case – of forming alliances or mergers with banks and/or asset management companies in order to strengthen their product base, gain size for economies of scale and link distribution routes to asset management products. Therefore, it should been seen in a positive light rather than a negative light.

ERNST WELTEKE

President, Bundesbank

INTERVIEW BY HANNFRIED VON HINDENBURG

Real life has delivered an opening for our conversation that could barely have been more apt. At the start of March, Deutsche Bank and Dresdner Bank announced a merger that will create the world's biggest bank in terms of assets. The merger failed, but clearly the pace of consolidation in the banking sector has accelerated. Will mergers of the size anticipated by the planned tie-up create the sort of global banking giant that could threaten the world's financial system? Has the pace of consolidation in the banking sector reached the point where we now have banks that are too big to fail?

It is clear that the question of 'too big to fail' would have reached a new dimension with the merger of Deutsche and Dresdner Banks to form the world's largest institution. But one must also add that, from the point of view of the supervisory authorities, there is generally *no* institution that is too big to go bankrupt. The responsibility must lie with the management of the individual institution.

The Bundesbank has often warned that the creation of banks that are too big to fail could yield major dangers. Is the Bundesbank warning against mega-mergers?

No, you cannot say that. Our warnings to do with the abolition of the individual national currencies, which takes away the need for fragmented money and capital markets. We now have a single money and capital market and that fosters a tendency to create larger institutions as well.

And if, on the other hand, we consider the trends towards more investment banking and securitization that are emanating from the English-speaking countries, it has to be said that those institutions, which in the past benefited from interest rate margins, are today faced with enormous competitive pressures. They need a very different customer profile to offset the enormous costs required for information technology.

You already referred to the impact of the euro. Looking further into the future – what changes do you believe the euro will bring for the banking sector? Will we see the same kind of consolidation in Europe as in the United States?

One cannot say for sure. But the would-be merger of Dresdner and Deutsche Bank represents to an extent a departure from our highly praised universal banking system. The two banks planned to spin off their retail business and either list it on the bourse with Deutsche Bank 24 or transfer it to Allianz. This last would give rise to an insurance company, which would then have an extensive network of bank branches – a totally new form of institution. Even though this did not happen in the end, it is clear that the trend towards such institutions is still in place and may materialize eventually.

How should the financial market regulators deal with this? Do we need a reorientation?

The supervisory authorities need to be coordinated at the European level. We need a level playing field. We need single standards. It is certainly also important that, in view of the continuing breakdown of the divisions between securities operations, insurance and traditional bank business, the supervisory authorities for these activities must cooperate closely with one another. They may even have to be integrated in the long run.

Could you elaborate on that? What would such an integration look like? Would it have to be at the European level?

That might ultimately be the case, but it is not necessary from today's perspective. Today, the main issues are cooperation and the creation of joint, single standards which are applicable everywhere. Backing a Europe-wide merger of banking, insurance and securities supervisory authorities would mean creating a huge bureaucracy, which, in my view, would not be any better equipped to do the job than is the case today.

Would it be regulatory overkill?

Yes, from today's point of view. And no one seriously wants that. We observe two trends at the moment. The first is the trend to take regulatory issues out of the central banks' hands. That is the British model – the Financial Services Authority, with its Chairman Howard Davies, who is also a proponent of this model.

We, as central bankers, on the other hand, argue that we need the information that flows in as a result of our market activities and our supervisory activities in order to fulfil our monetary policy role. We, as central bankers, would find it difficult to guarantee financial stability if we were cut off from the supervisory role.

In Germany, this means for me that we initially need something along the lines of a joint forum for the three supervisory authorities – Bundesbank, Bundesaufsichtsamt für das Kreditwesen, Bundesaufsichtsamt für den Wertpapierhandel. In the longer term we may discuss the alternative of bringing these three authorities under the roof of the Deutsche Bundesbank.

You are referring to the current dispute between the German finance ministry and the Bundesbank and your opposition to German Finance Minister Hans Eichel's plans to take debt management and banking supervision out of the sphere of the Bundesbank and transfer them to other authorities. Why do you believe that the Bundesbank is in such a good position to perform this supervisory role?

Our exchange with the Finance Minister is by no means a dispute, but a useful discussion and exchange of views. As for your question, the central banks are in a good position to take on the supervisory role as they command tremendous respect in almost all countries. In the Federal Republic, the public holds both the Bundesbank and the Constitutional Court in the highest esteem. I believe we should make use of the public's respect for and trust in the Bundesbank as an institution to ensure that monetary and financial stability are guaranteed. The public has already placed its trust in the institution. There is no need to set up a new agency or establish a new authority, which would have to begin by winning this trust.

The Bundesbank is represented in all of Germany's regions. We have the staff and the capabilities. This is what makes me think we are well suited to fulfil all duties within the financial arena and will continue to be so.

But the problem for the central banks surely is that they, in principle, are charged with the task of dealing with systemic crises through bailing out institutions which become illiquid or insolvent. Yet, on the other hand, they are prevented from stating this publicly for fear that the institutions would rest on their laurels in the knowledge that there is a safety net. The catchword is 'moral hazard'. Is this a particular problem faced by central banks that other institutions do not face?

The fact that a crisis involving systemic risk demands a response from the central banks is precisely the reason why we need to be involved in the supervisory process. We look at it all the other way around. Direct supervision means that the central banks have important information at their disposal for crisis prevention and solution.

May I ask again, independently of the question of who takes on the supervisory role: Is the fact that there is no express admission that 'We will bail you out if you run into problems' a necessary constructive ambiguity? Or how can one handle this dilemma?

You said it yourself. We need to do all we can to avoid situations involving moral hazard and if one says openly that one considers certain institutions too big to fail, then those institutions could abandon sufficient risk control and may be tempted to engage in excessively risky business activities.

We have very good deposit guarantee schemes in Germany, set up by the banking associations. In addition, we have the Liquiditätskonsortialbank (Liko-Bank), which is financed by the banking industry, and the Bundesbank. We effectively have a system where, in the event of a failure, the banking system bears the brunt and not just the taxpayer.

I would like to come back to the Europe problem in this respect. The Bundesbank would like to see the German system, for example, the Liko-Bank, at the European level. How can one best deal with the diversity in Europe? There are various competing supervisory authorities within the European countries and between the countries. How is it possible to create Europe-wide supervision and regulation. Should it not lie with the European Central Bank?

“We look at it all the other way around. Direct supervision means that the central banks have important information at their disposal for crisis prevention and solution.”

That would mean that a gigantic supervisory apparatus would need to be installed at the ECB. We already have the Banking Supervisory Committee within the European system of central banks. All the European Union central banks –

in this instance it is not only the Euro-system central banks, those in monetary union, but all EU central banks – are represented in this Banking Supervisory Committee. This is a body which, if a European institution were to run into problems, could be convened within hours and could then decide what was to be done. Of course, certain formalities would need to be observed by the Banking Supervisory Committee and it would need to have a mandate from all governments and states to act as crisis manager if the situation arose.

I think that [such a mandate] would be a step in the right direction. That would leave the supervisory role directly at the national government level, but would also create a body that would be there to respond immediately if a cross-border problem were to arise, without needing to raise the whole system to a higher level than that of the national states.

> “Divisions between insurance and banking supervision and securities trading houses are blurring, which means that duplication of work should be avoided. Creating a joint committee could be a first step to pave the way for an intermeshing of supervisory activities in the longer term.”

I think that [raising the whole system to a supranational level] would make little sense, as there are relatively few institutions that have a risk exposure extending beyond national borders. The majority of German credit institutions, including the savings and cooperative banks, would not create problems beyond national borders. I therefore think there is no need for a new European-wide authority. The Banking Supervisory Committee should be given a mandate and otherwise supervision should be left at the national level.

The changes in the financial markets are creating totally new institutions, as you have already mentioned, which are grouping different task areas under a single roof. One example is the Allianz group, which is increasingly moving into banking. Do we need special supervision for such conglomerates?

I do not want to go into more detail on the question of whether it needs more specialist supervision or a link-up between the individual financial supervisory authorities. But I think we should take a first step by ensuring that these supervisory bodies at least coordinate with each other and define their areas of activity. The would-be merger between Dresdner Bank and Deutsche Bank, with its impact on Allianz and Munich Re, would have demonstrated that the divisions between insurance and banking supervision and securities trading houses are becoming blurred, which means that duplication of work should be avoided. Creating a joint committee could be a first step towards paving the way for an intermeshing of supervisory activities in the longer term.

If we turn to the banking sector itself. As you have already said, the number of cross-border institutions and mergers is still limited. We have seen one big Swiss merger and the German one failed. This is amazing given the context of globalization and the introduction of the euro. Why, in your view, does the sector continue to be essentially structured along national lines?

There are still considerable legal and cultural differences which have to be overcome. There are national reservations in the case of takeovers. I could well imagine that if it had not been Deutsche Bank buying Bankers' Trust but Bankers' Trust buying Deutsche Bank or Morgan Grenfell buying Deutsche Bank and not Deutsche Bank buying Morgan Grenfell, or if Dresdner had not bought Kleinwort Benson but the other way around, we would have had a major debate in Germany about the takeover of institutions which are seen as national. That is not only a problem in Germany, but it is the same, in France and Italy, just to mention these two. We saw the same thing in the consolidation of the French banking industry. And when Deutsche Telekom wanted to take a foothold in Italy, we saw the united efforts undertaken to prevent it.

It is noticeable that Anglo-Saxon countries and companies are more accepting of such takeovers from abroad . . .

I think there really are cultural differences. America and England clearly demonstrate a much higher degree of public openness with respect to international perspective than is the case on the Continent. In some areas, we may not have done enough yet to overcome our national state mindset.

Could the central banks do anything to make cross-border mergers easier? Could they help to change the culture?

The Bundesbank basically has no influence on this. We conduct monetary policy – that policy is neutral for competition. We do not promote it; neither do we obstruct it; I do not know in what way we could create a more favourable environment for cross-border mergers.

Perhaps with EU-wide takeover laws?

We are not involved in that. Laws are made in Berlin or Brussels. We take a position on them, but we are trying to use our influence within the ECB to remove the restrictions that continue to exist, which persist in the cross-border markets due to outmoded regulations, legal matters or tradition, so that we can establish a unified capital market. There are often conflicts of interest and competition problems playing into this, but we are doing what we can to get Europe-wide rules of play. When they are in place, that will naturally, in turn, favour Europe-wide cross-border mergers in the banking sector.

PETER WUFFLI

Chief Executive Officer, UBS Asset Management

INTERVIEW BY ALICE RATCLIFFE

What will happen when the demographics shift and the current baby boom generation starts to draw down savings for retirement?

There are two fundamental theories regarding this issue. One speculates that the selling of financial assets by the baby boomer generation, to fund their consumption, will be the most dominating economic force, thereby creating significant asset deflation. This is expected to begin about 2010. The other theory argues that such deflation will not occur for two main reasons. First, the savings propensity of this retiring generation is higher than that of the younger generations. There is a likelihood that they will not spend a great portion of the wealth they have accumulated or, at least, they will have a higher proportion of savings than the current active generation. Secondly, we see societies emerging with much more intense savings needs and with very different demographic profiles than the traditional baby boomers. Some examples are the Latin American countries, like Brazil, Mexico and Argentina, as well as India and China. Given these trends, proponents of this theory expect that the global capital markets will achieve equilibrium and that dramatic deflation in asset prices is unlikely.

Irrespective of these longer term considerations, our assumption for the next ten years is continued growth in global financial assets. Further, clients' needs and requirements will continue to become more differentiated, according to their specific liability profiles, and we expect to see much more proliferation of different client-specific asset/liability and asset allocation parameters. Additionally, we are attentive to the growing phenomenon of 'instividualization' and realize that future efforts will combine individual and institutional approaches.

All this makes for a significant and continued attractiveness of the asset management industries, because of the need for sophisticated problem-solving capabilities in portfolio management. At the same time, it makes the industry challenging; it raises entry barriers and makes it more challenging to be a winning partner.

Where is it becoming challenging?

Generally we see that institutions, rather than coming to us and saying, 'We want a mandate in global bonds' or 'US real estate', instead come to us asking for help of a more strategic sort. They come to us and say, 'We have a specific liability structure that needs a specific solution' – for example, a structure that is constant over the next few years or a liability structure which is characterized by closed funds with significant surplus. They want to see different strategic options for coping with less attractive market return opportunities over the next several years. Some want assistance with risk control scenarios or contingency planning, where basically they ask us to help set parameters or want advice for taking bets on certain market trends. So, they want solutions to relatively complex portfolio management problems which go far beyond just 'plain vanilla' money management.

The same holds true for financial intermediaries such as medium-sized banks and life insurance companies that have very specific requests for products which fit their clients' needs. This includes, for example, capital preservation portfolios where people are able to gain some upside return, but give part of the upside away for protection of the capital. It may also include structuring devices, educational training or marketing support. So, they seek answers and solutions to relatively complex needs of our clients. Obviously, they usually have to do with asset management, but they also often require several additional services.

“Generally institutions … come to us and say, 'We have a specific liability structure that needs a specific solution.' … So, they want solutions to relatively complex portfolio management problems which go far beyond just 'plain vanilla' money management.”

Are you expecting more industry-wide consolidation?

We see several forces that will favour continued consolidation. I would specifically emphasize three. One of them is certainly globalization – globalization of client needs on the one hand, and of assets and asset classes on the other. Big corporations are integrating more and more of the management of their pension plans across the world. They want global relationships, which obviously requires their partner to have a global presence. This by itself will require consolidation.

As we know, the industry has traditionally been local, not global. Therefore, if you look at investment managers' market shares in various markets, you do not find any player with leading market share in all of them. We come relatively close to it, with a significant share in the US with Brinson Partners, in the UK with Phillips & Drew and with a significant share in Switzerland, Australia and Japan, but the competition is still very much local. That will most likely change in the future.

Managing asset classes, particularly equities, also will require a much more global view. It is rather obvious that you should not compare Nestlé with UBS or Novartis. One should compare Novartis with Merck and Glaxo, and UBS with J. P. Morgan or Morgan Stanley or Goldman Sachs or Merrill Lynch. However, the backbone of a lot of investment decision making is still local in nature. We have local indices, local stock market infrastructure and many local analysts. The practical implications for firms are huge. It basically means that you need globally integrated teams, organized by sectors. Coordinating and managing these teams and processes is a great challenge and we have begun to expand our efforts to address this issue. I think we are among the first, but it will take several years until this is firmly in the minds of institutional investors.

The second reason I believe consolidation will continue is based on the breadth of resources needed to solve client problems of the sort that we have discussed. Breadth is needed in terms of portfolio consulting, education, marketing and the fund-structuring capabilities necessary within portfolio management. You also must be conversant in several asset classes and that means you need dedicated specialists. There is a certain minimum scale needed for these to be credible specialist competences.

That leads into the third factor, which is also tied to size and resources, and that is talent development. People with a lot of talent want to work with other talented people. You need to have that strength, a certain global scope and a certain level of breadth in order to attract, retain and motivate the most talented people.

So, I think there are forces that support size, scale and global reach. It is clear that this does not imply a need for large bureaucratically led rigid organizational structures. I think the challenge will be to capture the benefits of size, while at the same time staying alert, entrepreneurial, client-centric and global in thinking. That is the kind of model we are trying to follow: a management style which reinforces values of partnership, of collegiality and of teamwork.

I think we have a good basis with our various building blocks in the asset management business group, Brinson Partners, Phillips & Drew, O'Connor GAM and the mutual funds area. We already have those cultural values firmly in place. For example, we do not have a divisional headquarters. Yes, I am physically located in Chicago, but I am often on the road, splitting time between various local offices. Our business committee meets every three weeks by video and telephone, with people joining from Australia, London, Zurich and Chicago. We do not have big central divisional staffs. We basically draw upon the capabilities of our individual business areas, where everybody has an entrepreneurial mandate. Yes, size and scale are important, but it requires a very specific management style to retain the benefits and advantages of a small client-focused organization.

“I think there are forces that support size, scale and global reach. . . . I think the challenge will be to capture the benefits of size, while at the same time staying alert, entrepreneurial, client-centric and global in thinking.”

Can you see any future for small boutiques in the business?

Of course, I think there will always be boutiques. In the end, this is a people business, no question about it. I think there will always be boutiques which have either a specific concept, or which are built around very specific, charismatic personalities. What will be very difficult to maintain in the future is a position in the middle where you have a strong, heavy infrastructure in one market – geographically, for example, or in one asset class or specific capability – but where you may not have the breadth to address the various needs of a client's franchise, and I think this will be a relatively difficult thing for some firms to manage.

At the start of this conversation, we spoke of the size needed to do business. Do you see an ideal number of large players that the market can support?

> “I think in Europe we will see that the strong relationship-based traditional networks, operating on a national scale, will be eroded. We will see specialists operating globally, in a globally competitive environment, gaining market share.”

I think this industry is certainly behind compared to the degree of globalization that the investment banking industry has reached. The investment banking industry, over the past several years, has been dominated by a relatively small number of players active in literally every major market. I think this is not yet reality in the asset management industry, but I think we see some of these same trends developing.

Any idea of the large firms which could be left, say, five years from now?

We will aspire to be one of them. And I think that the answer to that question is very much tied to your question about industry consolidation.

How will the asset management landscape develop in Europe?

I think in Europe we will also see – as in the investment banking industry – that the strong relationship-based traditional networks, operating on a national scale, will be eroded. We will see specialists operating globally, in a globally competitive environment, gaining market share. This will result from clients demanding specialists with professional resources and the ability to harness the synergies of an integrated global platform. That will put purely national players at a structural disadvantage. I think the trend here is clear. The question is, how quickly will this process take place and that is a very difficult thing to forecast. It also depends on the legislative velocity of the various markets in Europe – allowing for things like defined contribution plans, for example, which obviously creates a push for a more competitive industry than one dominated by a defined benefit structure.

So, it depends on the velocity of this break-up of the traditional network-based national models, and how quickly they are replaced with models favouring global specialization and focus, but in the longer term we should expect a globally competitive setting with, perhaps, ten or so leading global players dominating the industry.

FRANK ZARB

Chairman and Chief Executive Officer,
National Association of Securities Dealers (NASD)

INTERVIEW BY CAL MANKOWSKI

My question is whether the people are depending too much on stock markets to go up and up as they've done for the last five years at extraordinary rates. According to the ICI/SIA, almost half of the people own stocks even directly or indirectly. Are people getting too dependent on the stock market?

It's a worrisome dynamic – it's positive and it's worrisome. It's positive in that what really is happening is Main Street has put on a merge with Wall Street and that has implications with respect to our society as well as the economy because the obvious question is, 'What kind of liquidity does this add to the system when all these people and their 401Ks and the retirement plans participate?' The question is, what does it do to the characteristic of the equities market in a society?

When I started in this business as a very young man in a back office as a clerk, it was a bunch of fat cats that sold stocks and bonds to other fat cats. That was it. That was the extent of the business. And you went to a good school and your daddy had money and became a partner in a firm and a partner was a customer's man. A customer's man was a guy who sold stocks and bonds to his father's rich friends.

Now, given the trend of our society, today that wouldn't exist; I mean, it would die. So, it's a really important change that's happened here in that average people can participate. That has a political implication because now when you argue political or legislative questions that relate to the stock market, you have to change your views. In the old days, when we debated capital gains in Washington, the guys against it said, 'You're only giving money to the rich guys' and the guys that were for it said, 'Well, you got to give money to this sector because they generate the jobs.' Now, the average family has to pay capital gains tax. That has a political implication. If you're a Congressman, you have to start to think about that before you open your mouth about where you come out on that question.

Having said all of that, it is a major issue with respect to education of the new investor – and they need to understand the risks of the marketplace. That's really all you can do. You certainly regulate the way we regulate, step up regulation and you add technology to regulation – market surveillance becomes a premium. These are fast-moving markets, you have to be able to watch them, and you do have to worry on a continuing basis about whether or not investors are being told of the risks that they undertake. And that I have to hold the industry responsible for. If you're in the securities business and you sell stocks and bonds to people, you have some responsibility to let them know that this kind of investment has this kind of risk. That's why, for day trading, we have pushed hard for the firms that specialize in day trading, that they're up-front in explaining to the customer what the risks are in day trading. Once the customer understands all of the risks, then that's got to happen. Yes, it is something that we always are concerned with and markets correct and, when they correct, people will have lesser value and if they've been taught properly and they've invested with quality, they'll sit and, in the long term, they'll be in great shape. It's a long way to answer a small question.

Part of the drive to higher prices has been the baby boomer generation saving for retirement through new types of plans. Will there be a problem when these boomers seek to withdraw money as they get into retirement?

I think you'll find, first of all, these retirement funds will stay employed. They'll probably be more sophisticated and stay employed in the marketplace because they're more sophisticated and their children will be coming along. That's another generation now being trained in the household that owns securities, which, when I grew up, my family never saw a stock, ever; I had no idea what it was like. I never saw a stock certificate until I went to work in the securities industry and didn't have the slightest idea how it worked. Today, young people have the benefit of their mother and father looking at the stock tables in the morning paper and looking up a company and talking about it – it is a different dynamic.

“It is a major issue with respect to education of the new investor – and they need to understand the risks of the marketplace. That's really all you can do.”

In another area, we've seen some legislation go through Washington changing the financial services industry, and consolidation of the firms has been proceeding. As these ever-larger financial service organizations are formed, how does this affect the venues that we have in the United States for trading stocks?

“ The antique look at a marketplace said, 'Anybody who wants to buy or sell that stock must come to this building while we're open. In our re-take, we have said that our companies should be able to take advantage of pools of liquidity elsewhere in the world when they're open and we are closed. ”

It changes everything. It changes the core of the business. It changes the structure of the business. It needs to be changed carefully because, as I said at the Senate hearing, I haven't seen one piece of analytics that says, 'Here's a model and the model shows that if we trade this way, with this kind of book, it will trade better, worse or what.' So, I think we have to be a little careful when we give the facts, but, having said that, change will happen.

The fundamental change that we have been in the front of, and I'm sure that people don't appreciate it, we're trying to change the role of the stock market. When we bought the American Stock Exchange, we said to the American Stock Exchange, 'You are not a small New York Stock Exchange. You are a very unique institution so take advantage of your strengths.' Now they have structured product and options and they're building new business with being different. Better product, lesser cost and they get some business. Now, having said that, we also reinvented, we as an institution, along with our issuers and our market-makers, the way we look at our role. The old antique look at a marketplace said, 'Come here to this building, bring us your listing, do your IPO, and we'll trade your stock here through a specialist or whatever other system. And anybody who wants to buy or sell that stock must come to this building while we're open, physically or electronically, to buy that stock. If they don't come to this building while we're open, they can't buy or sell that stock.' Now that's lousy for the issuer and not very good for the investor. In our re-take of it, we have said that our companies should be able to take advantage of pools of liquidity elsewhere in the world when they're open and we are closed and our investor should have a better opportunity to acquire stocks of other companies so that our pools of liquidity can enjoy this bigger range of products, which sounds very simple, but is a very major change. It says that when we finish Nasdaq Japan and it is up and running at the end of 2000, before the end of 2000, Microsoft and Intel will start trading in Tokyo at 9pm our time, New York time. It's an interesting kind of economic valuation because we're saying we're willing to give up part of our revenue because that Japanese investor is going to not have to come here – he can buy that stock in Japan when Japan is open. Obviously, you can only do that with the largest stocks that have enough liquidity. Our position has been, that's correct, we are going to give up some of that revenue. But, two things: we're going to own a piece of that Nasdaq Japan, so we get the revenue there. Secondly, there are going to be a lot more investors participating in Microsoft than we've ever had before because their pool of liquidity is so large, so, we'll increase the size of that pie and we'll come out ahead of where we started. So, the argument that we shouldn't allow that to happen because we're giving up revenues, that's bunk. That's a problem for a traditional stock exchange because they have people on the floor who bought a seat and have an equity stake, and they don't have a partnership in Tokyo where they can get part of the revenues or expand their revenues, so it becomes kind of a political problem for the older institutions, which I'm sure they'll overcome because they have to. That's a fundamental change in the way markets work and it's probably the most dramatic and fundamental change that we've seen in recent years and will have the most impact.

Presumably some of the big institutions here would find a reason to trade over there when the trading takes place there. Would the regulation be the same, as it would affect them when they're here?

For the most part, regulations are very similar. We have to comply with local regulations wherever we are, so that the administrative finance standard needs to be adhered to in Japan. Ours are probably the most rigid in the world, so if ours were adopted, that's fine. When their companies trade here, they have to comply with our standards.

For a long time, the United States has had two competing market systems – the auction market and the dealer system. Do you think we will continue to have two systems indefinitely?

I think there are going to be two systems, but the two are merging together. They're getting to be more and more similar, adopting similar aspects to each other. The larger capitalized companies, in my opinion, trade better in a multimarket-maker environment. Microsoft and Intel prove that they just do better when they have 30, 40 or 50 market-makers that make a market and compete for the order. There are, however, some block trading characteristics that seem to work better with an individual specialist. I think smaller cap stocks sometimes need the benefit of being adopted by an individual that will sponsor that company and worry about it and make sure that the liquidity is always there. It'll kind of sort itself out.

That almost changes things around quite a bit from what we had many years ago when the smaller companies were on the dealer market.

It changes completely around. The guy who first raised that publicly with me was Greg Maffei, who was then the CFO of Microsoft – he has now gone off to head some company in Nova Scotia. Greg Maffei, at a dinner party at Bill Gates' home, was asked a question by one of the companies that were there – I forgot who it was – and he had been looking at this question from an issuer standpoint. He said the way it should really work is the big caps should be on Nasdaq and the small caps should be on the stock exchange, which obviously I didn't argue with.

Now, a big change has been ECNs. Some people have been saying the ECNs have been making the Nasdaq look a little bit more like the stock exchange in some ways. What role will they play?

The ECNs are a part of our market. They're all members. They run their trade through our market, so it doesn't affect our market share. They allow a lot of things to take place that we didn't allow as traditional markets. The existing markets didn't anticipate the requirements for internalization and didn't jump ahead of the curve. The technology that we're introducing is now before the SEC. The ECN model will change somewhat, although they're still aggregators of orders and they're pools of liquidity. They do form a system for certain aspects of internalization when that benefits the investor. My own view is that if we do our job properly – and the New York Stock Exchange does it job properly – there will be a lesser role for new ECNs in the market. That doesn't mean we are going to put them out of business; they will be there in a different role.

As the systems change, what should be the proper regulatory model, in whatever direction it goes? Between the self-regulatory function and the SEC's role, what do you think will work best?

The balance works pretty well now. The SEC oversees the self-regulator; the self-regulator has the responsibility to really do the detailed everyday regulation, which we do. I guess NASD is the biggest regulator in the world. I think it works pretty well. I think we have to step up our investment in technology regulation because, as technology trading gets to be such a big business, we need to keep up with our technology overseeing. There is an argument that says that the New York Stock Exchange regulators and Nasdaq regulators should merge and you have one central self-regulator. If done properly, that could be a big asset to the industry because it eliminates one regulator and it allows things to happen more efficiently. Getting rid of one regulator is always a good idea in my opinion. It has to be done properly because if it becomes simply a proxy for the SEC or cat's paw for the SEC, then that doesn't work well, so it would have to be structured and governed like a real self-regulator.

When you refer to technology regulation, what would be an example?

Well, our audit trail mechanism that we installed in the last year or so – where we now, through electronics, can monitor an order wherever it is, virtually every second of its journey, so that, if anything goes wrong, we know exactly where it was and who did it – that's using technology to do that. We're more and more using technology when we go in to examine a member firm by being able to use software to look at their records rather than have to go through a lot of paper. The day-to-day market watch – being able to watch movements in companies and prices and have a kick-out of exceptions while they are happening so a guy can get on the phone and say, 'What's going on with your company?' – and things that we haven't even mentioned.

“It'll always be the 2 or 3 per cent that are overextended – you know, gone too crazy in terms of margins and what they have lent customers and, when the market breaks, their capital is insufficient. We try to watch those and catch them before they become a problem.”

To go into another area, we saw some market shocks in 1997 and 1998. Are you concerned that, as financial institutions get bigger and bigger, there could be a problem that has a systemic effect?

I think that's less and less of a problem – the industry getting so much bigger. The bigger firms are well-regulated, they're well-managed. Smaller firms, generally speaking, are run by businesspeople who live by their wits and they are smart guys and honest guys and we always have 2 or 3 per cent that we have to weed out. It'll always be the 2 or 3 per cent that are overextended – you know, gone too crazy in terms of margins and what they have lent customers and, when the market breaks, their capital is insufficient. We try to watch those and catch them before they become a problem. I don't see a major issue here.

“Nasdaq is a state of mind; it's a stock market with an attitude. It is made up of members who make markets and provide liquidity and take risks and understand the new economy.”

You wouldn't see a need for more regulation in that area?

I think Long-Term Capital has given everybody a cause to look and I think the conclusion was that people who lent Long-Term Capital money should have been asking a lot more questions. I think everybody learned their lesson. The system also absorbed the problem and called on others to participate. When we had a problem in the Sixties – we had a similar period to this period – it overwhelmed the industry with paper and we would have to close one half a day a week and one day a week as an industry to catch up to the paperwork. The industry accommodated the problem and, when you have a real market shock, usually you have enough cushion. When the Iraq war broke out, that was a market shock, but the system handled it.

Some people say the hedge funds report less and there should be more disclosure there.

I'm always in favour of disclosure in any case. I will always come out in favour of disclosure, but it is an area that needs to be looked at by the Federal regulators.

Nasdaq has become a brand in people's minds closely related to technology. How important is the Nasdaq brand and how has it been transformed in the last few years and what do you think the potential of it is?

The brand is very important and it rings around the world now. Somebody did a survey and found that Nasdaq was the best-known stock market in London. It's incredible. So the brand is very important. It's important to our international expansion. It's important here. It's important to also recognize that, while technology companies have been in the forefront of the new economy and they have been part of our marketplace, there are some great companies that are on Nasdaq that are not technology – Staples, Starbucks. Nasdaq is a state of mind; it's a stock market with an attitude. It is made up of members who make markets and provide liquidity and take risks and understand the new economy. It's made up of issuers – a typical profile of a Nasdaq issuer is that the leadership are people that push the edge of the envelope, who challenge the status quo. They move out from where they were and continue to push out from where they were. Staples has reinvented the way people buy office supplies; Starbucks is the inventor of the way people buy coffee. So that, if you look at Nasdaq – all the issuers I've met – the leadership, I think, are people who push the edge of the envelope. That means we have a lot in common – we and they. I have met the guy who is running Palm Pilot this morning. This guy is not going to be satisfied to stay still, and the Chairman of 3Com was there, who is also the parent. He's not going to be willing to stay still. He and I talked about some of the next innovations and where they're headed internationally and what we can do together internationally. Just remember that Nasdaq is a stock market with an attitude, and that tells the story.

The next question has to do with the big change that the industry faces for decimalization. How big a challenge is that and how does it compare with some of the things that we've had before?

It's a big challenge because it comes at a time when the industry has changed so dramatically. It is more than simply running tests, changing clocks, changing software, changing hardware. This comes at a time – our volume on the Nasdaq marketplace, a year and half ago, when we were first talking about decimals, we were running about 700–800 million shares a day trading, and we were planning peaks for 1.2 billion, because you have to plan for the peaks – you live on the peak. We are now averaging 1.6 billion, 1.7 billion. We were over 2 billion this week. Probably more than once this week we'll be over 2 billion, and we're planning for 3 billion share peaks, but, more than that, our message traffic associated with that new volume has increased 4 times, which means that you have a lot more retail orders making up the volume, a lot more quote traffic, so the size of the wire which we thought was huge 3 years ago when we planned – we planned for a 2 billion share day – going to 4 billion, we thought that that was outrageous. Now we're looking at, potentially, a 3 billion share day this year. Now, when you bring in decimals, by definition, decimals add huge amounts of traffic to that, so it's a real challenge and my position with the Congress and with the SEC has been, 'Stop, look, measure before we do anything.' Let's understand what we are doing. We'll have decimals, but we have to do it in an orderly way, in a way that accommodates the new volume that's going to add to the volume that's already gone up so much. What other business could have gone up more than double its volume in 18 months and not have problems? Well, we've gone up that much in 18 months and we have had no problems, but, when you go to decimals, we not only have to accommodate decimals, we have to cover headroom, to worry about peaks, and I think that we need to take a very hard look at that.

There's a certain schedule that's been laid out for implementing it. Do you think that it should be modified?

I think it's too aggressive – I've said that publicly. I think everybody who sponsors it wants to keep the heat on. That's fine, but it's too aggressive and we shouldn't just close our eyes and pull a switch and then pay the piper.

Following up on decimalization, do you think it's wise to move to minimum price variation quickly?

Well, I know this industry and the SEC will probably try and keep their nickels for enough time to measure the impact of pennies, but this industry will go pennies in a blink. It becomes a competitive question.

Some people have said it would put pressure on the profits of the member firms?

It will change spreads. It will change spreads and it will change the profit model and that's not ever a good reason not to do things, because it accommodates the investor – the pie gets bigger and bigger and bigger. When we got rid of fixed commissions, everybody predicted doomsday, but the fact of getting rid of the commissions really helped make us what we are today.

Some people say that when companies like Schwab match customer orders internally, they don't get the chance to trade with these customers. Some institutions say, 'I'd like to buy or sell to those customers, but I only see that after the fact.' Is this internalization a real debate?

It's a debate because internalization, if it's done to the benefit of the investor, it works. If it's not done to the benefit of the investor, it doesn't work, so, there is going to be the debate. If I, as investor, can get as good a price as there is because you two have internalized, I'm satisfied. If I am an investor and get a worse price because you two have internalized, and I could have gone to a central market, I'm going to be very upset. So, the internalization process needs to be governed by the people who internalize or they're going to lose their business and should.

Could there be some time in the future when the Nasdaq and the New York Stock Exchange could become one?

That concept has kicked around now for years and every once in a while it raises its head – some member firms like the idea and some of them hate the idea. Some say it would be economically beneficial – there will be lesser costs, we'll be able to have one place to go to get all of our business done and we'll stop all of this competitive stuff. Others say, because we compete, we provide better service to the membership and better service to issuers. It's a public policy debate more than an economic merger debate and would require the government of the United States to be four-square in front of it and for it and I suspect some day there'll be a very, very serious look at it. Conversations, discussions, but never – I've never seen a very honest look at what it would mean if we did.

I think, as I say, no one has ever done the analytics for if we did go ahead. No one has ever done the analytics that say, 'Here is what the model would look like.' Until you have that, I don't think anybody should have an opinion. But I do know that it is something that would have to be led by the government.

INDEX